Joe's Blasts

Facing Leukemia With Courage, Hope, Humor, and Acceptance

Joseph Seeley

Terri,

Joe will come alive again in these pages. I hope you enjoy visiting with him. May his words bring you hope, joy, and more than a few belly laughs. Joe loved his Quaker "family." We treasure the support the community provided during his illness. "Enjoy the blueberries!"

Peace, Jan Seeley

Published by Team J Books

Printed in the United States of America.

Questions regarding the content of this book should be addressed to
Jan Colarusso Seeley
jan.c.seeley@gmail.com

Project manager: Jan Colarusso Seeley
Interior design: Angie Snyder
Cover design and interior layout: Judy Henderson
Copyeditor/proofreader: Ray Vallese
Printed by: Versa Press, Inc.

About the cover: Half a cup of blueberries harvested daily from three small but mature blueberry bushes in his backyard made a classy upgrade to Joe Seeley's breakfast—and put a smile on his face. Inset photo: bone marrow cells, including the acute myeloid leukemia blasts that were Joe's foe during his illness.

Bone marrow photo credit: VashiDonsk at the English language Wikipedia

ISBN 978-0-692-79949-9

Enjoy the blueberries.

Karl, Joe, Lauren, and Mara Seeley, July 2012

JOSEPH T. SEELEY

2/23/60 - 10/13/12

JOE WANTED US TO
ENJOY THE
BLUEBERRIES

Joseph Seeley memorial bench,
Crystal Lake Park, Urbana, Illinois

Table of Contents

Foreword

To be an oncologist is to have a unique and often quite intimate view of another's life. As doctors treating life-threatening leukemias and other malignancies, we are challenged to experience the disease from the offensive side—using chemotherapy combinations designed to put disease into remission, below any level of detection, and to treat serious bacterial and fungal infections that can threaten a patient's life as much as the underlying cancer. The intensity of these treatments fosters deep relationships between the doctors and their patients/families. When a patient is under active therapy, the pace of the relationship quickens, often requiring daily conversations in which the risks versus benefits of a particular approach are debated and considered. Patients and families are asked to participate as partners in their care along with the doctors and nurses, further solidifying their relationships. Analyses of daily laboratory studies and bone marrow biopsies are discussed at length. If a patient worsens, or if a relapse is detected, the conversations take a more serious tone and become long discussions of balances in care with quality of life.

This intimate relationship affords the physician a close view of the patient's life and his/her relationships. We meet spouses, children, extended families, and friends. We learn about the effect of the disease on the patient, the spouse, the children, the parents, and others. Cancer has a domino effect. It affects the lives of all those related to the patient, and the physician observes these effects, but is often unable to influence the negative impact of the planned care. We observe the financial drain, the strain on spouses and caregivers, and the emotional impact on all, but, being focused on the disease and its immediate medical consequences, we have less influence on these untoward consequences. Cancer is also a roller-coaster, with patients and families hanging on every blood count result and laboratory value. Their moods move with the results. When values are reassuring, hopes soar; when results indicate disease, aspirations plummet. It is an exhausting and harrowing ride.

My relationship with Joe began as they often do—between myself, the leukemia doctor, and my patient, in this case, one with aplastic anemia progressed to acute myeloid leukemia. My primary focus began as it always does—on the disease. Joe's journey began as it always does—on achieving a remission from leukemia. Since our medical center was several hours away from his home, Joe came to see us by himself or accompanied by his wife, Jan. As Joe's disease progressed, I met his parents. I spoke to his sisters, his sons, and his friends as his disease began to require daily phone calls. Over time, I became familiar with these people who made up Joe's life. I learned of his life before leukemia, his interests and hobbies. I saw the effects of his treatment, not just physical, but on all those who were part of his life. This was an intimate, privileged view of another's world, and it made losing Joe all the more difficult, because I saw the legacy of his disease on others.

Joe's book, *Joe's Blasts*, gives its readers a rare view of his life with cancer. The title in and of itself says so much: it is a play on words, reflecting Joe's clever sense of humor. "Blasts" is the word we use as doctors to describe leukemia cells. Joe's book is a daily, sometimes hourly account of his fight against those cells. At the same time, it is a shout-out to the world of his experiences, his wishes, and his reactions to setbacks. Rarely do those outside of medicine get such a close-up view of a patient's fight against his disease.

Joe's words are reflective of the experiences of many patients with cancer—the lengthy fight, sometimes victorious. This is Joe's story of his struggle against the blasts that ultimately took his life. It is at times difficult to read, as he suffered, but ultimately, it is rewarding for its love of life itself.

—Lucy A. Godley, professor, Section of Hematology/Oncology
at the University of Chicago

Preface

Early in our marriage, Joe dubbed us "Team J." When we worked together on a project—especially our collaboration on the Christie Clinic Illinois Marathon—Joe loved to call us by that nickname. I was always the "shorter half of Team J." In the spirit of that partnership, it seems appropriate that I write this brief preface to Joe's book. That *Joe's Blasts* has become a book would please Joe immensely, I think. He hinted at that possibility in his last post.

The blog started as a single entry the day after Joe entered the University of Chicago Medical Center for treatment in January 2011 and ended up spanning 21 months. Joe shared intimate details of his journey with unflinching honesty, laugh-out-loud humor, and a gentle grace. He let us experience with him the exhilarating highs and harrowing lows of his leukemia roller-coaster ride. And in doing so, he transformed us.

As my college classmate Julia Reidhead notes, *Joe's Blasts* "is also the story of an athlete who faces increasing physical limitation and illness with great grace, and of a coach who models courage and decency." For Joe, the good news was, there was a treadmill on the leukemia floor.

Joe had many blog followers all over the world, including some nurses, doctors, and administrators at the hospital. His blog caught the attention of the then-new hospital president, Sharon O'Keefe. Sharon not only started reading the blog but also visited Joe a few times in the hospital, eager for feedback on his experience. Between Joe's first and second extensive hospitalizations, some impactful non-medical changes were implemented at the hospital—not coincidentally, I believe—in the exact areas Joe wrote constructively about in his blog.

The first step needed to turn Joe's blog into a book was dividing his story into logical pieces. To provide context for each of the resulting five sections, family members wrote introductions. I am indebted to Joe's parents, Bob and Char; his sisters Mara and Lauren; his brother Karl; and our son Jake for these contributions. Joe's brilliant doctor, Lucy Godley, wrote the foreword, and college best friend, Maggi Smeal, penned the afterword.

—*Jan Colarusso Seeley, the shorter half of Team J*

Part 1

Good News, Bad News

When we pick up Joe's book to read, our eyes brim with tears. Then, reading, we have the wonderful sensation that he is alive again. There is his courageous humor in the face of a terrible disease, the determination that he Will. Not. Lose. As a patient, his insider's view of the hospital experience continues a lifelong instinct to make the world better in any way he could.

When we put the book down, the tears are back.

Through nearly two years of struggle, with the constant hope of remission and the foreshadowing of loss, we came to know Joe more deeply as he recorded what was happening to him, how his world had changed, his reflections.

His narrative spoke to old friends, colleagues, distant relatives, people he barely knew, and some he didn't know at all. It was a transformative experience for Joe, and for many followers of his "blasts."

Perhaps it will speak to still others.

—Bob and Char Seeley, Joe's parents

Char, Joe, and Bob: Carle Hospital, August 2012

Good News, Bad News

The good news is, there is a treadmill.
The bad news is, I don't get to run outside for a month.

The good news is, my room has windows all along one wall.
The bad news is, my view is the side of the next building.

The good news is, this isn't my eventual room.
The bad news is, my next room has a similar view.

The good news is, I can wear pajamas all day.
The bad news is, I could get used to that.

The good news is, next year's end-of-year letter won't sound like a rerun of the last few.
The bad news is, saying "end-of-year" feels like tempting fate.

The good news is, plenty of time to read or draw.
The bad news is, plenty of time to worry.

The good news is, I have great support from family, friends, and work.
The bad news is, I can't think of any clever downside to go on this line.

The good news is, I feel perfectly healthy.
The bad news is, the bone marrow biopsy says I'm not.

The good news is, I'm in one of the best facilities in the world for treating AML.
The bad news is, I'm being treated for AML.

The good news is, there is a treadmill.

Posted by Joseph Seeley at 6:32 AM

"This will come as a shock."

A brief timeline, for the curious.

▶ Late 2004, I was rejected while trying to donate blood due to anemia. Upon further inspection, all my blood counts were low, and I was diagnosed with aplastic anemia by doctors at the University of Chicago. This was most likely a side effect of a medication (sulfasalazine) I had been taking since 1988 to control ulcerative colitis. The condition wasn't so severe as to require treatment, but it did merit careful watching. Went off sulfasalazine, blood counts improved, though they never came all the way back.

▶ Late 2010, my regular blood test raises a red flag, which leads to a consultation with a hematologist at Carle, which leads to a referral back to the University of Chicago. No noteworthy symptoms.

▶ January 3—Meet some doctors at U of C. Based on history and most recent blood work, a biopsy is in order. Maybe the aplastic anemia is getting worse, maybe it's something else. Not super urgent. The next biopsy opening is January 18, and the next follow-up appointment opening (Mondays only) is January 24. The lack of urgency is comforting.

▶ January 4—Call from U of C. They now have a biopsy opening Thursday or Friday. I take one. I'm thinking, "How convenient."

▶ January 7—Biopsy. Typically there's no analysis over the weekend, but we can and do move the follow-up appointment up one week to January 17. Later that night, call from the doctor telling me that they will be analyzing the biopsy over the weekend after all, and so we could follow up the coming Monday if I want to. I'm thinking, "What fantastic customer service," though it occurs to me that perhaps things are more urgent than the doctors are letting on. Jan will be out of town on business, but (coincidentally) my mom is in Chicago visiting her brother. This means I will have a second person with me to receive the diagnosis.

▶ January 10, afternoon—"This will come as a shock. You have acute leukemia." They started suspecting leukemia based on the January 3 blood work, and it was confirmed by the bone marrow biopsy. The doctors were pretty surprised, but not as surprised as I was. I feel fine! "You could enter the hospital tonight." Umm, I definitely need a little more time to get ready, and I have a teenage son alone at home. It was great to have my mom there, though unfortunately the "kiss the booboo to make it better" cure was not deemed effective.

▶ January 10, evening—The drive home alone to Champaign was not as rough as I thought it would be. For the first time in my life, I had reason to say, "Sports talk radio is a blessing." The hosts and the callers were all so certain about the outcomes of the upcoming NFL playoffs that it's a wonder we even need to play the games, and as long as I paid attention to them, I was fine. When I started visualizing the difficult conversations I was about to have when I got home, I got a little shaky. But then Brian from Bolingbrook would weigh in on why the Bears had better be careful about the Seahawks, and I would be under control again. Maybe I should look into developing an app that plays sports talk, to be used therapeutically as a mental and emotional anesthetic.

▶ January 12—Admitted to the hospital.

▶ January 13—Starting chemotherapy, 10 days after my first consultation.

I'll describe the treatment plan in another post.

Posted by Joseph Seeley at 3:33 PM

Friday, January 14, 2011

Transport

The most unsettling part of the experience so far has not been the sometimes painful poking and pricking. What makes me shudder is the phrase, "I've put in a call to Transport."

The first 24 hours included a bunch of scans and a procedure (installing a multipurpose port just below my right clavicle). This meant having to travel all over the hospital complex, and such travel is managed by the Transport team.

First up was a heart test. Chemotherapy can weaken the heart muscle, so they want a baseline to compare to later. I'm getting ready to walk over to the testing with the Transport guy, but I see he has a wheelchair and expects me to get in it. Fine. Off we go.

It's a long walk/ride. I'm on the sixth floor of one hospital, and we're headed to the basement of another. It feels awkward to be taking such a long trip with somebody and not talk, so I try to make small talk. "How far do you think you walk in a day?" Unfortunately, I'm not very good at that, so it's just more awkward when the chit-chat dies.

Also awkward: riding elevators. Normally, if there are just a few people in an elevator, we arrange ourselves so that we're all side by side, facing the door and maybe turned a little bit toward each other. When people get on, we typically acknowledge them with at least a nod. Hospital elevators are long and narrow (to accommodate hospital beds), and they have doors front and back. We roll in and start going down to the basement. We stop and another person gets rolled in, behind me. There are now four people in the elevator—two patients and two pushers—and we're lined up in single file facing a door. It feels weird, not being able to see the other passengers and not being in control of what I can see.

We eventually arrive at the site of the first test. My transporter rolls me next to a wall in a unit with curtained bays on both sides, locks my wheels, and takes off. Soon, a technician shows up and wheels me into the room. We do our test on equipment being run by a Macintosh Power PC 8100 (which Wikipedia tells me was introduced in 1994). I remark on the age of the computer, and the tech sighs. They're praying the computer doesn't die, because they no longer have the disks (for the testing software, I assume).

The test is quick, the tech wheels me back out to the corridor, locks my wheels, brings me a cup of water, and says, "I've put in a call to Transport."

Then he's gone. It's kind of late, and the unit appears deserted. Did everybody go home? There's the medical background noise of pumping, whirring, beeping, but no voices. The curtains move slightly, as if there were a breeze. But we're in a basement, so maybe it's ghosts—the ghosts of patients left behind at the end of the day. About 30 minutes in, a staffer walks by. I ask how long one should expect to wait for a ride. She's not sure, but she thinks maybe because it's so late, there are fewer Transporters available, so it could take 30 minutes. Or more. I have no watch, but I'm pretty sure nearly an hour passes in all... just me and my chair and the medical white noise.

It turns out that being pushed in a wheelchair has cast a debilitating spell on me. I have gone from athlete to invalid in a single ride. I have finished my cup of water, and there is still no sign of Transport, or anyone else. I keep looking around for a staff member who can refill my cup. Suddenly I remember ... I can walk! It's a miracle! I walk down to the end of unit, where I saw a water cooler.

As I approach, a large man lumbers into the unit from a different corridor, also headed for the water. He gets there first. He sits down next to the dispenser, catching his breath. I wait. He recovers enough to get some water, and then I get mine. He's slumped in the chair next to the cooler, I'm looking at the familiar collection of outdated (yet somehow timeless!) women's and golfing magazines. The tech pokes his head out of his office and says, "Still here, Mr. Seeley?" The huffing and puffing man looks up and asks, "Are you Mr. Seeley? I thought you were still in testing." It turns out that he is my transporter for going back to my room. I think "I thought you were still in testing" is code for "I was resting in the back room to recover from walking all the way over here."

I'm concerned. As soon as we start wheeling, he starts wheezing. At one point, in a tunnel between hospitals, the floor has a very slight dip. We go into it with a little speed from the downhill portion, but we're losing steam quickly as we climb out. "I think I can. I think I can." We barely make it out. I'm thinking maybe we should switch places. "So, how far do you think you walk in a day?" "Too damn far, that's for sure."

Back to my room two hours after I left—10 minutes of testing, 110 minutes of travel or waiting to travel. My nurse doesn't think there are any more tests for the night, so I order dinner. Baked fish, red beans and rice, side salad, apple, orange, pudding. Then we learn I'm going for more tests, and I leave in a chair just as my meal arrives, at 7:00.

This time we're going for CT scans and x-rays, looking for infections in the sinuses and lungs. Yet another transporter, more elevator rides. Dropped off at the CT place, go right into the test, back into the chair. "I've put in a call to Transport."

And then the tech is gone, and I'm hanging out by myself again, this time in the CT room. Ten minutes later the tech comes back, unlocks my wheels, and says, "I'll just take you to x-ray myself."

At the x-ray place, I get dropped by a reception desk, but (naturally) my back is to the receptionists. Kind of a long wait, during which the Rush Limbaugh fan behind the desk tries to explain to his colleague, a young black woman, why she should not vote for the "Dumbocrats. Get it? I call them the Dumbocrats. Because they're so dumb." She is not persuaded, because she already doesn't vote for the Democrats, or anybody else. Because "they just do what they want to do, no matter who you vote for." (I can't say she's totally wrong about that.) The conversation keeps going on behind me, the passionately misinformed trying to persuade the ignorantly uninterested that it's really the Dumbocrats who are the party of the rich people. Like most fans of talk radio talking points, he has a lot of numbers, like the number of Goldman Sachs alumni advising Obama on economic matters. (OK, I can't say he's totally wrong about that.)

An x-ray tech comes to rescue me. In, out, back to the reception desk. "I've put in a call to Transport."

I have another epiphany. I'm on wheels! I unlock the wheels and entertain myself by carving figure 8s in front of the reception desk until Transport finally shows up. I get back to my room at 9. The dinner is, surprisingly, still warm and, not surprisingly, not very good. But no more Transport for the night. Yay!

Posted by Joseph Seeley at 11:10 AM

Saturday, January 15, 2011

Treatment Plan

A summary of the treatment plan:

1. Induce remission through chemotherapy. We're trying to kill nearly all the cells in my marrow.

2. Recover in the hospital. I'll receive transfusions to make up for the blood cells I'm no longer creating myself. I'll need to be in the hospital for several weeks after chemo, to give my marrow a chance to grow back and take over blood production. Hopefully, my marrow comes back with no detectable signs of leukemia.

3. When I'm sufficiently recovered, I leave the hospital for a couple of weeks to continue recovering. I have heard that I might have to stay in Chicago and that I might be able to go home. It depends in part how the various blood counts are doing. I'll be very vulnerable to infection, so I'll need to stay somewhat cocooned.

4. Another round of chemotherapy. This time, we're trying to clear out the marrow to make room for healthy cells from my sister Mara, who (luckily for me) is an ideal match. At some point, she will come to Chicago and spend a week or two, the end result of which is a collection of some healthy stem cells from her blood.

5. Transplant. This is done by transfusion. Mara's healthy cells are delighted to find all this unoccupied space in my bones, and they move in. If there are any lingering leukemic cells, the new cells will destroy them.

6. More recovery, first in the hospital, then out.

Posted by Joseph Seeley at 6:17 PM

Second Day of Chemo

Still no nausea, but somewhat tired. Slept through the first half of the Steelers/Ravens game, as did the Steelers. Probably a combination of the chemo and the interrupted sleep (speaking for myself—can't speak for the Steelers).

The doctors say I'm responding as I should to the chemo. Blood counts are starting to fall, but blood chemistry remains good.

I took a long walk up and down the corridors of this and other connected hospitals. It's a big complex, but I have exhausted the terrain. Tomorrow I might get clearance to use the treadmill—I'm not usually a treadmill fan, but under the circumstances, it'll be a great improvement.

Posted by Joseph Seeley at 6:25 PM

Sunday, January 16, 2011

Cruel Irony

The good news is, I am the target of this wonderful outpouring of support, the kind that could manifest itself as cookies and other baked goods—and there are some outstanding bakers in this group. I also have unlimited access to a large dessert menu from room service—ice cream, pudding, cobbler, milkshakes, cookies, brownies...

The bad news is, the chemotherapy has shifted my tastes such that the sweeter something is, the less appealing it is.

That just doesn't seem fair.

Posted by Joseph Seeley at 10:48 AM

Monday, January 17, 2011

Hooked Up

When under stress, we find ourselves doing things that are out of character. In my case, I have hooked up with a pole dancer named "Ivy."

Paradoxically, she's a five-footer who is taller than I am.

We've become very attached.

We're practically inseparable.

We've been sleeping together every night.

Jan is not happy.

Paradoxically, she's a five-footer
who is taller than I am.

Jan is not happy.

Posted by Joseph Seeley at 10:22 AM

Tuesday, January 18, 2011

So Far, So Good

I'm in my fifth day of chemotherapy. I'm not feeling any ill effects, but it is having the desired effect on my blood counts (pushing them down). The only time I have felt nauseous was during the Patriots-Jets game, but that passed.

As I mentioned, the blood counts are dropping as they should. Platelets are extremely low, leading to very easy bruising and bleeding. While out walking a few days ago, I kicked the feet of Ivy, my pole dancer partner, once with each foot. I now star in my own production of *Joseph and the Amazing Technicolor DreamToes*.

My neutrophil count is also extremely low. Neutrophils are one of the types of white blood cells, so I am extremely vulnerable to infection. Whenever I leave my room, I need to wear a mask. Eventually, I'll move to a wing where the rooms have two sets of doors and positive air pressure, so that potentially contaminated air from the corridor doesn't get in.

Posted by Joseph Seeley at 7:11 AM

Wednesday, January 19, 2011

Suggestive Clothing

Those who know me will not be surprised to learn that I value practical and clean much more than neat. Jan occasionally has to send me back upstairs to avoid going to work sporting my terrorist look or my "what two-year-old dressed you?" look. I don't believe that clothes make the man—our acts define us, not our clothes.

However, I am noticing the power of what I wear to affect how I feel about myself, which can affect how I act. When I was "wearing" a wheelchair, I started thinking like an invalid and briefly forgot I could walk. This morning, wearing a hospital gown and lying in a hospital bed, when some doctors left my light on after their 7 a.m. visit, I was ready to page the nurse to turn it off before remembering that four steps is still well within my abilities. When I wear pajamas, I feel less feeble than when I wear the hospital gown, and when I wear running clothes, I feel pretty normal.

Yesterday, free of Jan's fashion guidance, I did a corridor walk in what I considered a practical if mismatched ensemble: gown, socks, running shoes. The running shoes made a huge difference in how I felt walking, compared to the no-skid socks I had worn before. Sick people walk corridor halls with their IV poles while wearing socks. With my running shoes, I'm a healthy guy with leukemia. The gown is practical because it's the only thing that the hospital will wash, and I'm saving my running shorts for working out on the treadmill.

It was a good walk. In the shoes, I can go faster, and I can kick Ivy's feet without adding to my toe bruise collection. Occasionally I felt an unaccustomed breeze, which made me wonder if I was totally wrapped up. But I checked a couple of times, and I had the gown tied up as tightly as it gets. Not that I minded the sensation—I was thinking that maybe the Scots have a good idea with the kilts.

When I got back to my room, a nurse told me that she brought me an extra gown.

Me: What for?
Nurse: To wear like a cape over your first gown, on your walks.
Me: Why?
Nurse: I heard you were flashing.

Sorry, Jan!

Posted by Joseph Seeley at 7:25 AM

Thursday, January 20, 2011

Exciting New Weight Loss Miracle They Don't Want You to Know About!

I'm in a very good mood today, for no particular reason. Sunlight (finally) might be part of the reason. I had a (relatively) good night of sleep, which always helps. Yesterday's (mildly) sore throat has faded, which had me worried that I might be coming down with an infection.

This morning, I took another lengthy walk through the maze of corridors— still haven't found the cheese! I've become a regular sight in some of the far reaches of the sixth floor, and a few of the researchers and doctors and other staff greet me with some variation of "doing laps again, I see." One person offered a caution—stay out of a particular dead-end corridor, because they do animal research there, and who knows what diseases might be in the air. Helpful tip!

One of the advantages of being in Chicago (as opposed to, say, St. Louis) is that I have relatives here. I have already been visited by three cousins, on two separate evenings. Sam had the misfortune of being here while a second-year medical student practiced his history-taking technique, so Sam got to hear more than he wanted to about bowel movements, urination, and so, so much more. I'm hoping I can provide better entertainment to future cousin visits.

My medical question of the day is, why am I losing weight? Unfortunately, I missed my chance to ask the attending physician, because I was out walking when he and his posse stopped by. It is common to lose weight during or shortly after chemo, for various reasons: nausea, loss of appetite, vomiting, diarrhea. However, I have none of those symptoms. I have a couple of theories: At my in-hospital high weight, I was receiving the maximum amount of IV fluid, and I was constipated. (Feel free to make predictable "full of shit" jokes.) I figure that was good for a few pounds. When I asked the head nurse, she didn't sign on to my theories but gave two more possible explanations.

First, I'm probably eating less than I think, and less than I normally do. I don't have ready access to snacks, or to seconds, since I have to order everything and it takes about 45 minutes for it to arrive. So, there's no immediate second helping of jambalaya (I wish) or spur-of-the-moment cookie binge. This delay seems like it could be (or already is) part of a successful weight loss strategy.

Second, chemo can rev up the metabolism. (At least, I think that's what she said.) So, combined with not eating as much as usual, I could be running a calorie deficit. Please—don't try this at home!

Posted by Joseph Seeley at 2:01 PM

New Blood

I am, right now, receiving my first transfusion. Platelets, the blood cells that stop the bleeding. When they're low, you bruise easily and bleed more. Mine are at 10 (thousand), and we don't want them to get any lower.

Before I receive them, I need to hear about the risks from a doctor: fevers, chills, rigors (shakes); 1 in 2 million chance of HIV; 1 in 1.6 million chance of Hepatitis C; 1 in 150,000 chance of Hepatitis B. I'm signing anyway.

The platelets come in a clear plastic IV bag. It looks like the result of blending 2 T butterscotch pudding with 2 cups water. Takes about 10 minutes, and I'm good to go.

Off to run! No pudding for dessert tonight.

Posted by Joseph Seeley at 3:29 PM

Friday, January 21, 2011

Ivy and I Are Done

Yesterday, at 9 p.m., we officially broke up.

I will still hook up from time to time, for transfusions and possibly some medications, but for the most part I am a free man.

I had gotten fairly good at walking with the pole through the corridors and through doors, even developing a move I call the Seeley Spin to get over this one bit of carpet edging. Somehow, I never mastered the trip to the toilet and back to bed. I would get up, drag the pole five steps into the bathroom while avoiding the pole's power cord on the floor, do whatever needed doing, maneuver back to bed, and find that I had wrapped my IV line once (and occasionally twice) around the pole. Then, I would have to walk once (and occasionally twice) around the pole before I could get back into bed.

I felt like a feeble-minded dog who can't go five steps without wrapping his leash around his master.

Posted by Joseph Seeley at 6:36 AM

Saturday, January 22, 2011

New Room

The night chemo ended (Thursday) was also my last night in my initial room. When I was admitted, there were no free beds on the "leukemia" wing, so I started in a room on the "solid tumors" wing.

The nurse brought a wheelchair—shudder—and I loaded it with my small collection of stuff: backpack, books, pajamas, running shoes, some V8 juice (my way around the lack of any juices that aren't too sweet for my [current] tastes)...

I had been told that the rooms in the NW wing were larger, since they were doubles converted to singles. I was misinformed. My new room may be a converted double, but if so, it was converted by turning it into two singles and an anteroom. So, it's actually smaller. On the plus side, it does have an old wall-mounted HP computer, so that's something to look forward to in case my MacBook dies.

The anteroom is part of the enhanced sterility controls in this wing relative to the one I started on. Filtered air is constantly pumped into my room, and both my door and the anteroom door to the corridor remain closed. Whenever either door is opened, air flows out.

My windows face north, so I'll miss the direct sunlight my first room had. But the view is better: more sky, a variety of buildings, the main entrance to the medical center (always bustling), playground (empty—kids these days are such wimps about 10-degree temperatures).

I'm currently finishing my second platelet transfusion, with some red blood cells to follow. I can tell I'm running low on the latter. Yesterday, I was running/walking at 15:00/mile pace on the treadmill, thinking I was taking it sufficiently easy. Then I checked my pulse—160, which is too high for taking it easy. So I kept dialing down the speed until my pulse reached a more reasonable 140. Total workout: 31:28 for two miles. After my upcoming blood-doping session, who knows what I'll be capable of.

Update: Now receiving the red blood. It's going to be a few hours (two bags). The nurse asks how I'm doing, and I mention that I'm kind of sleepy. "Oh, that's the Benadryl. It makes you kind of mellow." Uh oh. I'm clinically mellow to begin with, so it looks like we'll be turning the mellow dial up to 11.

Posted by Joseph Seeley at 9:59 AM

Blood Doping Works

Yesterday, a 15:00/mile pace pushed my heart rate to 160.

Today, a 13:20/mile pace kept my heart rate at or below 140.

The difference? A couple of bags of blood.

Posted by Joseph Seeley at 5:20 PM

I Have It Easy

A lot of people have praised me for my positive attitude. It's a little embarrassing, because I don't think it's that praiseworthy.

Yes, I have a very serious medical condition, and I'm confined to a single short corridor on the sixth floor of a hospital a few hours away from home for at least a few more weeks, with an expected return stay that's even longer. Compared to where I was two weeks ago, this is a lot worse.

But compared to what some of my fellow patients are going through, my experience so far has been pretty sweet. As I write this, my neighbor to the west is repeatedly vomiting. (Note to self: Put on some loud music when lunch arrives.) I rarely see other patients, because most of them don't have the energy to get out of bed. Those who do get out onto the corridor are barely moving. One of the few patients I have seen on the exercise equipment looks like the skinnier of the two comic relief ghost pirates from the Pirates of the Caribbean moves—gaunt, sunken eyes, blotchy skin. I (so far) haven't had any negative side effects from my chemotherapy—appetite is fine, energy level is good.

And that's just the physical side. Financially, I have a strong health insurance policy, and a supportive employer with short- and long-term disability benefits and a willingness to let me telecommute as I am able, and savings to draw on if needed, and family to turn to if that's not enough. I'm sure there are others up here who, besides feeling physically terrible, are also tormented by financial worries.

Outside of the hospital, Jan has it rougher than I do. I have room service and people who clean my room and provide me with clean hospital gowns whenever I need them. Jan has her regular job(s), and she has to take on my share of the shopping, cooking, dishes, laundry, and day-to-day parenting that I would do if I were there. Plus, she worries about me.

It's easy to be positive when you aren't being tested.

Posted by Joseph Seeley at 12:05 PM

The Good Ship Lollipop

Last night was a largely typical night: Somnus Interruptus.

- ▶ Turn in around 10.
- ▶ Vitals check around midnight.
- ▶ Visit to the bathroom around 2.
- ▶ Visit again around 4.
- ▶ Vitals check a little later.
- ▶ Blood draw around 5.
- ▶ Morning pills around 6. Take advantage of being up for another bathroom visit.
- ▶ Vitals check around 8. I guess I might as well get up now.

For some reason, when I got back into bed after the 4 a.m. pit stop, I had the song "The Good Ship Lollipop" going through my head.

On the good ship Lollipop
It's a sweet trip to the candy shop

I was puzzled.

Where bon-bons play
On the sunny beach of Peppermint Bay.

Where in the world did this song come from?

See the sugar bowl do the Tootsie Roll
With the big bad devil's food cake.

I mentioned that it was a largely typical night. One thing that was different was a little abdominal pain.

And if you eat too much, oh, oh
You'll awake with a tummy ache!

Huh! My belly hurts, and somehow my mind dredges up a song with the words "tummy ache" in it? That's just weird. Does anyone have any better tummy ache songs to suggest?

Anyway, my tummy ache is gone now.

Uneventful day. Platelets down to 4, so I got another platelet transfusion. Now up to 21. Currently watching *Despicable Me*, courtesy of the recreational therapist.

Brother-in-law coming in for a visit this evening.

Posted by Joseph Seeley at 3:10 PM

Tuesday, January 25, 2011

A Medically Uneventful Day

Slept (relatively) well, feeling a little draggy due to low hemoglobin counts, had a good breakfast and lunch, did some work... Today's workout will be a low-key affair.

The morning medical posse stopped by to say everything looks good.

Jan had a great meeting this morning with an Urbana woman whose husband was treated for the same condition at this same hospital. That's going to be a good relationship to have.

My dad is arriving this afternoon and staying for the rest of the week. Also expecting a visit from a member of the U-C Quaker meeting.

Uneventful is good!

Posted by Joseph Seeley at 11:58 AM

Thursday, January 27, 2011

Tested (or, a Medically Eventful Day)

I missed a day of blogging. I was kind of busy. First busy with tests, but then mostly busy feeling like crap. All typical and expected stuff, according to the doctors and nurses. Feeling much better today, so I expect to fill in the exciting details as time allows.

Update 1:

Yesterday was so packed, I have to start at midnight. The NSA (nursing student aide) records my first noteworthy temperature (38.3 C, 100.9 F). A few hours earlier, the nurse had shared a story about a patient of hers who was happily up walking and two hours later needed help breathing, due to a galloping infection. Sweet dreams! And I have been told that once a fever reaches 38 C, we start to address it.

Me: That's kind of high.
NSA: Yes.
Me: Are we going to do anything about it?
NSA: I'll tell the nurse.
Me: (To myself—were you going to tell the nurse if I didn't ask you to?)

I wait... wait... close my eyes... wait...

1:15, I wake up to pee. I'm pretty sure the nurse hasn't been in. I wonder which of the following is true:

► The NSA forgot to tell the nurse.

► The NSA told the nurse, and the nurse didn't think it was important.

► The NSA told the nurse, the nurse thought it was important, and she just hasn't gotten around to my room yet. Did I mention that there are a lot of sick people here in the hospital?

I page the nursing station. "Can I help you?" "Yes, I'm wondering if my nurse was told about my fever and if she's going to come in." "I'll tell the nurse."

More waiting... 15 minutes... still wondering about the three possibilities above, because I have no idea what is going on outside my room. My dad (staying with me this week) heads out to the nursing station to see what's going on, and returns to report that the nurse is gathering supplies and will be coming in soon.

When the nurse arrives, the eventful day begins in earnest. Blood draws, to test for blood infections. Urine sample, to test for a urinary infection. We start several intravenous antibiotics, just in case there is a bacterial infection behind the fever. (Yes, this means Ivy and I were not as "done" as I thought. Instead, we were "done" in the manner of *Jersey Shore*'s relationship authorities Ronnie and Sammi.) Tylenol.

Maybe a little sleep. Then, chest x-ray, without leaving my bed—a mechanical dinosaur partially enters my room, cranes its neck over the foot of my bed, cocks its head to look at my chest, and *bzzzzt*.

Maybe a little more sleep. Vitals. The usual early morning tablets. Fever falling.

Breakfast time, feeling reasonable, but anticipating a need for a nap, both because of the disrupted sleep and because my hemoglobin count is below 8. I'll be getting blood later in the day, so I plan to work out after that.

But it didn't work out as planned.

Posted by Joseph Seeley at 7:28 AM

Friday, January 28, 2011

Tested (Part 2)

[First—Friday was fine. A little low on energy, but otherwise feeling fine. No fever since Wednesday, decent appetite, a good ride on the stationary bike. Platelet and red blood transfusions, plus continued antibiotics.]

Wednesday morning—fever diminished, and pretty uneventful.

Except for the bone marrow biopsy. Roughly 12 days after the start of chemo, they check the contents of the bone marrow to see what effect the chemo has had. I lie face down on my bed, tastefully flashing the doctor. A shot of local anesthetic, and then the doctor works a very thin and strong needle into my hip bone. It's a lot of work for the doctor, and mostly just a numbed pressure for me.

(When I had the biopsy earlier in the month that led to my diagnosis, the doctor—a different one than this episode—had to lower the bed so he could put more of his weight into it, and he ended up bending the first needle. Runner's bones are hard.)

Eventually the doctor works the needle through the bone's cortex and into the marrow. The marrow isn't numb, so I can tell the doctor she's there. She sucks out a bit of liquid from the marrow. It's a short, sharp pain that passes quickly.

Step two is essentially a core sample of the bone and marrow, working the same spot, but with a fatter needle allowing them to remove a thin plug of bone and marrow. Again, lots of work by the doctor, mostly numbed pressure for me, except right at the end when they get to the good part.

Then they bandage me up, tell me to keep pressure on it by lying or sitting in bed for an hour—which I assure them I can manage.

I order a new (for me) item off the menu—chicken and cheese enchilada— and I decide to give the chocolate chip cookie a try, since I think my sweet aversion might be fading.

(to be continued)

Posted by Joseph Seeley at 8:36 PM

Saturday, January 29, 2011

Tested (Part 3)

The midday vitals check on Wednesday showed the fever returning. I was feeling kind of draggy and hoping the two bags of blood scheduled for the afternoon would perk me up. Took a little nap.

Around 3, I start coughing. I have coughed off and on since arriving at the hospital. The air is extremely dry, and I have had a little bit of post-nasal drip, so the back of my throat is occasionally tickled or irritated. The doctors always ask if the cough brings anything up, and it (so far) hasn't. Some coughing is actually good for the lungs, helping to keep the air passages open and defending against lung infections. It's also good to take extremely deep breaths, for the same reason.

(Warning: NSFM [Not Safe For Mealtime])

This round of coughing is different, triggered from deeper down the throat. Next thing I know, I have figuratively tossed my literal cookies. But just the cookies. On the floor between the bed and the bathroom. I page the nurse to report my achievement. Since the chemo started, the doctors have been asking about nausea and vomiting, and I have had nothing to share. Now, I may have finally earned my Vomit merit badge. It wasn't very impressive, but it should count.

The nurse eventually comes in, cleans up the floor, offers me an anti-nausea medication (although I am not nauseous) that will make me (even more) groggy. I accept. More napping.

At the afternoon vitals check, my fever is up to 39 (102.2 F). (Surely high enough to earn the Fever merit badge.) We do another round of blood and urine samples, to re-run the pre-dawn tests.

At 6, more deep coughing. Chicken and cheese enchiladas!

At bedtime, the fever is up to 39.9 (103.8 F). Normally, high fevers are accompanied by aching muscles, but not this one. I'm guessing it's because I am not in condition to mount the kind of inflammatory response that causes the aching. More Tylenol, and the nurse packs me in cold ice packs—one under each thigh, one in each armpit, an ice pack behind my neck. They feel great. It occurs to me that there is a commercial opportunity in a pillow that you could set to a desired temperature.

By midnight, the fever is down, and it has yet to return. None of the tests turned up any infections, and it's not unusual for chemo patients to have unexplained fevers.

And so ended a very busy day. Lots of tests, a couple of merit badges. It's been mercifully quiet since then.

Posted by Joseph Seeley at 7:23 AM

Sunday, January 30, 2011

I Thought That Was a Good Thing

During my first day, undergoing a lot of tests, technicians and nurses kept taking my pulse. Almost every time, they would ask, "Is your heart rate normally that low?" Yes, when I'm lying in bed, breathing slowly, my pulse is usually in the low 50s. Sometimes, it's even in the high 40s. I'm a runner.

This morning, a tech wheeled in an EKG machine, hooked up leads to my chest, shoulder, arms, and legs, took a reading, and left. A little later the nurse came in and said there was some concern about my heart rate. During the 4:00 a.m. vitals check, my heart rate had been 48, and at 8:00 it was 49. She said they might move me to a different unit, one with telemetry, which means I would be hooked up permanently to a heart rate monitor.

"Does the unit have a treadmill?"

(Chuckle) "They don't use a treadmill on that unit."

That got my heart rate up. Here I had been proud of and encouraged by my low heart rates, and now there was a chance that having a low heart rate would cost me the ability to run.

Fortunately, the doctors are interpreting my low overnight heart rate as a return to a post-chemo normal, so it doesn't look like I'll have to move.

Posted by Joseph Seeley at 8:41 AM

Bad Hair Day

I often have what many would call Bad Hair Days. In the interest of not being judgmental, I claim my hair isn't actually *bad* on these days, just *misguided*. Your hair might be similarly misbehaved if it went to bed wet.

Anyway, my hair has been having an increasingly hard time lately. Chemotherapy attacks rapidly dividing cells. The target is cancerous cells, but the collateral damage is bone marrow cells, cells lining the digestive tract (frequently leading to diarrhea), cells growing your nails (making them brittle and rough), and cells growing your hair (causing your hair to fall out).

I had been seeing signs the last few days that I was about to earn my Hair Loss badge: seeing more hairs on my pillow upon waking; whiskers coming off in my hand; hair balls the size of a small rodent on the shower drain...

You can't quit, Harry McHair. You're fired!

I now have even less hair than my dad! (Thanks for the trim, Dad!)

As you can see, I still have facial hair. However, my eyebrow has already thinned to the point that it looks like I have two eyebrows. Anyway, I think this look works for me.

I'm also losing hair on my arms, chest, legs, and ... elsewhere. (Sorry, no pictures.) Soon enough, it's all going to be gone. Naked as a mole rat.

I think it's the loss of eyebrows that really gives cancer patients the cancer patient look.

Fortunately, my family's got me covered.

Posted by Joseph Seeley at 3:39 PM   Thanks, Jan!

Monday, January 31, 2011

It's All About the Blasts (plus, Good News)

Leukemia is a cancer affecting the white blood cells, also called leukocytes. In a person with leukemia, new leukocytes fail to mature properly. Immature leukocytes are called lymphoblasts, or "blasts" for short. Instead of maturing and assuming their role defending us against infection, the leukemic blasts remain immature and keep multiplying.

Eventually, the oversupply of blasts interferes with the production of normal red blood cells (carry oxygen), platelets (stop bleeding), and/or neutrophils (a specific type of white blood cell that fights bacteria). It was a drop in neutrophils that sounded the first alarm in my case, the presence of a few blasts in my blood that caused the doctors to move more quickly than they originally planned, and the high percentage of blasts in my marrow that confirmed the diagnosis of acute myeloid leukemia.

The bone marrow biopsy that I had last Wednesday was to see, on a preliminary basis, whether the chemotherapy had the desired effect. First, we want to see that most of the cells in the marrow have been killed. Second, we want the percentage of blasts in the remaining cells to be quite low. Some of the remaining blasts might be leukemic cells still dying, or healthy blasts just being born—I don't think you ever have no blasts.

And the results are in—it's just a preliminary reading, but they're as good as they can be.

Or, to put it another way, **they're as good as they can be!**

We'll be checking again after my marrow has had a chance to recover, but for now there's no reason to think I'm not on the right track.

Posted by Joseph Seeley at 7:03 PM

Tuesday, February 1, 2011

Nurses

A lot of you already know this, and I suspected that it was true, but this has been my first opportunity to see firsthand that nurses are fantastic people. The nurses on this unit (and my previous one) are on 12-hour shifts, so I have had quite a few in my three weeks here. Young and old, male and female, from all over the world—each, in his or her own way, friendly, caring, reassuring. Despite the occasionally dignity-robbing details of hospital life—Tuesdays are Fecal Swab Day!—they are good at maintaining patient dignity.

Nurses have different relationships with the hospital. There are staff nurses permanently affiliated with the hospital, traveling nurses who affiliate with a hospital for some period of time and then move on to another, and agency nurses who fill nursing gaps as needed. Staff nurses have priority over traveling nurses, who have priority over agency nurses, so the night shift has a higher proportion of traveling and agency nurses.

Today, as the Blizzard of the Century shuts down Chicago, the nurses are preparing to be hospital-bound for a day or two or three, working even longer shifts to make up for the staff that can't make it to the hospital. And they seem pretty upbeat about it— this is what has to be done to take care of patients, so that's what they'll do. (I can hear the wind howling outside, and the building is creaking under the force of the wind.)

= = =

The level of nursing care has been so good that the one exception took me by surprise. She was an older nurse, a new face (to me), and she came into my room as the evening shift was starting, to introduce herself. Unlike any of the other nurses, she was wearing a yellow isolation gown. I knew that some patients were so vulnerable that anyone entering their rooms needed to wear these gowns, and my first thought was that I had entered that category. No, she reassured me, she just liked to be extra careful. That works for me!

A little later, she came in to disconnect me from Ivy so that I could take a shower. (We are pretty much hooked up 24/7 again, since I started a course of antibiotics last week on Fever/Vomit Day.) Besides disconnecting, preparing for a shower also involves putting the three lumens of my Hickman Triple Lumen into a plastic bag and then taping the bag over the dressing that covers the entry point into my chest. She didn't seem clear on the process, but I walked her through it. When she was done, I realized she hadn't worn gloves, and I had a feeling that nurses always wore gloves when working with my IV lines. Maybe it wasn't as important when disconnecting...

The Hickman Triple Lumen, bagged for a shower.

After my shower, I called her back to reconnect me. I was relieved to see she had gloves and wipes. That relief was short-lived. She had trouble opening the little packets containing the wipes, didn't fully unfold the wipes, dropped one of the wipes... I made her redo some of the disinfecting of the connectors, because the first pass seemed like going through the motions. I noticed that she was wearing large gloves even though she had small hands. This meant she had long flaps dangling off the ends of her fingers, which I thought might explain why she was having trouble holding things. I told her that if she needed smaller gloves, there were three boxes, in different sizes, mounted right inside my door. She explained that she wore the large gloves because her rheumatoid arthritis was so bad that she couldn't put on the gloves that fit. Arthritis! That explained a lot. Her hands were preventing her from doing her job, and I knew she (anyone) would have a hard time recognizing and accepting that.

As soon as she left, I hit the call button on my multipurpose remote control —call, light, TV on/off, volume, channel up/down, and caption and radio buttons that remain mysterious to me. "How can I help you?" "May I speak with the charge nurse?"

The charge nurse came right in. I recounted my experience so far with the nurse who had been assigned to me, how inconsistent that experience had been with the rest of my nursing care, and how uncomfortable it made me. I noticed that my voice was shaking. "Would you be more comfortable if someone else took care of you for the rest of the night?" Absolutely. (Though I'm nervous for any other patients in her care.) The charge nurse said she would take over my care for the night and talk with my (now) ex-nurse, who was an agency nurse and therefore not known to her. I learned the next day that this nurse will not be back.

I want to thank all the friends who have stressed the importance of looking out for yourself and dealing with anything that makes you uncomfortable about your care, as well as making sure I knew that my greatest risk right now is infection due to faulty care. Without that priming, I'm not sure I would have called out my nurse. Ideally, I would have stopped her the instant I saw her having trouble with her fine motor skills, but it took me a little while to process what was going on and stir myself to action. If there's a next time, I think I'll be ready.

Posted by Joseph Seeley at 6:16 PM

Wednesday, February 2, 2011

SnOMGeddon

Hospital operations have been pared down to essential staff. The nurses, doctors, techs, and others whose shifts were ending around 8:00 last night got to work extra-long shifts and then spend the night. The outpatient clinic is closed. My lunch, which normally I could expect to receive within 45 minutes of ordering, is coming up on 90 minutes.

At the storm's daytime snowfall peak, visibility was less than half a block.

There were times last night when the building was creaking, and the lights flickered from time to time. Fortunately, we never had to switch to backup power.

Not much to report on the medical front. I'm in the chemo recovery phase. Platelets need replenishing every couple of days. Hemoglobin is holding steady, so I haven't had a red blood transfusion in a while. (And I ran 3 miles yesterday, easily.) Neutrophils are close to zero. The neutrophils are the limiting factor with respect to leaving the hospital. Without them, I am close to defenseless against bacterial infection. Sometime in the next two or three weeks, the doctors expect them to rebound sufficiently. What happens after that is still unclear, in particular how quickly we move to the transplant phase. I hope to learn more this week, when the hospital and clinic are back up and running at full strength and can answer questions.

Update: As was true for many, the storm interfered with my workout plans. Stranded nurses used the lounge with the tread-mill as a dormitory, so I had to walk the corridor instead. 35 lengths per mile. 3 miles. Running on a treadmill never looked so good.

Posted by Joseph Seeley
at 11:56 AM

Friday, February 4, 2011

Care Package

One aspect of this illness that chokes me up is all the offers of support, both for me and for my family. Prayers, wishes, meals, cards, calls, books, e-mails ... It's beyond heartwarming.

Not pictured—cards, V-Jerky, gas cards to pay for Jan's trips up to Chicago, restaurant gift certificates to simplify some dinners, iTunes card...

Thank you!

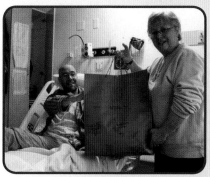

Jan delivered a large bag of goodies from my colleagues at Human Kinetics.

The pirate hat is popular with the staff on the corridor.

Curse you, Red Baron!

I wore this hat on my trip to the fifth floor of an adjacent hospital. It was a long trip, so the hat got a lot of exposure and a lot of smiles.

Scrabble Flash is great, although Paul consistently outscores me.

Reading material... The Avengers, The Nation, and MacLife. Who do they think I am?

Posted by Joseph Seeley at 6:11 PM

Sunday, February 6, 2011

Waiting

Early every morning, I have some blood drawn. If I'm lucky, this blood draw coincides with the 4:00 a.m. vitals check. The main information we're looking at is my blood counts. The chemotherapy knocked out the cells in the bone marrow that create new blood cells. Until I am able to create new cells in sufficient numbers, my counts will keep falling as older blood cells die.

When my platelet count falls below 10, I get a platelet transfusion. When my hemoglobin falls below 8, I get a red blood transfusion. My white blood cell count has been close to zero for weeks, but you generally don't transfuse white blood cells. (I think that's because they have such short life spans that it's not worthwhile.)

At some point, my marrow will start generating blood cells. The attending physician who was just in my room this morning expects this to happen around the end of this week. If that's the case, I could be heading home as soon as next weekend, or maybe a little after. Then I would continue to recover at home for a week or two before coming back here for the stem cell transplant. At this point, it's just a waiting game—blood draw in the early morning, report later in the morning, repeat the next day.

Speaking of transplants, my sister Mara is coming into town this Tuesday to begin her part in this adventure. She'll undergo some tests on Wednesday. Assuming those tests go well, she will start Neupogen injections to boost the number of stem cells in her blood, so that they can be harvested for me. That harvest is scheduled for February 21 or 22. Mara can expect some or all of the following side effects from taking Neupogen:

► redness, swelling, bruising, itching or a lump in the place where the medication was injected

► bone, joint, or muscle pain

► headache

► nosebleeds

Thanks, Mara!

Posted by Joseph Seeley at 8:40 AM

Monday, February 7, 2011

Waiting...

Nothing new on the blood counts... platelets at 10 this morning, so I got more platelets; hemoglobin at 8.6, so I didn't get red blood.

My sister Lauren started her visit last night. The staff had no trouble identifying her as my sister. Today, Lauren freed me from the confines of the hospital menu and brought me a black bean burger and a pecan roll from the Au Bon Pain downstairs. The pecan roll was followed shortly by a food coma.

Tomorrow, both Lauren and Mara will be in town. It's an infusion of sisters! I have it on good authority that Mara is bringing chocolate, along with her awesome stem cells.

Posted by Joseph Seeley at 7:13 PM

Tuesday, February 8, 2011

Transfusion of Sisterly Love

Counts

Platelets: 14 (after transfusion yesterday)

Hemoglobin: 8.1 (probably getting a transfusion tomorrow)

Neutrophils: too few to count

Monocytes: 4%, up from 1% the day before

This last number is a whiff of a glimmer of a hint of the start of the rebound. Maybe tomorrow I'll be up to a glimmer of a hint.

= = =

My sister Lauren has been visiting since Sunday evening, and she's leaving tomorrow. My sister Mara arrived this afternoon. Mara got a ride to the hospital from the airport from my cousin Jessica. Thanks, Jess!

Posted by Joseph Seeley at 7:43 PM

Mara, Lauren, and Jessica

Mara brought a few treats, including this essential accessory for my pirate cap.

Also, lots of chocolate, including a tiny chocolate mouse, perched on my hand.

Where did the mouse go?

Wednesday, February 9, 2011

Rash

Counts

Platelets: 8 (so I got a platelet transfusion)

Hemoglobin: 7.8 (so, as expected, I also got a blood transfusion today)

Neutrophils: still too few to count

Monocytes: 4%, same as the day before

= = =

Mara began her local participation in the transplant process. She met with the doctor who will manage her donation, and she took some tests: blood tests, EKG, chest x-ray. There will be more tests tomorrow, which is also Mara's birthday. Happy birthday, Mara!

Mara spent a good part of the afternoon at the Ronald McDonald House. The house is a place for families of child patients to stay close to their children, but guests of any patient in any University of Chicago hospital are welcome to use the daytime facilities —laundry, shower, kitchen, lounge. It's a wonderful place full of kind and helpful staff, and my dad and both sisters have all benefited from its offerings. They have all been so impressed that they want to put this Ronald McDonald House on their charity giving list.

To take advantage of having both sisters together, we had an early birthday with chocolate cupcakes. Don't be fooled by her youthful appearance and the number of candles. Mara is older than three.

Another benefit available to guests of patients is access to the campus athletic center for a discounted daily fee. For my sisters, this translates mainly into pool access, but they could use weights or the track or other fitness equipment if they wanted.

= = =

My medical excitement of the day is the appearance of a minor rash on my back. The daily posse wasn't sure what it was, so they requested a visit by a dermatologist, who also wasn't sure what it was, so she returned with a more experienced dermatologist. The older doctor thinks he knows what it is—a harmless, non-communicable virus—and they took a skin biopsy (nearly painless) for a test. I will get preliminary results tomorrow.

Posted by Joseph Seeley at 6:51 PM

Friday, February 11, 2011

A Sight for Sore Eyes

The posts are sparse these days because I have an eye infection that makes it uncomfortable to have my eyes open, and also makes it hard to read. The eye infection makes my eyes swollen and red, to the point that it makes other people's eyes water just to look at them. I will spare you pictures, at least for now.

There's still no movement on the blood counts. The doctor in charge of my treatment isn't worried. In fact, we might take advantage of the continuing low counts to go straight to transplant without the typical out-of-hospital interval between the remission phase and the transplant phase.

I'll write more when I can see more clearly.

Posted by Joseph Seeley at 4:09 PM

Saturday, February 12, 2011

The Eyes Have It

My eye infection (probably viral conjunctivitis) is slightly improved from yesterday. For example, the swelling below my eyes has gone down enough that the top of my cheek is no longer in my line of sight. Also, when I open my eyes after a nap, my cheek is no longer bathed in the liquid (tears, I assume) that used to pool under the eyelids. It is still more comfortable to have the eyes closed than open, but at least I can see relatively clearly.

The eyes themselves still look like a cartoon rendition of crazy-angry-sick-red eyes. The only part of my eye that is the normal color is the iris, though it looks odd surrounded by red. All those photos on which people use red-eye removal—maybe the red has to go somewhere, and I have a theory. I tried to find a picture online that captured my eyes at their worst—search for "conjunctivitis images" sometime when you haven't eaten recently—but none captured the swollen redness I managed.

Because of the infection, I have been cast out of the corridor I was on. Many of the patients there have received a stem cell transplant and are extremely vulnerable to infection. So I posed too much of a risk to them.

This is the beginning of the eye infection, before the eyeballs themselves swelled and turned a more hideous red, and before the face around the eyes swelled my eyes shut, making it impossible to take a picture.

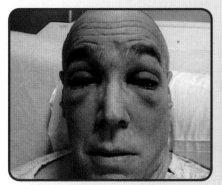 

Gradually, my eyelids and my face above the cheekbones began to swell. Later, Jan told me this look scared her the most.

Eventually, the swelling went down and I was left with these bruises. "You should see the other guy." Except you couldn't, because he was microscopic. But he sure packed a punch.

I tried various remedies. Unfortunately, the salad often arrived with only one cucumber slice.

This means I have lost access to the treadmill, which is quite a loss. Today I was back to walking the corridor (35 lengths to the mile). Disappointing, but I get it. When I am back on that floor as a transplant patient, I'll appreciate the precautions they take. The one advantage is that my room is a little larger.

Blood counts still haven't moved. Again, that's not necessarily bad—it may just mean that we move the transplant date up. I'm probably going to have a bone marrow biopsy on Monday to see if anything is going on inside the marrow that just hasn't yet shown up in the blood.

Posted by Joseph Seeley at 4:49 PM

Valentine's Day

On the positive side, I got to spend a good portion of this Valentine's Day with my sweetie. (And by that I mean Jan, in case anyone hasn't been staying current.) And I got in a walk and a shower.

On the negative side, I am a bag of woes:

1. Still no movement on the blood counts.

2. The whites of my eyes are still crimson (perhaps in honor of Valentine's Day). The swelling is gone, though there is still some irritation and blurry vision. Over the next few weeks, the "whites" of my eyes will transition from red to dark red to brown to yellow to white. I need to get some sunglasses. The swelling around my eyes has gone down, but I'm now sporting a couple of black eyes. As the dermatologist (see woe number 4 below) said, "How does the other guy look?"

3. I am usually intensely congested in the nose. The post-nasal drip is more like a flow, which is disgusting enough on its own. It also interferes with my breathing, which interferes with my sleeping. Occasionally, it leads to coughing, which occasionally leads to gagging.

4. This morning we noticed a couple of new dime-sized rashes on my lower legs. Dermatologists took a look, and then took a biopsy. Didn't seem concerned, but they want to figure out what it is.

5. I've got a sore spot in my gum.

6. I have some kind of infection on the tip of my left middle finger. The doctors have been monitoring it for a couple of weeks now, but for the first time it is painful to the touch, so it is probably going to merit closer scrutiny.

7. My appetite is down. I partially blame the food, which, to put it charitably, is not nearly as good as they think it is. But there's clearly more than that at work, since I have made it only halfway through the first of several delicious chocolate bars that Mara brought me almost a week ago. Normally, I could happily eat a bar a day.

Other than that, best Valentine's Day ever!

Posted by Joseph Seeley at 6:08 PM

It Never Always Gets Worse

My friend Jim Yost told me about a mantra that ultrarunners tell themselves. Ultrarunners do crazy things like run 100 miles through mountains and deserts, or run for six days straight. As you might imagine, these runners go through some very rough, dark patches. The mantra Jim told me was, "It never always gets worse." So, even if it just keeps getting harder and more painful through miles 60, 70, 80, eventually you reach a point where it no longer gets worse, and maybe it even gets a little better.

That mantra has been working for me lately. I may not feel good on Thursday, and Friday might be worse than Thursday, and so on, and so on. But I know that someday will be better than the day before. Like today! Appetite is better, eyes are ugly but functional, post-nasal flow is down to a post-nasal drip, and I had my first non-feverish reading in days.

My reward for feeling better is another bone marrow biopsy and a batch of CT and x-ray scans, checking out my sinuses, teeth, and lungs. In part, the scans are to look for a fever explanation, but they also provide baseline measures for evaluating my post-transplant. The biopsy will help them decide whether to recommend going straight to transplant or to go with the more typical schedule of leaving the hospital for a week or two before getting the transplant.

The biopsy already happened. It was pretty much like last time, but it took a lot longer. The doctor got a great workout. I got another pain in the butt. (Hip, really, but that doesn't sound as good.) I'm about to be turned over to Transport to get some CT scans. If you don't hear from me in a day, tell them to search the basement for a guy wearing a pirate cap.

Posted by Joseph Seeley at 12:03 PM

The Return of Transport

Blood counts: no news is no news—still not going anywhere. Expecting news from the marrow biopsy tomorrow.

Mile 1—15:02

Mile 2—14:39 (negative splits!)

= = =

[This is not my first encounter with Transport since my memorable introduction to their ways, and in a few follow-up posts I want to write about some of my (also memorable) other trips. But those can wait, and this is current.]

On Tuesday, I had a bunch of tests scheduled for the afternoon. Which means, in hospital time, sometime before midnight.

First was the bone marrow biopsy at noon, to be followed shortly by CT scans of chest and sinuses, to be followed by x-rays of my teeth. All but the biopsy were to look for possible explanations for my fevers and also make sure I am fit for transplant in case we go with the more condensed schedule.

The bone marrow biopsy was done at 12:50. It didn't make sense to order lunch, since CT scans were imminent, so I snacked from my stash, recently enhanced with treats from Great Harvest. (Thanks, Lisa!)

A scant two hours later, Transport arrived to take me down to CT. She had a rolling gurney, so instead of wheeling with my IV pole, she moved my one active pump from the pole to the gurney. Off we went to CT. I waited a while in the CT reception area, and then the tech came for me.

The CT scanner is a favorite of mine. It's a big off-white donut surrounding a sliding bed. Once you're on the bed, the machinery inside the donut starts spinning, and you hear this low whirring that rises in pitch as the machine speeds up. Through a clear window running around the inner waist of the donut, you can see the innards spinning faster and faster around you. Then a robotic female voice tells you to breathe in and hold your breath, and you feel like you're about to be launched through a 1950s vision of twenty-first century teleportation technology. Who knows where you'll end up, or if you'll arrive in one piece?

So far, I have always ended up roughly back where I started.

Then it was off to the CT reception area to wait for Transport. The nurse made a phone call that prioritized me. I thought she was just being nice, but then I found out that patients with certain vulnerabilities (like my inability to fight bacteria) get rushed back to their rooms as soon as possible, to minimize their exposure to dangerous hospital air.

My pump started beeping. After a few failed attempts to solve the problem by adjusting the settings and maybe some other things, the nurse solved the problem by turning off the pump. This did not disturb me as much as it might have, since it was just a very slow saline drip. Then, the nurse wheeled me out into the hall where I joined a few other patients, a little after 4:00. This felt familiar.

One man was dressed in street clothes, and he was agitated because they hadn't taken him in for his 3:00 scan, and now it was after 4:00, and he thought he had been forgotten. Outsiders and their sense of time... so cute!

The other man was in a wheelchair and wearing a gown—an insider. We talked. He said he thought that he had been there for a couple of hours waiting for his ride back to his room, though he couldn't be sure. I told him my Transport story (very abridged). He was scared that he had been disconnected from his pumps two hours ago for a "short" trip to CT and who knows what was or wasn't happening inside his body that should or should not be happening because of that.

I felt terrible.

Then Transport showed up. Yay! This poor man could finally get back to his room and some peace of mind. But, no. Transport was here for the prioritized me. "Can you take him first?" "No, I got your name."

I felt worse.

As Transport wheeled me away, I hollered, "Somebody get this man back to his room!" Like that would help, but it was all I could think of.

I complained to my transporter about how people sometimes get left for way too long. She agreed that it happened, but I didn't get the feeling she felt it was a problem.

Back at my room, my transporter moved the pump from the bed to my IV pole, and I'm thinking that's it for the day, it being so close to suppertime. Familiar concepts of time die hard.

I went to plug my IV pole back into the wall, but I could not. The pump had been reattached in a way that left only a few feet of power cord free, which was barely enough to reach the outlet and far short of the amount of leash I need. I summoned help. The nurse took a long, bewildered, disgusted look at the vertical tangle of power cords, pumps, and tubing, and then started dismantling a good portion of it. It took her about 10 minutes to get it the way she wanted it, which was much neater than it was when I left the room, but that's kind of how she is. Which I appreciate in a nurse.

Not too long after the nurse left, I had a visitor: the Patient Transportation Manager.

(to be continued)

Posted by Joseph Seeley at 7:41 PM

The Return of Transport (cont.)

The manager had heard about my most recent experience, presumably from my nurse, and wanted to hear about it from me. I told her about the transfer of the pump, the ride down, the reasonable wait for me, the unreasonable wait for Wheelchair Guy, and the mismanaged return of the pump.

She asked me about whether a line had been nearly pulled out, which made me wonder what the nurse had told her. I assured her that my line had not come close to being ripped out of my chest, and that my personal transport experience had been good except for the pump at the end. (I later learned that she and the nurse both understood the problem to be that the pump end of a line had been almost detached from the pump.)

I shifted to the bigger and widely acknowledged problem, which I had personally experienced early in my stay: patients often wait too long to get back to their room. We're sick, we're scared, we have no idea how long we're going to wait, we worry that we have slipped through the cracks—leaving us in a corridor or waiting area puts a lot of stress on a body that already has too much.

The response was manager-speak: we hear you, bear with us, we're working on it, we have our good days and bad days, she was very sorry for my experience. She left me her name and number, in case I wanted to talk again.

It was now close to dinnertime, so I figured the teeth x-ray had been pushed to Wednesday. I had dinner. I talked to family on the phone. I had a great walk, right at the change of shift, so all the nurses and assistants were out in the halls preparing their carts. It's crowded, but they appreciate the effort I'm making. They start giving each other grief about how they should be able to walk a mile if Mr. Seeley can walk two. "Without hemoglobin," I remind them (not technically true).

Back to my room, relax, talk to Jan, getting ready for bed...

[*Knock on the door*]

"Transport here to take you to x-ray."

At 10:15?! (Oh, right. Hospital time.)

Anyway, best transport yet. Taken to x-ray, transporter waited while I had my procedure, and I was back to my room by 10:45.

Postscript: Just talked with the manager. The target maximum wait time is 2 hours.

Posted by Joseph Seeley at 2:51 PM

An Incredible Tease

Counts: We don't even talk about counts anymore when the doctors come around. Too little going on in the counts, and too much going on elsewhere.

Mile 1—14:33
Mile 2—14:39

As I walk toward the nighttime windows at the west end of the corridor, I am walking toward my own reflection coming at me, so I visually feel like I'm striding along at a superhuman sub-7:30 pace. Right near the end, the lighting is such that I become silhouetted. With my bald head, yellow smock, blue gloves, and (I know) bright red eyes, I am a powerful and terrifying figure who Will. Not. Lose. At least in my own mind. Which is where it matters.

Not negative splits tonight, though they would have been had I not decided to slow down as a precaution. The elevated pulse was hurting the site of Wednesday night's Midnight Surprise Emergency Oral Surgery, so I backed down to a pace that didn't hurt the surgery site.

The Midnight What?!, I can hear you asking.

Oh, that casual aside only scratches the surface of what has gone on the last couple of days, which I wanted to record more promptly but was unable to make the time for. And not for you, but for myself. I want to get as much of it down as I can, but I know rest comes first. I'll get to it.

And so ends the incredible tease.

Current status: Feeling good. Surgery appears to have been successful. Mara has started her injections and cells will be harvested Monday. Still no decision on when it will be best to transplant.

You've missed a lot, but it's not clear anything significant has changed.

Posted by Joseph Seeley at 8:05 PM

Friday, February 18, 2011

If the Cancer Doesn't Kill You...

It's taken me over a month to realize it—I've had a few distractions—but it is challenging to order a single day's worth of nutritious meals off of the menu, let alone enough meals to get a patient through an extended stay like my own. By nutritious, I mean meals that follow current dietary guidelines.

I can't find the menu right now, but I believe the only whole grain sources on the menu are Cheerios, Bran Flakes, oatmeal, apple bran muffins, and whole wheat bread. Some of these are only nominal whole grain sources.

The only significant non-animal protein sources are (highly sweetened) soy milk, (white) rice and beans, a soy-based fake chicken patty, and meatless chili. (For the chili and the beans, you would need to also order corn.) If you eat eggs and dairy, there are milk, cheese, cottage cheese, yogurt, and eggs.

I eat everything, so I don't have ethical or moral problems with my food choices here. However, I believe the menu fails to support current nutritional advice. Apparently, the menu is far better than it was a few years ago, which is disturbing to contemplate. My guess is that they increased the number of lean meat choices, most of which are decent or better—grilled chicken, baked fish, roast pork, roast turkey. The meatloaf is unreliable—the first time I tried it, moist and tasty. The last time, and it will be the last time—grey and gristly.

Personally, I have been constipated most of my time here, despite eating fruit and/or vegetables at every meal, and despite a steady dose of stool softeners.

I'm sure it's the lack of fiber, at least relative to what I typically eat. Perhaps it was coincidental, but my first normal bowel movement in a long time came the day after my mom brought me some lentil soup from outside. It is crazy to constipate patients with your menu and then prescribe stool softeners (or laxatives) to fix the problem you created.

I spoke with an unsympathetic dietitian yesterday about the situation. First, she pointed out that Nutrition and Food Service are completely separate departments and have no interaction. (Brilliant!) She argued that most patients need as much protein as possible, so that's why there are so many meat choices and so few non-meat choices. Also, they get very few complaints about the food, and they have to serve what people like. It's also true that most patients are not in the hospital as long as I have been and will be, so they aren't going to be as bothered by limited choices. And lots of people in this country are obviously happy with salty, low-quality meat- and starch-heavy meals, or Bob Evans and Denny's would go out of business. But I would still expect a hospital to at least make it possible to order meals that comply with current nutritional recommendations and maybe even use hospitalization as an opportunity to help people consider some healthier food choices for the long term.

I hear I'm getting a visit from the Food Service side today. I will try to be tactful.

Posted by Joseph Seeley at 6:31 AM

Saturday, February 19, 2011

But Wait. There's More!

Host: Well, Joe, let's review what you have won so far: a stay (of indeterminate length) at the Bernard Mitchell Resort, hot and sweaty nights (but not the good kind), interrupted sleep, chemotherapy, mouth sores, rashes, hair loss, weight loss, gagging, 4 a.m. bloodlettings, guided tours (of indeterminate length) of the medical center, and unlimited meals from a very limited menu.

But now you have *also* won...

....a new MONIA!!

[*Audience applauds madly.*]

Joe (to himself): This is the worst game show concept ever.

= = =

Tuesday afternoon...

I had sinus and chest CT scans mid-afternoon, trying to identify an explanation for my persistent fever. Later in the afternoon, one of my doctors comes in, without her usual smile. "I'm sorry. You have pneumonia."

Pneumonia is a terrifying prospect for a patient with a compromised immune system. It can get out of control quickly, and it can kill you. Every day, multiple times a day, doctors and nurses check my breathing with their stethoscopes. It's always clear. Patients are encouraged to breathe deeply and to cough, both ways of making your lungs a less hospitable place for pneumonia.

I was surprised. I have had pneumonia, and it knocked me out. Trouble breathing, incredible muscle aches. I had none of those symptoms. I think, because my immune system is currently ineffective, I can't mount the inflammatory response that produces the typical symptoms.

The plan is to adjust medications and monitor. The good news is I'm already receiving the kinds of medications I would be put on, so in effect we have already been treating it. If it's viral, we just have to wait it out.

I'm finally feeling well enough to walk. After dinner, I put on my smock, gloves, and mask. I'm a little unsteady standing up, and I feel weak.

When I begin the walk, I am moving slowly. I am lightheaded. I feel like a sick person. And a scared person. And I'm angry at this stream of illnesses and conditions. Walking is my way to fight back. As I'm strolling, then walking, then striding up and down the hall, I have this refrain going through my mind, one word per step:

I will
beat you
I will
beat you
I will
beat you
I will
beat you
I will
beat you

The longer I walk, the stronger I feel. By the end of the walk, I feel practically normal. I have had runs that left me feeling good, but I have never had one that took me from feeling sick to feeling healthy.

Posted by Joseph Seeley at 10:35 AM

No News IS Good News

When I don't make a blog post for the day, that has typically meant things were not going well. In those cases, no news had meant bad news.

Today, there is no significant news to report, which is good news. I enjoy uneventful days.

Having been freed yesterday afternoon from the contact restrictions that confined me to the corridor and, when out of the room, to a mask, smock over my gown, and gloves, I am back to running (walking) the larger sixth-floor maze. Last night, I covered roughly 2 miles (based on time).

Tonight, I used what I knew of my walking pace to determine a half-mile course through the non-patient part of the sixth floor. My first attempt was about 30 seconds short, so I added a leg down a dead-end corridor. The second pass came out just about right. Then I jogged the third lap and walked the fourth.

Posted by Joseph Seeley at 7:58 PM

Sunday, February 20, 2011

Whipsaw Days (Part 1)

[*Wednesday morning, February 16*]

Tuesday ended with a diagnosis of pneumonia. Wednesday morning, I get to see pictures. (There's an app for that!) The good news was that its shape suggested that it was a fungal pneumonia, which is generally not as aggressive as bacterial. I mention the sore spot on my gum, which they look at. "We'll keep an eye on that."

Mom comes! She's in town to see her brother Fred, in his final days, but also to see me.

The Posse comes in. No news. "Any pain?" "Well, I have this sore spot on my gum." Mouth sores are common with chemotherapy, so they look but are not concerned.

Lunch, including lentil soup my mom brings up from the Au Bon Pain downstairs. I am about 10 bites into the soup when there is a knock on the door.

In comes a nurse from ENT (eye nose throat), wheeling a tall cart with tubes, drawers, and a monitor. *Imagine a movie in which the hero has been captured and is being held in a room. The door opens, and in comes a new character wheeling a cart. You don't even have to see the contents of the cart to know what's coming—torture.* It's kind of like that in the hospital room. When an unfamiliar face comes to your room with a large toolbox, there will be procedures.

The nurse explains that the CT scans showed lots of crud in my sinuses. Could be no big deal, could be a big problem; residue from chronic sinusitis, or a sign of an active infection. For the first day in many, my nasal passages are completely clear.

I abandon my lunch, get onto my bed, and submit to a very close, detailed scoping tour of my nasal passages. First, the nurse sprays a couple of numbing agents up each nostril. Then, she sticks a flexible scope up one nostril and in much farther than I thought one could go. There are multiple cavities to explore, on each side. I could watch on the monitor, but I go with the ever-popular if-I-can't-see-it-maybe-it's-not-really-happening strategy. The nurse is looking for dark crusty stuff in particular, which if found could be very serious.

My mom, however, has a front-row seat and, with less personal involvement, is able to watch. She says the insides of my nasal cavities look amazingly clean and empty. (Thanks, Mom!) Fortunately, the nurse confirms that this is not just the biased opinion of a loving mother—no dark crusty stuff, barely enough mucus to take a sample. All clear on the sinus front.

Back to lunch and just some more hanging out with my mom, relieved that the pneumonia didn't look serious and that my sinuses did not appear to be harboring any killer organisms.

(See Part 2 on pages 49–50.)

Posted by Joseph Seeley at 8:24 PM

Moving Day

Now that I am not considered a threat to the rest of the patients on the leukemia wing, they want to move me back. In fact, last night, at around 9:45 they wanted to move me some time that night. I persuaded them that me sleeping was more important than me getting into a new room on Saturday night rather than Sunday morning.

Sunday brought a lot of visitors—cousins Mindy, Paula, and Jana; my mom; Mara; Jan; and Paul. Not all at once, but there was some overlap. I am now in position to provide my own whole grains and fibers.

A little before noon, my nurse came to tell me I would be moving soon. I had been talking with anyone who would listen about my strong desire to get one of the bigger rooms on the floor. I had been in a regular room and in a small one, and the small was pretty cramped, especially with a visitor. This floor only has large and small, and I wanted to hold out for a large one, given the time I had already served in the small one, plus the length of my stay so far and yet to come. The nurse tells me I am getting one of the large rooms.

With the help of family, I pack up all my stuff and we waited. Around 3:00, someone came by with a wheelchair (to carry stuff, not me). We parade off of South and down the hall to North. Going down the hall. Rolling and parading into my new SMALL room! I stamp my feet, hold my breath, explain how special I am, and get the person in charge to agree (with only a little eye-rolling) to put me in one of the larger rooms. Fortunately, one is coming available within the hour. My nurse who had told me I was getting a larger room stopped by, and she was not happy to hear about the attempted room switcheroo. "I am going to speak with someone about that."

Since my now ex-new room is too small to host the number of visitors I had, we hang out in the lounge with the exercise equipment. We keep getting updates on the room—it's empty, we've ordered a cleaning STAT, we're still waiting for the cleaners, the cleaners are in there, it's almost ready.

Around 5:30, I get to move in. The room feels twice as large as the one they were prepared to move me into. It's fantastic.

Posted by Joseph Seeley at 8:57 PM

D-Day (Sort of)

Today is Donation Day for Mara. She just sent me an e-mail from the clinic next door saying it is going well and she is feeling good. Based on the pace of collection, she'll go back in tomorrow to finish providing the number of cells we want.

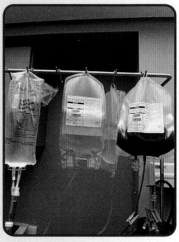

Mara's stem cells

My own D-Day—when Mara's forces storm onto the hopefully deserted beaches inside my marrow—is undecided.

There are tradeoffs between proceeding immediately with the transplant and waiting. I am still recovering from several infections, and you want to go into transplant with as few infections as possible. My neutrophils are finally showing some signs of recovery, which increases my ability to take care of the infections I do have. The last four days of absolute neutrophil count have been 40, 40, 60, 100. They were showing glimmers more than a week ago, but then the infections shifted my body's energies. So, the longer we wait, the more vanquished my current infections will be. On the other hand, the longer we wait, the more opportunity there is for another infection to take advantage of my weakened immune system.

To try to move things along, I am going to start my own course of Neupogen —the drug Mara took to boost stem cell production—tonight. If I'm lucky, I'll experience the bone pain that means I have so many stem cells in my marrow that they are bursting.

Update: Mara stopped by. She's feeling tired, but otherwise OK after six hours tethered to the harvesting contraption. She is glad she didn't have to earn her Bedpan Badge.

Posted by Joseph Seeley at 2:02 PM

Whipsaw Days (Part 2)

(See Part 1 on pages 45–46.)

[Wednesday afternoon, February 16]

In the early afternoon, a doctor from ENT (~~eye~~ ear nose throat) comes by to look at the gum sore. She takes a full history—from a feeling five days before that I had burned the roof of my mouth on hot cocoa (completely plausible) through the current "hot spot" on the tongue side of the upper left set of teeth, about half-way back. She looks at it, says it's probably fine, but she will return with a more senior doctor to check it out.

Relief. It's probably fine.

A doctor from ID (infectious diseases) comes by to confirm that my pneumonia is almost certainly fungal. There is no way to be absolutely sure without surgically taking a sample of the lung tissue, and there is no way to do that safely in my condition, so we're going to go with how it looks on the CT scan. Fungal pneumonia is generally less worrisome than bacterial, and does not inherently pose an obstacle to a transplant. It does take a long time to clear up.

More relief. I don't have a pneumonia that's going to run wild.

The first ENT doctor returns with her more senior colleague. He approaches with a swab and asks me to open my mouth.

"I'm just going to take a look..."

"OW!!!"

"... and poke at it."

All that expensive and extensive schooling, yet the doctor has trouble with the basic temporal sequencing concept of Before. *Before* you do something to a patient, tell him what and why. If it's going to hurt, tell him how much and how long. BEFORE. Perhaps some remedial training from Bert and Ernie would be helpful.

Now he's casting about the room for "any sharp object I can use to take a piece." Happily (?), the other doctor has some sterile scissors in her pocket. He approaches with the scissors, but I'm ready this time.

"Stop. What are you going to do?"

"I'm going to take a small piece of tissue from the infected site so that we can analyze it more closely."

"How much is it going to hurt?"

"About as much as when I poked it."

I can handle that—after all, I just did. And, perhaps because I know what's coming, it hurts less.

His preliminary conclusion: it's probably nothing, maybe some gingivitis from overly aggressive tooth brushing. But there is a dangerous fungus that spreads very rapidly that he needs to rule out. He says he is "99.9% certain" it is not that, but he will not sleep unless he has ruled it out completely through a culture.

I have a relaxed, though not a very good dinner. I have pneumonia, but it's not a bad one. I have a gum sore, but it's probably no big deal. I play some online Scrabble, answer some e-mail, go for a walk, have a shower, get ready for bed.

There is a knock on the door.

Posted by Joseph Seeley at 4:38 PM

Tuesday, February 22, 2011

Whipsaw Days (Part 3)

First, a riddle that arrived on a postcard from my brother who is spending the year in Prague with his family. (Lots of wonderful writing and photos on their blog, written by my sister-in-law Kate.) The riddle itself is from my eight-year-old nephew Ben.

Q: Why can't you hear a pterodactyl go to the bathroom? (Answer at the bottom of the post.)

= = =

(See Part 1 on pages 45–46 and Part 2 on pages 49–50.)

[*Wednesday night, February 16*]

There is a knock on the door. It's one of the ENT doctors. I need to have surgery. Tomorrow? No, right now. That explains the gurney outside my door.

The biopsy they took from my mouth in the afternoon did indicate that there was a fungus involved. Too soon to know what kind of fungus, but there is one in particular that they can take no chances with, the one that keeps the ENT doctors up at night until they rule it out or eradicate it. She describes it as "very aggressive." I later learn that this means "can kill you in a day," but "very aggressive" provides plenty of dark room for the imagination.

The doctor offers to speak with my wife. I think it's better if Jan hears it from me, so I put off the call while I learn more. The plan is to cut away the inflamed tissue on my upper palate to see how much fungus is hiding underneath it. They can't say how much tissue they will need to remove or how long the procedure will take. If the fungus appears to be contained within the inflamed tissue, then they're done once that tissue is excised. If it has spread deeper into the palate, they will remove more. If it has spread to the teeth, they will remove teeth. If to the jaw, remove part of the jaw. (There would be reconstructive surgery later to replace whatever gets removed.)

Since they don't know how much they're going to do until they start doing it, they can't say how long it will take. I might be back up in my room by 3 a.m., I might be recovering in the intensive care unit at 8 a.m., I might still be in the operating room at 8 a.m. It all depends on what they find when they make their first cuts and how far they have to go to feel that they have gotten it all.

Time to call Jan to let her know that I may not be in a position to give her the daily morning "I'm awake" text/call, and why. She is on my phone's speaker as I review the plan, with the doctor present. As I start getting to the removal of teeth, Jan indicates she's heard enough detail. Jan gets a phone number for being able to contact the ENT team, and they get her number in case they need to contact her.

I say good night to Jan, but a far different good night than she deserves on her birthday. (Sorry, Jan.) I know she's not going to sleep tonight.

I'm sitting on the edge of my bed, putting on my slippers, head bowed, shoulders rhythmically convulsing.

"I know," says the doctor sympathetically, "it's a lot to take in all at once."

But I'm not crying. I'm laughing (ruefully) at the absurd perfection of this ending to the day, with all its ups and downs. *Of course* we needed one more twist to make the day complete.

Transport has been waiting outside the room, patiently. He greets me by name with a Mexican accent and a smile. I prepare my room for this unexpected absence: put away attractive small items, lock up laptop. Once I'm on the gurney, he positions himself so he can talk with me, which he does. Talks about how much he loves his job, loves learning about the patients he moves, likes to check in on them after their procedures. He was happy that he was stuck at the hospital for 5 days during the blizzard, that's how much he loves his job. He is from Acapulco. I tell him I have visited Acapulco, "y yo vivía en México cuando yo tenía quince años." "Ah, we must talk of Mexico and Acapulco. Good luck, Mr. Seeley, and I will see you again." That is how Transport is supposed to work. For the duration of the trip, I feel less stress than I felt just before and much less than I am about to feel. He is a healer.

"Welcome to the OR Recovery Room."

"Oh, finished already? You guys are very good."

No, the recovery room is also where we prepare for the surgery.

There are some introductions, who's going to do what. A few minutes in they realize I'm under an isolation order, which means they all should have on an extra layer of stuff—gloves, masks, smocks—before I came in and potentially contaminated them. "Wasn't that information in the order?"

"There was no order." "How can there not be an order?" It's kind of too late, since I've already been wheeled in and some have already interacted with me, but they scramble to put on the gear. Not building confidence.

It feels like a hospital TV show cast—loose banter among staff. More serious than *Scrubs*, less intellectual than *House*.

"Is this your first surgery?"

"Yes."

(Someone yards away) "Vir-gin!"

I have received a bunch of platelets and blood already today, and I'm going to get more. My platelet counts have hovered around 10, and you want at least 50 to feel comfortable cutting someone open. I'm close, but more is coming.

A doctor tells me the side effects of a medication I'll be receiving: shakes, chills, sweats, kidney malfunction. Also, a risk of anesthesia so close to eating—unavoidable, since this is an emergency—is vomiting into your lungs and then contracting a deadly pneumonia. But they have a way to minimize the risk by pressing on the voice box as I'm going under, so I shouldn't be alarmed if I feel that happening. It sounds very uncomfortable, as I'm picturing that they are manually collapsing my voice box, but they demonstrate and I realize it's not something I need to worry about.

For the first time since my diagnosis, I have a Mortality Moment. They're going to be slicing open my head, from the inside of my mouth. The surgery could go wrong, and I could die. I could vomit into my lungs, and I could die. The surgery could fail to get all the fungus, and I could die. I might not leave the hospital alive. The OR might be the last thing I remember in my life.

But probably not, and the moment passes.

I sign a bunch of waivers. There's a lot of fancy words about risks and side effects, but it all boils down to, "Do you want to live?" "Yes."

Off we go to the OR. I am torn between wanting to see my surroundings, for documentation, and wanting to close my eyes and go to my happy place. Oh no! I haven't picked a happy place! I'm flipping through mental brochures at the Happy Place Travel Agency. In a hammock on a tropical beach. Floating in a magical cenote in the Yucatan peninsula. Basking on the rocks at the top of a New England mountain. Hurry! Pick one! The building is on fire and is about to collapse!

Not working!

I try a smiling Jan gazing lovingly down at me. It's corny, but there are pink and red valentines scattered behind her. It's powerful stuff, and it is briefly calming. I think, not only is she helping me now, but I'll be able to tell her afterward how gazing up at her sustained me through the surgery. "You're having surgery?! What are they doing to you?! Oh, God, please don't die!"

NOT WORKING!

I have no idea where it comes from, but now I see what I would see if I were riding a bumblebee circling a foot or two over Moroccan mosaics. Rhythmic, sinuous, infinite—not bad for a last-minute happy place entry.

But I'm still feeling those side effects they mentioned: shakes, chills, sweats, teeth chattering.

"So, that medication with the side effects you were telling me about? Have we started it?"

"No, that medication starts after the procedure."

"Oh, so these symptoms are just from fear. Thanks."

"Don't worry, we have something for that."

The last thing I remember hearing is, "At least one of those teeth is coming out."

Fade to black.

= = =

Q: Why can't you hear a pterodactyl go to the bathroom?

A: Because the "p" is silent.

Posted by Joseph Seeley at 9:02 PM

Wednesday, February 23, 2011

Whipsaw Days (Part 4)

(See Part 1 on pages 45–46, Part 2 on pages 49–50, and Part 3 on pages 50–54.)

[*Sometime in the very early morning, Thursday, February 17.*]

I remember nothing of the operation. (Thanks, anesthesiologist!) The first thing I remember, I'm being wheeled to OR recovery. I've had anesthesia before, and I know that, much to Jan's amusement, I keep asking the same questions over and over. I try to show my medical sophistication by asking, "Have I been asking a lot of questions over and over?" "Yes," replies the nearest person. "Including that one. By the way, your limit is six." I don't know what they do when you reach the limit.

While I'm in this forgetful state, they're telling me (I later confirm) that they were able to get all the fungus without getting as far as the teeth. They need to check what they took to make sure there are clean margins—the outer edges of the excision show no trace of fungus, indicating that it is entirely contained in the removed tissue—but they are pretty sure they have succeeded. I have a small depression in the roof of my left palate, right by the teeth. If my palate were a fairway, it would be a sand trap up against the stone wall lining that side of the green.

It's the very early hours of Thursday morning. I'm going to be back in my bed by 3 a.m. Incredibly thirsty. Plastic oxygen mask on, which is hot and wet and uncomfortable. Mask comes off. I get to dab my tongue with wet sponge swabs, but not too many. I also get to figure out how to pee into a handheld urinal while sitting up on the gurney with my legs sticking forward, still not fully coherent. Amazed I don't make a mess.

Back up to my room. Some pain meds, some Ambien, hoping to sleep a little later than usual.

6:30, maybe 7:00, the Junior Posse comes in, somewhat flustered. They had been taken by surprise by the emergency surgery. (I know how they feel!) How was I feeling? Could they look? My mouth is a tourist attraction.

A little later ... Word from someone (ENT?) confirming that everything looks great—didn't see anything left behind during the operation, didn't see any fungus on the margin of the tissue removed. Relief.

Need some rest. Can't eat, because I don't know what I am allowed to eat with the recent remodeling of my mouth. Someone will find out.

Relief. Resting. Reporting to family. I feel like I have made it through every test.

In an hour or so, in comes the Senior Posse, with a bad vibe. "How do you feel?" "Apprehensive?" "That's appropriate, in these circumstances." The ENTs want to go back in on Friday. They are 99.9% sure they got it all, there is no evidence that they didn't get it all, but that remaining .1% that could quickly explode is going to keep gnawing at them. Until when, I wonder? Until the surgeons have gnawed off any teeth or bit of jawbone that could be harboring these terroristic molds and fungi? 100% solutions are generally bad ideas.

So, a return, non-emergency surgery is planned for Friday. Emotional low point of this Grand Life Detour, so far. The last surgery was scary, and the fact that they feel they need to go back is scary. I think I should talk to some supportive people, which inevitably will make me cry, but I'm also exhausted. Napping wins over crying.

Still no word on what I can eat. Haven't eaten since 5 p.m. yesterday. Finally someone tells me all I have to do is call Food Service, and they'll tell me what I can eat. The doctors communicate with Food Service, not with the nurses or patients. I'm on a soft food diet—applesauce, yogurt, gelatin, ice cream (mistake! the surgery site is very sensitive to heat and cold!).

A little later the ENT anaesthetist is in to talk about how it went last time, so they can adjust for tomorrow. She can't tell me what they're actually planning to do this time, and I emphasize that I want that information ahead of time. She'll see what she can do.

Followed immediately by ID Guy, talking about various scary fungi for a while before I realize he's delivering good news. I definitely don't have the Monster Fungus Mucormycosis, which terrifies the medical establishment and would justify a return visit to the OR. I probably have a more common and more easily managed aspergillus, or something like it, my medications have been changed to address this finding, and he's surprised that there is a follow-up surgery planned. I emphasize the importance of ID and ENT communicating with each other and with my main team, so we make sure the left hand is not exorcising a demon the right hand has proved does not exist. They will be talking, and I should hear from some doctors before the end of the day.

Sometime during the afternoon, during one of the doctor visits, my transport angel from last night pokes his head in to see how I'm doing, as he promised he would.

After 5, which in my mind is the end of the day, still no word. In hospital time, the end of the day may be closer to 11:59. I ask the nurse if she has heard anything, or if she sees anything on my schedule. No. Maybe it's not happening!

5:30, call the leukemia nurse from the clinic to ask for some communication, leave voicemail.

6:30, head leukemia nurse in the hospital checks in. I don't think she's an emissary, just seeing how I'm doing, but she does have information. Everybody's been talking. (Good!) We're not on a quest to find more hidden mucormycosis, because we know it's not that. ENT just likes to revisit their work, to make extra sure they were as excellent as they thought they were originally. It sounds like there's a low probability of more actual cutting, and there's definitely less risk from the anesthesia this time because we can plan for me to have an empty stomach. The nurse doesn't know if a decision has been made.

Dinner is something off the soft food menu—don't remember.

Around 10 (maybe earlier—still tired), go to bed. Still no surgery showing up on my chart. Hopeful relief. Fall asleep.

Midnight, vitals check, and word that I DO have surgery scheduled for tomorrow, but the time is not known. No drinking allowed starting now. I could get a 6:30 knock on the door, or it could be at 10:00. (More likely the latter, since this is a scheduled surgery.) "I'm going to need an Ambien."

The Ambien is not effective. I take advantage of being awake to take notes on the past crazy couple of days. I get a lot down. Eventually, I feel tired enough to sleep.

Friday, 4 a.m., vitals check, surgery is scheduled for 10:00 a.m. Not sleeping very well.

6:30 a.m., knock on the door. In comes the ENT team. They take a look at their handiwork inside my mouth, pronounce themselves satisfied, and say, "You don't need any more surgery."

After they leave the room, lying in my bed, I raise my hands over my head in the universal sign of celebration.

I Will

Beat You.

P.S. This is the last installment of Whipsaw Days. It's been a quiet ride since the pardon from follow-up surgery.

Posted by Joseph Seeley at 6:16 AM

A Happy Birthday

[*This post is going to be amended multiple times as I remember (or Jan reminds me of) gifts and kindnesses that I will surely forget to mention the first time through. It was an overwhelming (in a good way) and humbling outpouring of love and care.*]

The party started on Sunday, when Jan and Paul were visiting. They brought up a few items, some of which we opened then and some which we saved so I would have something to open on my birthday.

On Monday, Paul's best friend Andy came up with his mom Janelle. He had the day off from school, and he chose to use it supporting his friend and his friend's family. (Thanks, Andy!)

Tuesday, the day before my birthday, I got a visit from Shannon, a nurse in the neonatal unit here and the daughter of a colleague at HK. A card from the Zoll family, a card and gift card from the Finance department, and some excellent mint chocolates, which were delicious and are now gone.

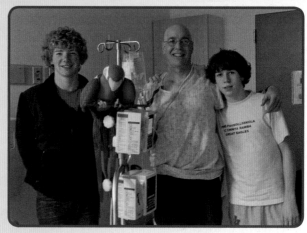

Andy, Joe, and Paul

Which brings me to today. Midnight vitals, "Happy Birthday, Mr. Seeley."

7 a.m., birthday greetings from Paul.

8 a.m., regular morning call from Jan.

"What would be the best birthday present?"

Hmmm. To magically not be sick would be great, but that's not in the cards.

"To not have anyone come at me with sharp objects?"

"OK. What else?"

"A surprise visitor?"

"Like who?"

"You." (You don't get to the twenty-fifth year of marriage without knowing the answer to that question.)

And in she walks, talking to me on the phone! Surprise!

Well, not entirely. She had guaranteed that the dirty running clothes she was taking away on Monday would be back by Wednesday, and we already knew from a previous shipment that UPS was not up to fulfilling that guarantee, so I knew *someone* was coming. And since I know her reasonably well, I figured Jan was a likely candidate, but I wasn't certain. Lucky me, I got my wish.

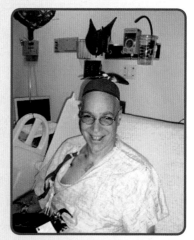

Jan came loaded with gifts from family and friends.

And there was lunch, courtesy of the Tech Group. The colors and lighting make the food look bland, but this Reuben sandwich, potato salad, coleslaw, and pickle

A propellor beanie to wear while doing website work.

A way to have a bad hair day,
even if I have no hair.

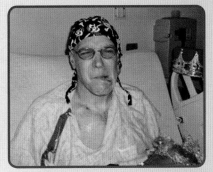

A pirate do-rag. I need to work
on my pirate face.

were delicious and was just what the doctor ordered, so to speak.

And cakes! One brought by Mom and Mara, one brought by Food Service.

I had a piece of cheesecake, my guests shared some pieces and took some when they left, I saved a piece for tomorrow, and nearly half of the cheesecake went to the nurses' station. Can't hurt!

Lunch courtesy of the Tech Group.

Not pictured: many cards and gift cards. Amazing homemade whole grain fig bars. A DVD of birthday greetings from HK colleagues. An oil change and tank of gas and new back wiper blade from Pro-Tech Motors.

All in all, a really, really great birthday. Thank you to all.

Note: When I have guests, I sit in the bed so they can use the chairs. And I always wear the hospital gown, because I can get a clean one whenever I want. But the combination makes me look more sickly than I feel.

Posted by Joseph Seeley at 3:47 PM

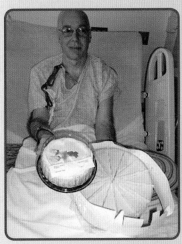

Hmmm. White cake from Food
Service or cheesecake from
The Cheesecake Factory?

Chocolate or Fungus?

This isn't a question about which I prefer.

I am a big mushroom fan—salads, omelets, soups, pizza—though I am not a mushroom connoisseur. I know the difference between a portobello and a shitake, but I have never gone out of my way to eat a porcini, oyster, chanterelle, or morel.

Still, as much as I like mushrooms, good chocolate, especially dark chocolate, is its own sanctified food group for me. (But please don't send me any more, at least not now. I have a hefty supply.) I am sure this is not a rare preference.

I look at mushrooms differently now. My fungal pneumonia and fungal oral infection have taken the "fun" out of fungus for me. Sure, some of them look cute and harmless and round and white there in the produce aisle, but other members of the family stalk hospitals looking for defenseless bodies to invade.

Which brings me to my tongue. The first time the ENT docs came to look at my gum sore, he recoiled a little when I stuck out my tongue.

"How long has your tongue looked like that?"

"Probably since I just finished a chocolate pudding."

He was OK with that, and proceeded with the investigation that eventually led to oral surgery. I took a picture, because I thought it was funny that it freaked him out a little. (He more than got revenge.)

Last night, at the end of a wonderful birthday, I had a couple of exquisite chocolates for dessert. (Thanks, Mara!)

When I was brushing my teeth a little later, I noticed that my tongue looked a lot like the picture above. Chocolate, I thought. I tried brushing my tongue— no change. The saline mouthwash I use had no effect. Upon closer inspection in the mirror, my tongue appeared to have a slightly spongy texture, but it was hard to say. The brown color was definitely *in* and not *on* the tongue.

I called the nurse to take a look, who put in a call to the night doctor, who wasn't sure what it was but prescribed an anti-fungal lozenge. Curse you, fiendish fungi!

I have to believe that this is a new development—that the initial brown tongue really was chocolate pudding, and that this current discoloration is something new. Doctors have been looking in my mouth several times a day over the last week, and surely they would have mentioned this discoloration.

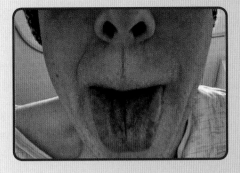

This morning, my tongue is still brown. It's clearly not a chocolate-coated tongue.

A quick Google tells me that Black Tongue is an unsightly (I'll say!) but harmless condition, sometimes caused by prolonged use of broad-spectrum antibiotics (which I am on). That's reassuring, but it's still gross.

Chocolate or fungus? In this case, probably neither, or maybe some of each.

Update: Apparently, I have had a brown tongue for at least a week. It's so common that nobody thought to mention it.

Posted by Joseph Seeley at 6:14 AM

The New New New New Plan

Once upon a time, the plan was induce remission, take a short break outside the hospital, and then return for a stem cell transplant. The break is good psychologically and physically. The physical part is that your own immune system can attack infections that may have taken advantage of its previously weakened state, providing a better starting point. The psychological advantages are obvious—being in a hospital is inherently stressful, even when nothing is going wrong.

I got half of the remission right—no detectable leukemia—but it's not remission unless the blood counts build back up. So a new plan was floated. It might make sense to go straight to transplant. As part of this plan, there was a potential plan to postpone Mara's donation by a couple of days so that my conditioning chemotherapy would end as her donation was ending and I could get fresh stem cells, not frozen.

Then the many doctors discussing my case decided that my infections argued against going straight to transplant, at least on a schedule tight enough to make it reasonable to extend Mara's schedule by a couple of days. So she was put back on her original schedule, and we're back to seeing if my counts start coming back once the infections are being managed.

This past Monday, the plan was to give me Neupogen for four days and see if that boosts my counts to leave-the-hospital levels. If not, go straight to transplant. If so, take a break. Decision to be made on Thursday.

On Tuesday, the doctors determine that they didn't get quite as many stem cells from Mara as they had hoped. Her age is a factor, as is the fact that I outweigh her by as much as I do. There's only so much she can give, and she gave it all. It's enough to do a transplant safely, but it might stretch out my recovery a little. This adds some weight to the take-a-break side of the scale. A break opens up the possibility of bringing Mara back for another donation round, after she recovers. A break, assuming my immune system is up to it, also gives my body a chance to keep beating down any infections I have, known and unknown. Decision day is still Thursday.

On Wednesday, the plan is to extend the Neupogen injections a full week and make a decision next Monday.

Today, the plan is to go straight to transplant. My counts are not moving as much as they hoped. I appear to have the current infections in check—several consecutive days without a fever, feeling good. Tomorrow, I start the conditioning round of chemotherapy. A week from Friday, transplant.

So that's The Plan. It is more firm than any previous plan, or choice of plans. It's basically back to Monday's plan, and we have arrived at Monday's plan's decision point.

I'm ready. I'm not worried about the psychological break I'm not going to get. I know what it's like to be at less than full psychological strength, and I'm far from there. I am strong right now. I'm a little concerned about the infections I'm clearing up, but I trust the doctors. Also, the longer we wait, especially in a hospital, the more likely I am to catch another infection. And, the sooner I get the transplant, the sooner I'm out of here.

Let's go!

Posted by Joseph Seeley at 3:23 PM

You Can't Unsalt Food

I know I don't know all the constraints the hospital Food Service operates under, and I know it can't cater to me. But I think there are a few simple changes that would be easy to implement, would raise the nutritional quality of the menu, and would be popular with enough patients to justify their addition.

Last week, I got a visit from Food Service—I think she was a manager. I don't know if it's because I have been asking twice daily for the Chipotle Black Bean Burrito (hidden on the gluten-free menu, for some reason), or if I was the target of a random sampling. (They do not have the burrito in stock, and I have promised to ask for it and make them check for it every day until it's in.)

I wanted to start with what was good about the menu—a decent variety of breakfast choices, a good selection of lean (meat and dairy) protein choices, a range of plain vegetables that are not overcooked, some fresh fruit. But the manager wanted to hear what I was unhappy about, so I told her what I would like to see.

1. Less salt. One of the reasons I have a hard time getting through meals is that they are too salty for my taste. I know many Americans are too fond of salt, so this high-salt diet may cater to the majority of patients. However, it is easy for patients to add salt to a dish if it isn't salty enough for them, but I can't unsalt a dish.

2. More whole grain fiber. The menu currently has Cheerios, Frosted Mini Wheats, granola, bran flakes, wheat bagel, whole wheat bread, and an apple bran muffin. These aren't bad options, but they are focused on breakfast, and some are only nominal sources of fiber. Consider adding: brown rice, multigrain wraps, multigrain chips.

3. More legumes. The menu currently has red beans and rice, and chili. (Both are too salty, of course.) Consider adding: baked beans, refried beans, bean burrito, black bean soup, lentil soup.

There is (theoretically) a bean burrito, but it's on the gluten-free menu that many patients (and some call-takers) don't realize is open to patients on a regular diet. Also, it has been out of stock since I started ordering it more than a week ago. This past Monday, I received a call back from a call-taker telling me the burritos would be in by Tuesday or Wednesday. As of Thursday night, still no burritos.

The manager also told me that there *are* baked beans on the menu. This is not true, if your definition of "on the menu" is "visible to a person looking at the menu." However, through some back-and-forth with one of the call-takers, I have determined that you can order "pork and beans," and you will receive what most of us would consider baked beans. So it's on the menu in the sense that you can order it if you know what to call it. It's a small side dish, so I have learned I should order two. There is also another hidden item, which the call-taker described as refried beans but turned out to be un-refried pinto beans in a tomato sauce. With a little ketchup and brown sugar, I made something close to baked beans. (There will be a later post containing the recipes I have come up with, using only items that I can order.)

Overall, my visitor from Food Service seemed interested in my feedback and open to suggestions. She took notes.

With the exception of the salt, I have been able to address my complaints by supplementing the Food Service offerings with outside food—bean and lentil soups, whole grain crackers, almond butter, Sun Chips, dried fruit, whole-grain cereals, homemade whole wheat fig bars (incredibly good). However, a patient should not have to go outside the hospital offerings to eat a healthy diet, so I'm hoping Food Service will make a few adjustments, someday.

Bon appetit!

Posted by Joseph Seeley at 6:23 AM

Visit From the President

Not that President, although that would be great. Anyone have some connections? I am in his hometown, after all. And I did vote for him, enthusiastically. And I do have some constructive suggestions. Of course.

No, I just had a good visit with the new president of the medical center that has been my home these last 6+ weeks.

I wrote her a welcome note, and urged her to consider non-medical dimensions (food service, patient transportation) in her stated goal of improving the patient experience.

She wrote back, and asked if she could come and talk with me about my observations and ideas. Of course!

It was a good talk. She asked about how I am doing, what I do for a living, and how my family is doing. And then we talked about the needs-improvement aspects of the patient experience, from my perspective.

She comes to this position from other hospitals that handle food and transportation better than they do here. So, not only does she know it can be better, but she knows specific ways that other hospitals have addressed these particular issues. Very encouraging!

It's also encouraging that the person at the very top, less than a week into a new job, values patient input enough to take time out of what has to be a very busy week to listen to a patient.

I hope to be out of here before the kinds of systemic changes required could be implemented, but I am optimistic that the full spectrum of patient care, and especially the non-medical but still health-related dimensions, is going to get better.

Posted by Joseph Seeley at 11:17 AM

Saturday, February 26, 2011

D-7

(FYI: The title read "D minus 7.")

Friday was D-7, which means next Friday is transplant day.

D-7 means a new set of helpful poisons start running through me, and I get a new team of in-patient doctors. I am now under the direct care of the transplant service. Same nurses, same great food.

(Note: I wrangled a not-on-the-menu bean and cheese tortilla out of Food Service last night, after getting bumped up a couple of levels in the call chain over my disappointment that we still don't have the Chipotle Black Bean Burrito, which is on the menu but perpetually out of stock. It was very good, and the manager personally delivered it. And left his card.)

My new chemo drugs...

Alemtuzumab (Campath) Possible side effects: itching, hives, swelling of face and hands, swelling or tingling in mouth or throat, chest tightness, trouble breathing; anxiety, restlessness, nervousness, trouble sleeping; change in quantity or frequency of urination; changes in vision; fast, pounding, or uneven heartbeat; fever, chills, cough, sore throat, body aches; lightheadedness, fainting; muscle pain, tenderness, weakness; numbness, tingling, or burning pain in arms, hands, legs, or feet; shortness of breath, cold sweat, bluish-colored skin; skin rash; sores or white patches on lips, mouth, throat; swelling of hands, ankles, feet; tremors; unusual bleeding or bruising; unusual tiredness or weakness; headache; loss of appetite; nausea, vomiting, diarrhea, stomach pain.

Campath is the only chemo drug I received on D-7, and the only side effect yesterday was a brief spell of chills.

Melphalan Possible side effects: itching, hives, swelling of face and hands, swelling or tingling in mouth or throat, chest tightness, trouble breathing; bloody or black, tarry stools; fast heartbeat; fever, chills, cough; lightheadedness, fainting; new lumps or growths under your skin; severe nausea and vomiting, seizure, or severe muscle stiffness; skin rash; sores or white patches on lips, mouth, throat; trouble breathing; unusual bleeding, bruising, or weakness; yellowing of your skin or the whites of your eyes.

Fludarabine Possible side effects: blood in your urine, pain in sides or joints; confusion, extreme tiredness, fainting, trouble seeing; cough, chest pain, trouble breathing; fever, chills, sore throat, other signs of infection; numbness, tingling, or burning pain in arms, hands, legs, or feet; skin rash; unusual bleeding, bruising, or weakness.

These drugs are so powerful, you don't even have to take them to feel some of their side effects. All you have to do is read about the side effects to lose your appetite, feel shortness of breath, or have a fast heartbeat. Don't worry. However, if reading the above causes tarry stools, please consult a doctor immediately.

D-7 brought my first visit with the transplant team of doctors. The attending physician gave me a lot of information. I'll have six days of chemo, on days D-7 to D-2. Most patients tolerate the chemo well, which means they do not experience that sickening list of side effects, or at least not much. On one of these days, I'll receive the one (I'm guessing Melphalan, from the listed side effects) that often causes mouth and throat sores. I've heard from other patients and from the attending that a six-hour course of oral cryotherapy (otherwise known as sucking on ice) is very effective at keeping this side effect at bay.

D-1 is a "rest" day in the sense that none of the chemo drugs are being administered. They're still coursing through your system and doing their work.

D Day, next Friday, is Transplant Day, sometimes referred to by patients as Second Birthday or ReBirthday.

Two birthdays in two weeks. How lucky is that?

Posted by Joseph Seeley at 5:01 AM

Recipes

Baked Beans

Order: 1 refried beans (they will be pinto beans in tomato sauce), 1-2 ketchup packets,
1 brown sugar, 1-2 pepper packets.

Add ketchup, sugar, and pepper to the beans, to taste. Mix.

Spicy Asian Noodles

Order: 1 plain spaghetti, 1 peanut butter, 1 soy sauce, 1 lemon juice, 1 honey, 2-3 hot sauce, 1 pepper packet, 1 scrambled egg, 1 broccoli, additional vegetables if desired, hot water, empty bowl.

With chicken and carrots.

Sauce: Put peanut butter in the bowl. Add soy sauce, 1/2 of the honey and 1 hot sauce. Stir and taste. Add honey and hot sauce to taste. Add hot water and stir until you reach the desired consistency.

Chop the scrambled egg. Put sauce and egg on the noodles. Mix. Add broccoli (and other vegetables, if desired) on top. Sprinkle with lemon juice and black pepper to taste.

Chicken, Bean, and Cheese Quesadillas

Order: grilled chicken breast, 2 pork and beans, 2 string cheese, 2 taco sauce, 2 corn or wheat tortillas, 1 sour cream (optional).

Slice the chicken into small strips. Shred the string cheese by hand. Cover half of each tortilla with chicken, beans, cheese, and taco sauce. Add half of the sour cream to each, if desired. Fold each tortilla over. Take the plate down to the nurse station and ask someone to microwave it for 30 seconds.

Assembled, not yet microwaved.

Chicken Stir Fry with Extra Vegetables

Order: stir fry (chicken with vegetables), broccoli, carrots, green beans.

Add extra vegetables to the stir fry. Mix.

Lemon Pepper Rice

Order: 1 white rice, 1 lemon packet, 1-2 pepper packets.

Add lemon, and pepper to taste. Mix.

Banana Cream Oatmeal (or Cream of Wheat)

Order: 1 oatmeal or cream of wheat, 1 banana, 1 vanilla ice cream, 1 brown sugar (optional).

Dice half of the banana. Add to the hot cereal and mix it in. Add 2 or 3 spoonfuls of ice cream. Optionally, sprinkle with brown sugar.

Mocha

Order: 1 coffee (regular or decaf), 1 packet hot chocolate (regular or sugar-free), 1 vanilla ice cream.

Mix the hot chocolate powder into the coffee. Stir. Add a spoonful or two of vanilla ice cream on top.

Posted by Joseph Seeley at 8:10 AM

D-6

I spend part of the morning getting to know my new Kindle. I had been hesitant about getting one, since I have no trouble not reading the books and magazines I already have. A Kindle could just be a more expensive way to not read. But a couple of chapters into my first book—*When You Are Engulfed in Flames*, by David Sedaris—I'm pretty excited about it.

I also get a visit from one of the Infectious Diseases doctors who was working on my infections last week. He says everything looks good on the infection front—no fevers, the pneumonic blob in my lungs is smaller. He hasn't heard about the sinus scan.

In the early afternoon, I get a visit from a Champaign friend and his son, who is a school soccer teammate of Paul's. They are up in the Chicago area for soccer training and made a significant detour to stop by. Get some good Kindle tips. (Thanks, Rob and Randall!)

During their visit, the attending physician stops by to confirm that all of yesterday's tests came back with good news, including an improved sinus state and a clean bill of health on the heart sonogram.

Near the end of the chemo drip, I notice a slight tightening of my breathing passages. It reminds me of when you step out into really cold weather, and your airway hasn't yet adjusted. It is not alarming, but it is one of the side effects that we're supposed to make known immediately. I let the nurse know, and she says she will let the doctor know.

A little later, I notice a slight itch on my upper back. I reach to give a light scratch, and realize that my skin is bumpy. Another page, another nurse. I'm thinking, this must be those hives I've been reading about. She confirms.

Luckily, they are not tormentingly itchy.

Doctor comes in to check on me. Prescribes a few things: Benadryl, Pepcid, and some kind of steroid.

Someone brings in a nebulizer to ease the breathing, which never got very tight and was already easing on its own. I can't tell if the nebulizer makes a difference.

As soon as the nebulization is done, in rolls a portable echocardiogram machine, to see how my heart is doing.

Haven't received the echocardio-gram report, yet.

I wonder which side effects have signed up for D-5.

Around 6:00, I head for the tread-mill for my first Kindle-enhanced run. It's a great combination. I can push the font size up to a point that allows me to read while run-ning, and the page turning buttons are easy to hit while running. I still occasionally go forward a page when I want to go back, be-cause I expect the go-back button to mirror on the left the go-for-ward button on the right. Instead, both left and right sides have little go-back buttons above larger go-forward buttons. Overall, it does make the time pass more quickly.

So *that's* what hives look like. Sexy!

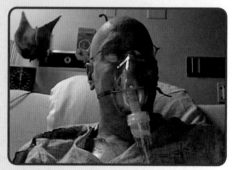

I think I have hives on my dome.
Also sexy!

My treadmill distance is 3.2, 2 miles of it running at a little over 14 min/mile pace. I run or walk at whatever pace will get my heart rate to 140, and today that was 14:15. Since my pneumonia diag-nosis, I think I have only missed one day of running or walking. Today's was the longest and fast-est since before the Bad Week. Probably a combination of being

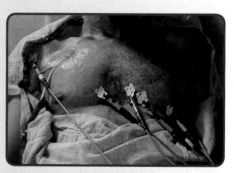

No comment.

further recovered, getting two bags of blood yesterday, and having a Kindle.

Now, I'm waiting for Food Service to deliver the ingredients for Spicy Asian Noodles.

Later, a few phone calls, maybe some online Scrabble, and then a contest between *Saturday Night Live* and Ambien. My money is on Ambien.

Posted by Joseph Seeley at 5:58 PM

Name the Parrot

After my colleagues sent me a pirate cap, to cover up my then soon-to-be and now bald head, sister Mara decided she had to bring an essential accessory.

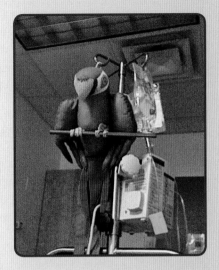

He or she (I'll say "it" for now) perches on the IV pole and is therefore my nearly constant companion. The nurses don't mind, and some specifically mention that they like it. On my last transport to a procedure, a couple of days ago, I was greeted by name by someone coming up behind me into the elevator.

"How did you know it was me?" I asked, already knowing the answer. "I think a little bird told her," said someone else already on the elevator. (I was wearing the pirate do-rag, too, so I was all gussied up for the trip.)

Several people have asked what the parrot's name is. I don't know.

I have thought of one name, relevant but twisted, but I don't want to bias this very intelligent and creative audience by sharing it, yet.

The floor is now open for nominations. You may justify your nomination or let its brilliance speak for itself. Unlike the parrot, which is mute.

= = =

A note on the comment mechanism: quite a few people have had trouble leaving comments, including me. My workaround is to select the profile (even if already selected), then select Preview, and repeat those two steps until a preview appears. Then, within the Preview box, there is an option to post. Once I see the preview, the post option within the preview always works. If that process doesn't work for you, you can also send me an e-mail and I will post it for you, or you could try using a different browser.

Posted by Joseph Seeley at 6:20 AM

D-5

A good night of sleep, maybe the best I've had here. The only disruptions were the midnight and 4 a.m. vitals checks.

Today, the doctors are taking several measures to head off a repeat of yesterday's (relatively mild) side effects. I will receive ahead of time some of the medications I got yesterday to relieve the hives and chest tightness, and I will receive the Campath over eight hours instead of four.

My brown tongue is less brown—there is less brown overall, and some of the remaining brown is more coffee-colored than chocolate-colored.

A visit from the attending around midday, who clears up some minor misunderstandings I had. The heart sonogram I had on Friday was the echocardiogram, while the picture of my chest covered in leads [on page 70] was an EKG. The results of both are, in her words, "boring." Which means "good."

The other misunderstanding I had was about the number of stem cells collected. All along, I have been hearing numbers like 3 million (ideal + backup) cells, 2 million (ideal), 1.7 million (what they actually collected). I was thinking that was the number of cells collected, which seems like a lot. But cells are really small, and those numbers describe many more cells than I thought, because they refer to the number of cells per kilogram of my weight.

I could raise the number of cells we have per kilogram by losing a lot of weight over the next five days, but I'm sure that's a bad idea.

Halfway through the eight-hour drip, still no side effects. Good lunch, completely from my personal provisions: lentil soup, almond butter on ak-mak crackers, dried peaches, a little chocolate, water.

A visit from Dave and Allison, once across-the-street neighbors so close we joked that we lived in one house with a road running through it. They moved to Oswego years ago, but we have stayed in touch and our oldest sons are still good friends. They brought some of David's famous sweet potato bread and some McIntosh apples, and fresh-squeezed orange juice from the Au Bon Pain downstairs. (Thanks, Dave and Allison!)

Seven hours into the drip, still no side effects.

Seven and a half hours in—spoke too soon. Mild hives on the lower arms. Getting some Benadryl and steroids.

Dinner off the menu—no cooking tonight. Chicken, stuffing, corn, grapes, and broccoli, which was erroneously banned but is allowed by a doctor's note. I went over this with the call-taker. She said it was fine. Dinner arrived later than the usual 45 minutes, with an apology and an explanation. They decided they had to make a call about the broccoli, to make sure, and it took a little while to clear up their confusion. I thanked her for her caution, and she left. I lifted the cover—no broccoli! I called Food Service, and they said they would send it right up. 45 minutes later, after I was done with dinner, the broccoli showed up. "Too late. But you can take my tray." I also had some of the sweet potato bread, warmed in the microwave. The nurse who warmed it was jealous.

Getting ready to go to sleep. Pretty restful day.

Posted by Joseph Seeley at 7:54 PM

Monday, February 28, 2011

D-4

So-so night of sleep. I'm getting a lot of liquid during the day intravenously, which means more frequent bathroom trips at night. Also, the early morning visits were not consolidated into one, so I was largely awake since 5 a.m.

Put in 3 miles on the treadmill before breakfast. I was already hooked up to an IV, so I had to wheel the pole across the hall with me. Which brings up an unexpected Kindle bonus—it fits exactly into the breast pocket on the hospital gown, leaving my hands free to wrangle myself and the pole through two doors and a very narrow passage to get out of my room.

The good news is, I got my run in.
The bad news is, I can't take a shower until the end of the day, because of the long drip time on my chemo (8 hours).

After my run, the nurse comes in. She's wearing a yellow isolation gown and blue gloves.

The good news is, Tuesday is no longer Rectal Swab Day.

The bad news is, I have the organism they have been swabbing for—which is why they have stopped looking for it—and I'm back to wearing gowns and gloves when I leave my room, and visitors have to wear the same when they come into the room. No mask for visitors. The organism is VRE (Vancomycin-Resistant Enterococci). Very common in hospitals. I am colonized, but not infected. No treatment for now, but it's one more thing to keep an eye on post-transplant. The new rules are going to make my runs much warmer, especially the gloves.

Some telecommuting. Working on a journals app for both iPhone and iPad. First iPad design!

Visit from someone to issue some tests as part of the morbidly named Co-Morbidity Study that I consented to participate in. I believe the point of the study is to assess pre- and post-transplant activity and fitness levels in transplant patients over 50 and to see how those levels correlate to ... various outcomes. There are a bunch of surveys I haven't filled out yet. This woman was here to administer a couple of physical tests: a grip strength test, and a 5-yard walk test. I believe I passed!

A glance at the first survey shows some questions that will be hard to answer. *Compared to one year ago, how would you rate your health in general right now?* The choices range from *Much better than one year ago* to *Much worse than one year ago*. What's the right answer? In most ways, I'm healthier than most of the staff. But I am being treated for acute myeloid leukemia, which I did not have a year ago.

Tried to order burritos for lunch. Couldn't get either the listed Chipotle Black Bean Burrito or the secret bean and cheese burrito I got a couple of nights ago. Time for a new recipe—Chicken, Bean, and Cheese Quesadillas. Delicious!

Good afternoon of telecommuting.

No side effects, as of one hour after the end of the chemo. Promising!

Dinner (baked fish, lemon-pepper rice, broccoli!, carrots, sweet potato bread).

Phone calls, e-mail, shower...

A good day!

Posted by Joseph Seeley at 6:37 PM

Tuesday, March 1, 2011

D-3

Around midnight, my lower legs are itching to the point that it is keeping me awake and tempting me sorely to scratch. They had been itchy before, and I thought it was just dry skin. But I had been putting skin lotion on them, and they aren't dry anymore. I ask the nurse for help—Benadryl to the rescue!

Good sleep until 5:00, then again until 6:30. With today's chemo schedule, I realize this is my best chance for a run and a shower, so I hit the treadmill.

With my VRE colonization, I now need to wear a yellow smock over my hospital gown and thin blue rubber gloves whenever I leave the room. It's a warm getup under any circumstances, but it's really hot when you're running. I manage a couple of miles, a little slower than yesterday. It's not the extra clothing; I'm just feeling less energetic. I predict I will be getting more blood today. When I get back to my room and take off the gloves, pooled sweat pours out of them onto the floor. Disgusting. However, it's still better than not running.

The shower in my room is weak. The water doesn't get very hot, perhaps to protect against scalding. There is hardly any water pressure, so it takes a long time—15-20 minutes—to get the soap off, and I'm not sure I ever get all of it off. Maybe that's why my legs are itchy.

Another bathroom peeve—the toilet paper is installed so that it dispenses from the bottom of the roll. Madness! Naturally, I have tried to fix it. Mysteriously, the toilet paper dispenser requires a key to open. I understand why my medications in the vestibule outside my room are locked down. They probably have a street value of hundreds of dollars and are being billed to insurance for thousands of dollars. But toilet paper? That's a black market I don't think I want to know about.

After my shower, I feel a slight pain in the middle of my chest, right under the sternum. Not alarming, but being the good patient I call the nurse. EKG machine shows up soon, but the pain is already gone by then. EKG results are boring. Might be acid reflux—I have been taking Nexium every morning, and this morning it wasn't included in my large collection of morning pills.

Some telecommuting, by phone and computer. Take a break/nap—combination of needing blood and the large hit of Benadryl I get before the chemo starts.

Lunch. More work. Still no side effects.

A couple of visits from the Infectious Disease doctors to make sure I'm still doing well and to assure me they are keeping track of all my test results, all of which look good to them. They ask me if I'm bored. (I'm not.) They ask how my appetite is, and I tell them I'm eating well. "Really? With our food?" I point out my pantry, which elicits knowing chuckles. Then I tell them about my recipes, which makes them laugh out loud. "You have to publish those recipes." Flattering, but really the hospital should just improve its menu.

More work. The end of the chemo. No side effects. Happily surprised!

Tomorrow, I get a different treatment, and I will need to keep my mouth as cold as possible for six and a half hours to prevent mouth sores: ice chips, popsicles, milkshakes, ice cream...

Watch the Fighting Illini lose another close road game. Not surprised!

9:45, still waiting for my platelets and blood. Not sure what the delay is. Maybe they're trying to create a perfect storm of nighttime disruptions.

Posted by Joseph Seeley at 7:47 PM

Wednesday, March 2, 2011

That Which Does Not Kill Us (or, The Name of the Parrot)

I am not an absolute believer in Nietzsche's statement—That which does not kill us makes us stronger—but I believe it is true far more often than not. (Come to think of it, I'm almost certain it's not in my nature to be an absolute believer in anything.)

Whether it was a "killer" workout or a mental depression, I have come out the other side better equipped to handle races, or life, than I was before.

Therefore, by one vote over all the other nominees, with only one vote cast, the winner is...

Leuk

(pronounced Luke)

Why name my companion after the monster who is the "you" in my internal marching chant, "I Will Beat You"?

This disease has been hard on me, my family, and my friends. There are more hard days to come, most likely. I wouldn't wish it on anyone. Not even Dick Cheney.

But the leukemia has also brought many gifts, and, as wonderful as they have been, I'm not talking about the tangible gifts like cards, chocolate, visits, hats, calls, money, chocolate, baked goods, hats, Kindle, chocolate, hats, fruit, books... I mean the intangible, lasting gifts of learning more about other people (all good) and about myself (some good; some not, but valuable nonetheless).

It would be great if we could receive such gifts without going through a crisis, but I don't think it works that way. We may need to be rubbed raw, beaten down, and opened up in order to be receptive.

So, three cheers for Leuk, cruel sneaky bastard who tried to kill me, but who I expect will end up laying the foundation for a better, richer life.

(Note to the Fates and other mythological entities from various cultural traditions who punish hubris: I am not declaring victory. I know it's not over. There is no need to assess an excessive celebration or unsportsmanlike conduct penalty in the form of, say, a nasty infection or some severe graft-vs.-host disease. I'm just saying—as much as this sucks, there's a lot of good coming out of it.)

Posted by Joseph Seeley at 7:42 AM

D-2

Slept solidly, but in small chunks. Midnight vitals and disconnect from the late-night blood transfusion. 2 a.m. bathroom break. 4 a.m. vitals check and weigh-in. 5 a.m. bloodletting and start of antibiotics IV drips. 5:30 switch to another antibiotic. 6:30 disconnect. Time to work out!

First, I drink some water and check to see if it's my turn in my online Scrabble games. It is! One opponent has played through the triple word score I had my eye on, leaving an E dangling out there to play on. I have BERRTTU. BRUTE? BUTTER? BUTTERER! What? How can that not be a word? One who butters. "When I grow up, I want to be a better butterer of bread." Hmm... REBUTTER! Bingo!

Off to the treadmill, in my gown and gloves. As I'm getting started, one lens falls out of my glasses. Over the last seven weeks, a screw has gradually loosened. The screw is still there, and the lens is fine, but it's going to be hard to read the Kindle while I run without glasses. But wait... I can increase the font size to the point that I've got about 20 words per page, and it works great. Bingo!

I stop by the nurse station after my workout, to see if they have a tiny screwdriver. They don't, but they think the gift shop sells them, and they can send someone down to get one. I'll sort that out later. I can read and use the computer without glasses, so I'm fine for now.

Back in my room, I realize I have cut the time too close. It's 8:00, I need to shower, I need to eat breakfast, and I need to start icing my mouth at 8:30. A shower takes 30 minutes: 5 to bag up the ports coming out of my chest; 5 to get wet, because the shower has as much water pressure as a handheld spray bottle; 15 to get the soap off, for the same reason; 5 to dry off with towels barely larger than a hand towel. Another puzzle... Aha! Today, I skip the soap. 15 minutes saved. Bingo!

Breakfast is oatmeal, banana, omelet, grape juice. I finish just in time.

And then the oral ice bath begins. It has been described as a chore that you have to make yourself stick to, but I really like to crunch ice. The only reason I don't do it more is that it's not very convenient. But here, it's as convenient as it can be. When I start running low, I press the red button and get more ice.

The drug itself is delivered quickly, but the side effects can set in over the next several hours. Until 4:00, my nurse tells me.

So, it's mouthful after mouthful of ice, for a total of seven and a half hours. The ice is perfect for crunching: pellets a little larger than jelly beans, lots of air in them. I spice up the day with a few treats: milkshake at 10:00, strawberry-banana smoothie at noon, two ice creams at 2:00. And then it's done. The only side effect was more than hourly trips to the bathroom.

I have a productive day of telecommuting, and the usual visit from the docs. It's not a posse anymore, just an attending and a fellow (I think). I ask about the week after transplant. The attending says the first week is when I may feel the worst. Diarrhea and tiredness are likely, but both typically come and go rather than beat on you all day.

In the afternoon, my nurse starts a new drip. "Have they told you about the Pro-Graft?" No. "Oh. Why don't they tell you these things?" Beats me. From now until I leave the hospital, I will be connected to the pole to receive this anti-rejection drug. I am allowed one 20-minute break per day, so I'll have to figure out when I can take that break and schedule my workout accordingly. I'm still not sure I can shower in 20 minutes, and I can't go with the no-soap option on a regular basis. Maybe they can adjust my water pressure.

My nurse also makes a trip to the gift shop, taking all of my money ($5) with her. It's enough, and I now have functioning glasses. Which could come in handy tonight, since Adrian, volunteer extraordinaire, brought *Black Adder Goes Forth*.

Expecting a relaxing evening. And tomorrow has nothing scheduled—no procedures, no chemicals.

Posted by Joseph Seeley at 4:39 PM

Thursday, March 3, 2011

D-1

A very good night of sleep, with some help from my little friend (Ambien). The usual disruptions, but I got over them quickly. The bloodletting was from the arm this time, but expertly done—barely felt it.

The nurse is going to work with me to get in the workout. She'll let me know when the bag changeover is coming, with more than an hour's notice, so I'll be able to finish running just before. We're going to look into fixing the water pressure, and it may be possible to detach the shower head from the wall.

Got a note from the editor of an internal medical center publication. She's doing a story about the new president and wants to quote some of the nice things I said about her on the blog. She's also going to give the name of the blog, so maybe some other folks here will take a look.

Lentils and couscous for lunch. (From my private pantry, of course.)

Excellent run. A little over 2 miles, and by the end I was running at a 13:40 pace. Would have run longer, but my drips end a little ahead of schedule.

We're trying to keep the disconnection time to under 20 minutes, so as soon as the pumps stop, I end my run, return to the room, and call the nurse.

She bags up the ports—I've been doing it myself lately, but it's faster if someone else does it. I have figured out how to remove the shower head from its wall track—something any two-year-old could do in a few minutes, though it took me seven weeks—and I'm hoping it helps a lot. It does. In, wet, soaped, rinsed, and out in 5:06! (Finally, a use for my running watch.) Towel off, put on hospital pants (faster than the spatial puzzle that is the hospital gown), call the nurse—9:47! She comes in, does some extra housekeeping on the lines and ports, and gets me connected and the pumps on -- 15:49! I didn't get a watch on the initial port-bagging phase, but it was surely less than 4 minutes, so I call it a win. Victory!

Without the extra line/port housekeeping, I think we will lower our time tomorrow.

Doctors come in, ask how I'm doing. Great! The transplant is scheduled for 2:00 p.m. (hospital time). Am I doing anything special for tomorrow's big event? Jan's coming up for a long weekend, but I hadn't been planning anything special.

The attending tells me about a "goofy" lady who was doing some Buddhist sand art during the transfusion. I won't be doing that, but it doesn't sound crazy to me. If you think it helps, there's a good chance that it does, even if not for the reason you think it does. Placebos, for example, are remarkably effective in many circumstances, with no side effects. Our belief that something is helping triggers the release of hormones and other chemicals that actually do help. There's nothing goofy about enlisting our own internal forces, through prayer or sand art or music or meditation or comedy, to assist the medical team. And maybe those methods work for the reasons that we believe they do, even if the doctors don't believe it.

A member of the Infectious Disease team pops in, partly to see how I'm doing, but also to ask if I have any ideas for making Ensure more palatable. A fellow patient is reduced to drinking that and is having a hard time getting it down. Fortunately (for me, not for the other patient), I have never had Ensure and have no ideas. Anyone? Make sure it's cold?

Another productive day of telecommuting. I build my first iPad prototype. I am slightly hampered by connectivity problems that keep me from reaching my network at work. Coincidentally, hospital IT staff was in the corridor when I emerged from my room to get hot water for my lentils, and they acknowledged they were having problems and would look into it.

I got a call around 5:00 letting me know they didn't see any problems at their end, and that they didn't officially support the kind of VPN access I've been using since I got here, and since it was the end of the day nothing could get fixed until tomorrow. But the woman calling gathered some information about my hardware and software and said she would try to cash in a favor tomorrow.

Five minutes later, my access was restored. Maybe they fixed something, or maybe they stopped fixing things and went home. Either way, I was able to check e-mail and enter my daily activity minutes in the Winter Fitness Challenge. Grand Prize: an iPad!

Dinner will be the Spicy Asian Noodles again, this time a little spicier and with grilled chicken.

Tonight: e-mail, some race web work, calls, a few sitcoms...

Tomorrow: D-0!

Posted by Joseph Seeley at 4:48 PM

Friday, March 4, 2011

The Day

I have been telling myself and others that today isn't that big a deal. It is transplant day, the one we have been counting down to. But when a lot of people hear "transplant," they're thinking surgery and organs. In my case, at 2:00 this afternoon, a bag of stem cells from sister Mara will quickly drip into me. I've been having fluids dripped into me and pulled out of me for seven weeks.

Sometimes there are immediate side effects, sometimes delayed. (One IV medication a couple of days ago came with a warning of brief but excruciating anal burning, unless administered very slowly. "Now, I know I have no medical training, but I do have a suggestion....")

For today's transplant/transfusion, there are no immediate side effects. The graft cells (Mara's) quickly head to my vacant marrow and start to make themselves at home. It takes some days. I may feel more tired than I have been. Eventually, infections have their shot at the defenseless body, and the graft cells may not play well with host organs, but initially things should be quiet.

So, I've been thinking of today as full of significance but without excitement.

However, my sleep tells me I'm not fooling myself. I had a poor night of sleep that I cannot blame on the staff. My "midnight" vitals check comes at 1:30, giving me a rare long initial round of sleep. Then I am mostly awake until 4:00. Not stressed, not tired. It is the wakeful vigilance of a seven-year-old on Christmas morning, opening his eyes at 2:30 to see if it's gotten light enough to count as morning so he can run downstairs and open one present. It's not. Not at 2:50, either. Or 3:30. Or 4:00. But then I do fall back asleep, perhaps because I'm back to the usual rhythm of being awakened every hour for a vitals check, drip change, or bloodletting.

Anyway, it is finally Christmas/Second Birthday morning, and it is a big deal, but I will be able to wait patiently until 2:00 to open my present.

Posted by Joseph Seeley at 6:27 AM

Mara to the Rescue

When I was diagnosed with aplastic anemia about six years ago, my two sisters had their blood typed for being potential stem cell donors. My brother was not tested, because he has the same intestinal condition that I do, though more severe. There is some thought that ulcerative colitis is an auto-immune disease, as are some types of aplastic anemia, and it makes little sense to trade one compromised immune system for another.

Sibling matches are the best donors for leukemia patients. Other cancer patients can receive their own stem cells. I need a brew that is hostile to any lurking leukemia cells (currently undetected, possibly non-existent, but you can't be sure), while also friendly enough not to pick fights with my liver or kidneys. My own cells would presumably leave my organs alone, but they might not go after my leukemia cells—Hey, that bro's gang colors indicate he's one of us. Let's go borrow a cigarette instead of beating him to death.

Anyway, it turned out that Mara was a match and Lauren was not. We might have predicted this, since Mara and I are almost twins—11.5 months apart, and, I think, we have always gotten along fairly well. When we were very little, she would aggressively defend me against neighborhood friends/bullies who were being mean to me. (Good training for today.) We have similar personalities—observant, analytical, introspective. It was her joining the high school track team that led me to join, with positive side effects that continue until today. I was intimidated by the thought of belonging to a real sports team, despite plenty of evidence that I was fast. But once Mara joined, it seemed safe enough to give it a try. We had some overlap in our social circles, which overlapped more when I stayed for an extra senior year and joined her graduating class. (No, I was not held back for academic reasons.)

Lauren and I had a more contentious and probably typical big brother/kid sister relationship. Part of that was surely age—four years apart, enough to make her a strange being rather than a peer. Part personality—Lauren is the most spirited and outgoing of the four siblings. (Naturally, such assessments are *relative*. In plenty of other families, Lauren would be the quiet one.) How did I torment her? Let me count the ways. Or, at least the two that get regular recountings at family gatherings. There were many more, petty and demeaning.

The more benign was when she was 5 and terrified that a monster was hiding under her bed, preventing her from getting out. Joe to the rescue! I volunteered to climb under the bed and give the all clear. "Looks good... Nothing here... Wait... Oh, no! There's something! It's got me! Aaahhhrrg!"

The more sinister incident involved a friend (maybe two) and me dangling Lauren out of a third-story window of our house. Partway out, all the way out? Don't recall. Lauren currently says, forgivingly, that she probably deserved it, but I can't remember (or imagine) an offense worthy of that treatment. (Sorry, Lauren!)

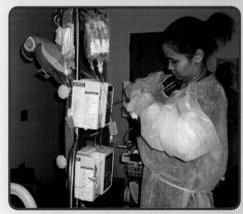

Anyway, the sisters had discussed the matching results and decided that it was probably for the best that Mara was the match. As much as Lauren loves me and has forgiven my youthful terrorism, she still

Getting started. Leuk pointedly turns his back on the proceedings.

could harbor revenge at a subconscious and sub-cellular level. Best to not take any chances.

= = =

Jan arrives a little after 11. I haven't seen her in nine days, which is the longest we have been apart since the first year we were married. She looks good! I don't notice that she's had a recent haircut, another measure that I'm functioning normally.

Everything gets checked multiple times. My name, after seven weeks, remains Joseph Seeley.

Premedication starts at 1:00. Benadryl, Atavan to calm me down—usually not a need of mine, but I'll take it—and a steroid. It gets hard to type straight. I eventually give up, and I am in and out of sleep until nearly 5:00. At some point, I helpfully wake up and pass along a piece of wisdom to Jan: "flash cards."

Jan keeps a log of the "action":
Transfusion start: 2:22
Second bag: 2:40
Third bag: 3:05
Fourth bag: 3:25
Done: 3:40
Joe conked out until 4:45.

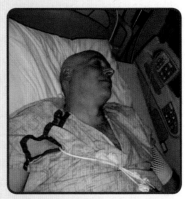

Most of the time, I am asleep.

= = =

We have joked that now I will be more in touch with my feminine side, since my blood will be my sister's. Since I already enjoy a number of activities that are conventionally but baselessly categorized as more womanly—gardening, cooking—it's not clear what that would look like. Maybe I won't get

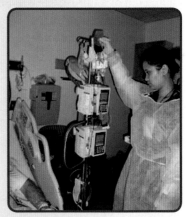

The nurse gets an arm workout by trying to enlist more gravity into the flow.

into many bar brawls going forward. Unless Mara has a dark side she's not sharing.

Seems like the whole thing went well. No reactions to the cells or to the pre-medications (other than drowsiness).

As hoped, a day with little drama and plenty of significance.

Posted by Joseph Seeley at 5:01 PM

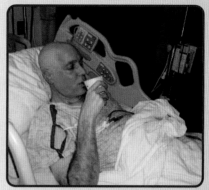

Finally up, and having a cold one to celebrate. (Ice water)

Saturday, March 5, 2011

D+1—Wonderfully Quiet

Quiet day. Excellent!

Jake is in for the weekend to visit, and Jan arrived (and slept over) yesterday.

Some website work in the morning, a 40-minute walk at 1:00, half-napping most of the afternoon, Thai food (from the outside) for dinner, some online Scrabble.

Something's going on inside, because I'm tired, but other than that I feel fine. I'll take it.

Posted by Joseph Seeley at 7:03 PM

Sunday, March 6, 2011

D+2

Similar pattern to the day as yesterday—feel pretty good through the morning, get in a workout just before one dose of ProGraft runs out so that I can get in a shower during the changeover to the next dose, then start to drag through the afternoon. Napping/reading...

Some nausea this afternoon—got a pill to help.

Had some more good food brought in for supper—salmon burger and cole-slaw.

Will probably go to sleep early tonight.

Posted by Joseph Seeley at 5:46 PM

Monday, March 7, 2011

Transport Follow-up

I have described the patient transportation system here as approaching dys-functional. In the interest of fairness, here is some nuance.

In my first account (see page 5), I mocked the musings ("Dumbocrats") of a person behind the desk at the x-ray waiting room. I had a second encounter with the same waiting room, and again Transport was lacking. My trip was supposed to be a round trip, which means my transporter waits for my brief procedure to be over and then immediately takes me back to my room before I am exposed to even more pathogens than are already at work on me. I came out of the procedure, and my transporter was gone. The x-ray tech took it upon herself to get me back up to my room. As we came to the elevator, Mr. Dumbocrats was there, having left his post to help me, my wheelchair, and my IV pole over the gap between the elevator and floor. And then he rode up, to help me off the elevator. The transportation system still broke down, and his political philosophy is still incomprehensible to me. But I have to give credit for seeing a need and going outside his job description to fill it. (Thanks, Limbaugh/Beck fan!)

In a later account (see page 37), I mentioned a visit from a transportation manager (probably assistant manager). Particularly alarming to me was learning that the target maximum waiting time was two hours. While I hoped I misheard, or she misspoke, I had nothing else to go on, and my own obser-vations had done nothing to make me doubt that number.

I had a more recent visit, from a different (probably assistant) manager. We reviewed my experiences and observations, and I asked about the target wait time again. This time, the answer was 30 minutes. I know (from personal experience) they're not hitting that number, but at least that is a reasonable target.

We talked about the problem with waiting: the patient is isolated, scared, and without information, and these conditions are harmful to patient health. I mentioned Mara's idea of equipping patients with pagers so that they can get in touch with their nurses. The manager pointed out that patients are never truly abandoned. There are always medical staff nearby, though they may be out of sight. Perhaps the x-ray or CT or other staff should take responsibility for checking in with patients left in their area.

I also learned that the dispatch system is not quite as primitive as I feared. I imagined (in my negative frame of mind) that a free transporter simply called in and got the next name on the list, which could lead to lots of inefficiencies depending on relative locations. I gather that there is a more sophisticated process, with patient and transporter location being factored in.

There is obviously lots of room for improvement, but the situation is not as bleak as I thought. Hurray.

Posted by Joseph Seeley at 1:15 PM

Tuesday, March 8, 2011

D+4—An Interrupted Nap

I had a great night of sleep. 9:30 to 7:30, with the least possible number of interruptions. Even my self-scheduled bathroom trips ended up coinciding with visits for vitals or medicine. Very efficient.

I was still tired when I woke up. I've been tired all day. Not a sick tired or a sore tired, just curl up in bed and close the eyes tired. This is normal a few days after transplant, exacerbated this morning by Benadryl as premedication for another platelet transfusion. The whole day has been more or less one long nap with occasional breaks for each end of the digestive tract. (Is there a limit to how long you can sleep and still call it a nap?)

Jan and Jake visited in the morning before heading back to Champaign after a good long weekend here.

I told the doctors about what great sleep I got the night before. On the way out, the fellow said he would try to arrange vital checks every two hours. It took me a moment to realize he was joking.

I had been observing to staff that I was running low on toilet paper, and the matter had been referred to housekeeping, but housekeeping did not have the same urgency about the matter as my bowels did. I didn't quite run out, but I could see the future and it wasn't pretty. When I later went out on the corridor, I asked a nurse for help, and he raided an empty patient room for me. Nurses are great.

= = =

Not a banner day for Food Service. This morning, after the call-taker expressed mild delight at my plan to put cut peaches instead of sugar on my oatmeal—"That sounds really good. I'll have to try that"—the tray arrives without peaches. Or silverware. I call. "We'll get that up as soon as possible." 45 minutes later, silverware, and peaches for my cold oatmeal. In the meantime, I eat my egg and sausage, and slice up a mango. (Thanks, Adrian.)

Lunch is great—leftover curry over noodles, from last night.

Snack—fried mozzarella sticks with marinara sauce and a mango smoothie. 45 minutes later, the snack arrives. The cheese sticks are pretty good. For some reason, I receive a single ounce of mango smoothie. Which, 45 minutes after it is poured into an uninsulated plastic cup, no longer qualifies as a smoothie. It is now a chug of warm mango syrup, which I can't bring myself to try. I know there are restrictions on what we can eat based on our condition, but I cannot imagine what would make one ounce of mango smoothie acceptable but a full cup a danger to my health.

Posted by Joseph Seeley at 3:02 PM

Wednesday, March 9, 2011

D+5—An Excellent Day

Unlike the previous morning, I wake up this morning actually feeling awake. I get exactly the breakfast I order, including, for the first time, a little bit of whipped cream with the waffles. (Third time's the charm, I guess.) I also top the waffles with marionberry fruit spread, an Oregon specialty delivered by my friend Jeff, who visited last evening and is in town for several more days.

I work on a website prototype, take a short nap, go for a walk, have lunch, take a shower, do some more work, have another nap. Jeff brings in some dinner, we start to catch up on... um... about three decades. It's a good day.

Last night, when ordering dinner, I unraveled the mystery of the single ounce of mango smoothie. The normal serving is 10 ounces, but the call-taker only managed the first digit while taking the order. So, the person filling the order was probably thinking, "Some of these patients have crazy requests, but whatever makes them happy..."

Today, I notice that I have three spare rolls of toilet paper in the bathroom, including the one I obtained myself. Had I overlooked two rolls during the Great Toilet Paper Panic of D+4? Or had housekeeping replenished my supply since then? Beats me.

Related to the Great Toilet Paper Panic was the fact that I was experiencing diarrhea. This could be the result of a bacterial infection, so they took a sample for that. It could also be a common side effect of chemotherapy. If it's bacterial, they'll add another antibiotic to my stew. If not, they'll give me Imodium. In the meantime, the nurses want to keep track of my bowel movements. "Just let me know when you have your next one." A few hours later... I have news to share. I press the red Nurse button on my universal control. "Can I help you?" "Uh..."—realizing that I am broadcasting this news to everyone within earshot of the nurse station—"... my nurse wanted to know when I had a bowel movement, and I just did." "Thank you. I'll let her know." (Are they snickering? Probably not.) No matter how formal the language, and no matter that I was merely following my nurse's request, I still feel like the toddler in potty training who runs down the hall yelling, "I made a poopie!" Except I don't get a little sticker.

It has been great having Jeff visit. We were friends, teammates, and fellow theater techs in high school and again in college, and best men at each other's weddings. And then ... not much contact. I knew he had moved to Oregon, but I didn't know his mother died until well after the fact. And even when I did find out, I didn't manage to get in touch. Bad friend! But as soon as he learned of my incarceration, he was proposing a visit. Good friend!

Which brings me back to why I named the parrot Leuk. Leukemia is horrible, but it has brought blessings along with the suffering. Renewing friendships, seeing how many people offer so many types of support, learning how valuable even the smallest gestures are, learning (therefore) ways I want to be better... priceless.

Posted by Joseph Seeley at 7:58 PM

Meanwhile, Across the Seas...

I have mentioned before that my brother Karl and his family are spending the academic year in the Czech Republic. He is teaching, and his wife Kate has been keeping a marvelous blog of the year, which is going to be a lasting treasure, especially for their sons (currently 6 and 8).

Posted by Joseph Seeley at 11:04 AM

D+6—On a Roll

Another good, uneventful day. Reasonable energy level. Took a nap and a walk. Jeff brought in pizza for dinner.

Got some platelets. I have virtually no white blood cells (expected at this point).

Getting ready for sleep.

Posted by Joseph Seeley at 7:27 PM

Relay for Life

We're coming up on Relay for Life time, all over the country. As I marvel at the sophistication and relative precision of the medical care I'm receiving, I'm keenly aware that the care is far better than it was five or ten years ago, thanks to all the research that has been done. A lot of funding for that research comes from Relay for Life and similar events.

If you're reading this, you know at least one person who is benefiting from that funding. You almost certainly know more than one, and some of you have yourselves been beneficiaries.

If you're reading this, you're already supporting me, and it helps. I love seeing comments, and even just seeing the names that pop up on the list of followers. I also know that there are many more people reading than are listed as official blog followers, and that helps, too. Connection is part of the cure.

If you're looking for a way to support future cancer patients, I encourage you to participate, physically and/or financially, in a Relay for Life. There is almost certainly one in your community.

Posted by Joseph Seeley at 7:51 PM

Friday, March 11, 2011

D+7

Not much to report here from TN655. Not quite as peppy as yesterday—being low on hemoglobin probably explains part of that. Blood counts still not moving—sometime next week is when we expect to see them climb. Got in a walk (cut short by a medication pump going off because its delivery was complete) and a shower.

I watched the critical 10 minutes of the Illinois-Michigan game, which was a perfect miniature of the entire season. "We can score at will, in many ways... This is boring... Let's stop playing this way... Will there be Rice Krispie Treats after the game?... Oh, crap. We lost, again."

Also watched a lot of CNN.

Posted by Joseph Seeley at 5:14 PM

Saturday, March 12, 2011

D+8—Nausea

The Infectious Disease docs wanted another stool sample and left a "hat" the night before that sits in the toilet bowl. At 6 in the morning, I get to make another public "I made a poopie" announcement. The nursing assistant who comes to process that hat's contents is very pleasant about her role, at one point saying, "Thank you so much." Um... you're welcome?

When I finally get up, I am nauseous. I request and receive a Compazine tablet. It doesn't help. We try some Zofran, which also doesn't help. More Zofran. A little better. I order and eat a late, bland breakfast, even though I don't feel like eating. Although it's the most nauseous I have felt during my 8+-week stay, I would rate it about a 4 on a scale of 10. Compared to how some people feel at this point in their treatment, I'm getting off lightly.

The doctors report that my white blood cell count is still beneath detection.

Jeff comes by a little after midday, with a St. Patrick's Day tam, and a necklace.

Midafternoon, I order a bland lunch— noodles with parmesan and a salad.

Jeff heads to the airport. We agree that we should get together before another two decades pass. Jeff has sweetened the prospect of visiting Oregon with some mouth-watering descriptions of the food he and his wife eat, either at home or in area restaurants.

The tam and necklace go so well with my gown, and with my nausea-hued face.

Shortly after Jeff leaves, Claire arrives. Claire was Jan's college roommate, and we spent a few days in Maine with her, her husband David, and their dog Marseilles last summer. Claire was giving a presentation in the Chicago area and was able to stay over the weekend to see me and (tomorrow) Jan.

Late afternoon, Claire leaves and I take a nap. The anti-nausea medicine is working well enough that I order a fairly normal dinner, though still on the bland side—baked fish, baked potato, broccoli.

Eventually to bed.

Posted by Joseph Seeley at 3:36 PM

Sunday, March 13, 2011

D+9—Counts!

Went to bed with both Ambien to help me sleep and Atavan (anti-nausea and pro-sleep). I sleep pretty well.

I have been on an every-8-hours Zofran regimen since yesterday. It's working—only barely nauseous when I wake up.

I get some Lasix because my blood pressure has been getting a little high, for me—150/80. This is a result of all the liquids dripping into me all day:

Prograf, vancomycin, meropenem, magnesium, platelets (sometimes), red blood (sometimes), more... The Lasix does bring my blood pressure down to more normal, for me—120/70. Lasix works by reducing the amount of fluid in your body, which means I have to pee every 30 minutes.

The doctors visit, with news! My white blood cell count is 300, indicating that the stem cells I received 9 days ago have settled into their new home and have been getting to work. Tomorrow's numbers will allow us to start narrowing in on a go-home date. (I later find out that the count was 200 yesterday, but the doctors had visited before the counts were available.)

Jan and Paul visit, with treats! Seltzer, McClintock fig bars, chopped nuts, golden raisins, a mass of cards. Claire also comes by, getting in a visit with her college roomie (and me).

Around 7 p.m., I go for a walk. With the two bags of blood I got today, I figure I should be pretty peppy. I'm wrong. 1.2 miles in 25 minutes, and it's hard. And the nausea is coming back. But at least I get some good laughs from my current Kindle reading, *A Walk in the Woods*.

Jan, Joe, and Claire

After my walk, it's time for my regularly scheduled Zofran. (Maybe that's why the nausea started to come back—I was jonesing for my next hit.)

Dinner, help Paul with some studying, do some Illinois Marathon data work, go to bed. Although, since I spent most of the day *in* bed—sitting up, usually—it would be more accurate to say that I put my Advanta™ 2 bed into the "Bed" position and turned out the light.

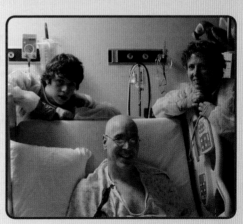

Paul, Joe, and Claire

Posted by Joseph Seeley at 9:02 PM

Monday, March 14, 2011

D+10—Generally Great, with a Side of Kvetching

A good night of sleep, perhaps helped by the new pillow Jan and Paul brought me yesterday, definitely helped by Ambien and Atavan. The hospital pillows are on the insubstantial side, which is actually OK with me. However, they are encased in plastic, for sanitary reasons, which means you always wake up with a clammy pillow under your head, even with a pillowcase between your face and the plastic. There have been nights that I assumed I had a high fever because my pillow was so damp, an assumption dispelled by the every-four-hours vitals check.

Breakfast was partially from my pantry (Kashi Honey Puffs, dried cherries, walnuts, golden raisins) and partially from Food Service (pepper, mushroom, onion, and cheese omelet).

Some work in the morning. The fellow comes by, with nothing much to say except that the WBC (white blood cell count) is 700. (200, 300, 700... I like the looks of that.) Above 4,000 and you can defend yourself (and leave the hospital).

I shave. I have some scattered whiskers below my nose, and some more on my chin. What they lack in numbers they have started to make up in length, and they're annoying. (On the plus side, maybe this means I'm through with the hair loss side effect of chemo.) I have to use an electric razor, for safety reasons. With such low platelets, a nick could bleed profusely. Also, with my white blood cell count so low, a nick is an infection risk I need to avoid. Knowing this would be the case, Jan had picked up an electric razor way back in January.

Twenty minutes into shaving a very small area of my face, I have made little progress. The razor buzzes convincingly as it passes over the whiskers, as if it were doing something, but the whiskers remain. Their numbers are slightly diminished, and some of the others are shorter than before, but I have essentially the same scraggly excuse for a mustache and soul patch that I started with. For all I know, the few whiskers that show up in the sink left my face on their own, to get away from the constant buzzing. Maybe Jan picked up a toy electric razor—"Shave like your dad! (Safe for kids 2 and up.)" Or maybe this is really a facial massage device, shaped like a razor to protect the fragile male ego—"Give yourself a facial massage, while looking like a man." But it's clearly not an effective razor. It wouldn't hurt a whisker.

Lunch from the pantry—lentil soup, marionberry jam on ak-mak crackers, seltzer, mango. More work in the afternoon. A nap.

The larger posse comes by in the afternoon, confirms the counts. I learn the following:

▶ WBC over 4,000 is one threshold for leaving the hospital.

▶ Sufficient platelet creation that I do not need daily transfusions is another threshold. Every two or three days is OK (though inconvenient). I might be there already.

▶ Red blood cell and hemoglobin counts are rarely an issue. If the other numbers are sufficient, these almost always are, too.

Also, upon leaving the hospital:

▶ Avoid houseplants. I can look at them from across a room, but I cannot be near them or care for them in any way. Soil contains fungi and bacteria, and I have already learned how much fun fungi can be.

▶ No gardening or yard work, at least through this summer, maybe into the fall. (Same issue as with houseplants, only worse.)

▶ Minimal sun exposure. Run early in the morning or late in the day, with a hat, with either full-length sun-blocking fabric or a high SPF sunblock.

There are many more restrictions, all contained in the Black Book, which Jan took home with her so she can begin preparing our house to not kill me. Thorough housecleaning, carpets cleaned (some replaced), drapes cleaned (or removed), plants removed... Lots to do, with, unfortunately—but also fortunately!—not much time to do it.

I provided a stool sample a couple of days ago, so I ask if the results are in. The doctors weren't aware of any results, and didn't even seem to be aware that the test had been run. Either there are no results to report, or whatever test was run came back negative and therefore didn't show up in red on my daily chart.

I did conduct my own ALOA (Arm's Length Olfactory Analysis) of the stool sample at the time of its creation, and I got the results immediately. Despite all the praise I have received for how I'm handling my condition and treatment—the grace, the courage, the wit—I can confirm that my shit does, in fact, still stink. A lot.

More work, 30 minutes on a bike, time to order dinner. My appetite is a little weak, so I think carefully about what appeals to me. The roast pork with gravy is pretty good, as is the bread dressing. Add some broccoli and corn, plus desserts from my pantry, and it should be a good dinner. I call Food Service. "Food Service. How can I help you?"

I'm not sure why so many of the call takers start the interaction this way. The only reason I would be calling is to order food, the only way you can help me is to take my order, and the only way you are going to allow me to order food is to ask for my name so you can verify who is calling from the room and determine my dietary restrictions, so really it would be better if you just asked for my name right up front.

For a while, I would answer the "How can I help you?" question with "I would like to order breakfast (/lunch/dinner/some food)." And they would inevitably ask, "First and last name, please." Now, I don't bother to answer the question and just tell them my name.

I start my order. Pork, dressing with gravy, broccoli... "I'm sorry. Broccoli is not allowed on an oncology diet." It is the case that the people in my condition are not supposed to eat *raw* berries and *raw* broccoli. However, neither of those items are on the menu. It is not possible to order raw broccoli or raw berries, yet somehow the system is programmed to prevent oncology patients from ordering *cooked* broccoli.

Many, many weeks ago, when my neutrophil counts first took their dive into oblivion, this same restriction had been imposed. When I asked the doctors about it, they said it made no sense and appended a note to my dietary plan saying that broccoli was OK. So I have happily been ordering broccoli every few days, both because I like broccoli and because it is the only member of the very nutritious cabbage family available, unless you count the 5 shreds of red cabbage in the tossed salad. (I don't.) I asked the call taker to check the notes. "I don't see any note about broccoli. Oh, and you can't have the bread dressing, either. I think it might have broccoli in it."

I am feeling stubborn, even angry, in the face of this capricious reimposition of an irrational restriction. "I'll call you back."

I press the big red Nurse button. "Is there a doctor available to clear up my dietary restrictions?" I feel guilty immediately. This is not exactly an emergency, and I could stomach mashed potatoes and green beans for tonight and address the problem tomorrow when the doctors come by on their regularly scheduled rounds. And I only have 15 minutes to get a reply, because the Food Service phone shuts down at 8:00.

At 7:55, with no doctorly intervention forthcoming, I call back to Food Service. "Thank you for calling Food Service. May I have your first and last name?" I inefficiently take a moment to thank her for the efficient way she answers calls, and then restart my order. I mention that I *wanted* to have broccoli but was for some reason being prevented. After some discussion, she agrees that a ban on raw broccoli should not block me from ordering cooked broccoli, and she provisionally allows me to order the bread dressing. She will find out why the dressing is blocked, and then send me either that or my backup of mashed potatoes.

When dinner arrives, it has beautiful, bright green broccoli. Also, the least appetizing glop of bread dressing I have ever seen—it looks like the fake food you sometimes see on display plates at lesser restaurants. It has a glossy sheen, and when I lift a forkful, the rest of it tries to come along for the ride. You win some, you lose some.

I see that I delivered several sides of kvetching, not just one. But it was still a great day. 700!

Posted by Joseph Seeley at 7:09 PM

Tuesday, March 15, 2011

D+11—A Joyful Pain

After midnight vitals, I have trouble getting back to sleep. This has been common, though the anti-dynamic duo of Ambien and Atavan have been fairly effective in the past, and I went to bed with both of them this night.

The problem this time is that I have these small aches, all over, but mostly in my legs. "*Now* what? Oh, wait... I've read about this... side effects Mara might (did) experience as the Neupogen puts stem cells into overdrive, and the marrow becomes crowded with new cells. That would be awesome!"

The pain isn't bad, but it's enough to keep me awake. Tylenol to the rescue, followed by a good, long sleep (by hospital standards).

When I wake up, I do some work for the race.

Breakfast is from Food Service, enhanced from the pantry: oatmeal with fruit cocktail (ordered peaches—close enough), dried cranberries, walnuts, whipped topping (because I'm a small-time hedonist); orange; hard-boiled egg; grape juice. I don't drink the grape juice straight—too sweet—but a little of it in a glass of ice water is refreshing.

Almost makes you wish you were here, right?

Some work, by phone and computer.

A call from my supervising physician. She sounds happy. She tells me my counts are looking great. Today's WBC is 1,400. (200, 300, 700, 1,400...) It's looking likely that I get to go home *this weekend*. (!) Another bit of good news is that, contrary to my expectations, my only guaranteed return visits to the clinic are Monday mornings. I may need to return more often if complications (such as an infection) appear, or if the regular Monday blood work turns up something that requires further testing.

A nurse comes in and tells me we are starting to shift some of the IV medications to tablet or capsule form, another necessary step before being able to leave. The countdown has definitely begun, though it is less determined than a rocket launch. It could go, "4, 4, 3, 2, 2, 1..."

The fellow brings me a copy of the Black Book.

Meanwhile, following the guidance of her copy of the Black Book, Jan has been arranging the housecleaning, the carpet-cleaning, the removal of couches, the purchase of couches. Also, co-directing a marathon and publishing a magazine. Yikes.

The attending stops by. Yes, the counts are good. (His guess for today had been 2,000, so he's 1 for 2 on predictions.) I mention that the information in the Black Book and the information from various medical staff is not consistent. Don't have any houseplants. Houseplants are OK, but not up close and not where you spend a lot of time.

We have already determined that the Black Book dietary information is outdated, but there are other issues. One page reads as if you can't shop, cook, or drive. Another page says to avoid grocery shopping. Yet another page says to shop when the store isn't crowded. (But it doesn't mention that you need to thoroughly wipe the shopping cart handles, which are cesspools in an easy-to-grab form.) Some passages are repeated often from one section to another. It may be relevant to display that information in multiple places, but it should be clearly identified as repeated information, because otherwise the reader tends to skip over it and may skip too far. Overall, the book reads like a committee product that lacked an editor, which seems pretty likely.

The attending asks if I would look through the book and provide feedback. You get three guesses as to my response, though if you need three for a yes/no question there's something wrong with your reasoning skills, and if you've been reading this blog, you only need one, and it shouldn't be a guess.

My dad arrives around noon. I have lunch and do some more work, for Human Kinetics and the race. Dad heads off to check into his lodging and to bring back dinner.

Feeling a little bit more of that joyful pain. During the day, it's not disruptive enough to bother asking for Tylenol.

1,400!

Posted by Joseph Seeley at 3:57 PM

Wednesday, March 16, 2011

D+12—Exponential Growth

At the very beginning of the day, which is to say just after midnight, one of my pump alarms goes off. This is no longer alarming to me, since I have learned what the different alarms mean.

There's the bird-like *dee-deet dee-deet* .... *dee-deet* that means the medication has been delivered. There's the *deet* .... *deet* ...... *deet* .... that means the battery is running low. And there's the *deeeeeeeeeeeeeeeeeeeeeeeeeeeeeeeee eeeeee* that sounds like a patient flatlining, if TV medical shows are to be believed. That one was alarming the first time I heard it, even though I was not hooked up to any machine that could evaluate whether I was dead or alive. The flatline alarm means the battery has run out of power.

Usually, the nurses work out the timing so an alarm does not go off in the middle of the night. Not this time, but this late night alarm isn't as disruptive as it might have been, since I still haven't fallen back asleep after vitals.

I press the Nurse button on the remote. I hear the click indicating the channel is open, and then the click indicating it's closed. I press the button again. "Can I help you?" "Yes, my pump alarm is going off." "I know. The nurse is on his way." She sounds annoyed that I called twice.

I realize that when she responded to my first page, she immediately heard the alarm, closed the channel, and dispatched my nurse. As far as she was concerned, she had solved my problem. However, since she did not respond *to me*, I had no way of knowing that.

This complete lack of verbal communication with the patient was the most extreme case of a more general problem with the Nurse button, a failure to let the patient know what is going on.

I don't have a very good night of sleep, but it's enough. Breakfast is good: oatmeal with bananas, dried cherries, walnuts, a little brown sugar, and a sprinkle of cinnamon; a cream cheese "omelet" (scrambled eggs that I wrap around some cream cheese); grape juice. I realize I should have ordered some milk for the oatmeal, and then realize there are drinks in the Nutrition Room on the floor. To the Nurse button!

click
"Can I help you?"
"Do we have milk in the Nutrition Room?"
"Yes."
"May I have some?"
"(unintelligible and cut off)" *click*

Nurse button, take two.

click
"Can I help you?"
"Could I please have some milk?"
"(unintelligible and cut off)" *click*

Nurse button, take three.

"Can I help you?" (Annoyed?)
"I'm sorry, but I have not been able to understand your answer the last two times. Could I please have some milk?"

"Yes."
click

(Thank you for holding the Talk button down for the entire duration of your response this time!)

The milk arrives. That was Not Easy.

Some work, some nap to make up for last night.

Doctors come. WBC = 2,700. (200, 300, 700, 1,400, 2,700...) Neutrophils are 2,200, which means I am officially not neutropenic anymore, and have some defense against bacteria. I am still very vulnerable to infection, because other parts of the immune system are not back yet, while still others are being suppressed by medication to reduce the chance for rejection. Medically, I could maybe go home Thursday, more likely Friday. Logistically, Saturday is the first day that works. So, barring a late-breaking infection, I'm going home Saturday. (!)

Dad comes, with lunch from Au Bon Pain. Some visiting, some more work.

I take care of some medical administration back home. For some reason, the rest of my family was assigned a new primary care physician earlier this year, as if we were new to the system, and as if Paul were an adult. I restore Paul to his pediatrician of 15+ years, Jan to her doctor of many years, and move Jake to a new doctor that comes highly recommended, since Jake is now too old for a pediatrician and we don't know anything about the doctor he had been assigned to. I also change my primary care physician to the same doctor as Jake, since I have lost confidence in my previous doctor.

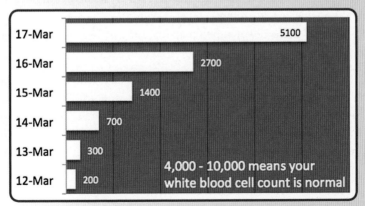

I used white for the bars, to symbolize white blood cells,
and red for the background, for blood in general.

On the home front, the stairs and upstairs hallway get new carpeting, which is great except that the installers leave 90 minutes' worth of cleanup, which the housecleaners have to take care of before getting to the cleaning they were planning to do today. The installers also leave a note: "Sorry for the inconvenience. Our vacuum broke." The manager is incredulous. According to him, installers don't travel with vacuums and would not leave a note. Note in hand, Jan later invites the manager to come see it, and to check out the quality of the installation while he's at it. Like she needs another hassle.

Dad heads off to the Art Institute. I do some more work, get in a 30-minute walk, and get disconnected from the IV pole. I will now take all medications orally. If I need electrolytes, I'll get reconnected, but not for long.

Dad returns with dinner—Black Bean Turkey Mango Brown Rice bowl, and a coconut chai, with dessert (oatmeal chocolate chip cookies) provided by sister Lauren and niece Isabel.

Dad heads off. E-mail, Facebook, blogging, get ready for bed.

2,700!

Posted by Joseph Seeley at 8:30 PM

Thursday, March 17, 2011

Communication Breakdown

There is room for improvement in the Nurse call system. We all have a big red button on our bedside remote, labeled *Nurse*. We have many different reasons to press it: need water, pump alarm going off, having trouble breathing, and so on.

Typically, the call is answered by the unit's secretary, who then (in theory) informs the appropriate person to take care of the request. Secretaries have more duties than just answering these calls, so sometimes they are away from the nurse station. In that case, somebody else will respond—could be a nurse, or an NSA (nursing student aide). If you're lucky, it's your nurse, and he or she says, "I'll be right there," and you know it's true. If it's anybody else, you enter a zone of uncertainty.

The initial response to pressing the button is inevitably, "Can I help you?" After you convey your request, you almost always hear, "I'll tell your nurse," and that's the last you hear from the secretary. Typically, the nurse comes by in a few minutes, so all is well.

However, there have been more than a handful of times that the nurse does not come in a few minutes. A few days ago, I called the nurse station about a pump alarm. "I'll tell your nurse." Fifteen minutes later, the alarm is still going off, and there's no nurse. I call again. "I'll tell your nurse." Five minutes later, the nurse comes, pleased at having timed her arrival just as the alarm was going off. When she hears that the alarm has been going off for 20 minutes, she is puzzled. She had not received a page after my first call. (She had received the second page, but mistook it for one about a patient she was attending at the time.)

My worst case, when I first started having a significant fever, required about 75 minutes and multiple requests for attention before there was any indication of a response, and that was only because my father went out into the hall to find out what was going on.

There was a small but extreme case of non-communication a few nights ago, where the responder never spoke, just opened the channel, heard the pump alarm, and closed the channel again, causing me to call again. He or she perhaps figured that the treatment I was receiving not only cured leukemia but also gave me mind-reading capabilities.

Earlier today, I called about a pump alarm, and the secretary hung up on me without saying anything (but did tell the nurse, who came shortly).

As I write this, I am 15 minutes past "I'll tell the nurse," with a pump alarm going off. Just called again. "I'll tell your nurse." I've been here long enough (9 weeks, 1 day) to know that all this alarm means is that my magnesium is done, and I don't need to worry, and I barely notice the alarm anymore because I have heard it so often.

The nurse comes in, 20 minutes after my first call. She did not receive a page after my first call. Earlier today, she walked past a patient room, heard the alarm, went in, asked if the patient had called, and learned the patient had called 20 minutes earlier. In that case, again, no page.

So, one problem is the secretary (or whoever receives the request from the patient) not actually following through on the promised response to tell the nurse.

Even if the nurse has been contacted, there is no guarantee that the nurse can respond right away. There are plenty of legitimate reasons that you might not get an immediate visit from your nurse: your alarm is less pressing than the needs of another patient at the moment, your nurse has been called away from the floor, the pagers aren't working...

Whatever the cause for the delay, *let the patient know.* It's common courtesy, and good customer service. "I'm sorry. Your nurse is with another patient right now and might not be there for 15 minutes." "I'm sorry. I paged your nurse but haven't heard back. I'll try again, and if I don't hear anything, I'll send in another nurse."

Because if we don't see a nurse within 5 minutes, we start wondering if you actually paged the nurse, and with good reason. In many cases, we're going to worry, and with good reason. Worry is bad for our health, so don't undermine the excellent medical care we're getting with your poor communication skills. Keep us informed, unless you know, for sure, that the nurse or whoever is about to walk into our room.

= = =

And another (minor) thing... I don't really understand "Can I help you?" as the standard response to the call button. I pressed a button that effectively means, "I need help." "Can I help you?" is not the right response. I'm constantly tempted to say, "I certainly hope so."

"How can I help you?" makes more sense, but maybe the hospital's supply of that question has been commandeered by Food Service so that they can get their calls off to an inefficient start by asking how they can help me instead of asking for my name, which they need before they can actually help me by taking my order.

I associate the phrase "Can I help you?" with either mixed or negative situations. There are the sales staff who approach you as you browse the offerings at a store, which is sometimes appreciated and sometimes not. I associate it even more with people who are actually saying, in a sarcastic way, "Stop invading my (expansively defined) space/bothering me/existing." Parents of teenagers may know what I'm talking about.

= = =

Of course, tone makes a big difference. And many of the secretaries say, "Can I help you?" with a tone that makes it clear they want to know how they can help you. These are the ones that often fulfill the request themselves, if it's not medical: bring you water, or a copy of your most recent labs, or a juice.

On the other hand, others convey annoyance, boredom, fatigue...

There is one secretary here who surpasses them all in her negative tone. Her rendition of "Can I help you?" is set to a melody familiar to parents.

It's the melody that usually goes with the lyrics "Do I have to?" So you feel like that's what she's really saying, despite the words.

This same secretary has a lot of trouble keeping her finger on the Talk button long enough to complete her response. So after you burden her with your unreasonable request for water, or pain relief, or breathing assistance, you might get the response, "OK, I'll (click)." You'll what? Forget to page my nurse? I'm sure you have better things to do than respond to patient requests for help, but once you've stirred yourself to listen to my plea, the least you can do is hold the button down for the whole 10 seconds (or less). If that's too hard, please get another job.

I do not have the knowledge to write this score. I could not even have told you how many lines on a staff. Original draft by my father, with help from Wikipedia. Final draft by me.

Posted by Joseph Seeley at 3:15 PM

D+13—Not At All Unlucky

It's nice sleeping without being tethered to an IV pole, although I have not had too much trouble with it. Only a few times have I wrapped the line around myself while sleeping. And visiting the bathroom is simpler. Initially, and for quite a few weeks, I made it harder on myself than it needed to be, by keeping the pole plugged in and navigating the five-footed pole around the power cord, to the bathroom and back. Inevitably, on the way back, I would end up maneuvering the pole's feet around the cord in such a way that I arrived at bedside with the lines wrapped once or twice around the pole. Then came the epiphany that just as I could unplug the pole and go for a walk, or run on the treadmill, I could do the same for these much shorter walks from bed to bathroom. (My mom always said I was smart.) I would have felt smarter if I had figured this out in week one, and I wouldn't have *had* to be smart if someone had passed along this tip when my IV life started.

Anyway, it's nice sleeping without the IV. Unfortunately, after an untethered 1:30 trip to the bathroom—and you would be surprised at how happy that sliver of freedom made me—I am not sleeping at 2:00 a.m. Instead, I am designing (in my head) an online system that would help Illinois Marathon entrants find available rooms in our area and surrounding communities. As it is, all of the race's partner hotels are telling callers that they are full, though we have some (probably outdated) information that a few of them, and some additional places, have rooms. So I'm building a system in my head in which area hotels directly update an online directory of availability, instead of the current weekly phone survey that is obsolete by the time we get the results. (My mom always said I was smart.)

But this isn't what I want to be doing at 2:00 in the morning. I realize I forgot to ask for my A&A (Ambien and Atavan) before going to bed. (Smart, but forgetful.) I get them now, and sleep until 7:30 with a brief interruption around 5:00 for vitals and a blood draw from the arm. Monday and Thursday mornings are the arm draw days. I'm *almost* wistful—this should be the last blood draw from my arm while in the hospital.

Is it my imagination, or does the air constantly pumped into my room, air that is normally dry to the point of causing nose bleeds, seem a little more moist today, and smell vaguely like spring? Could just be me anticipating breathing fresh air in a few days, for the first time in nine and a half weeks. Or it could be that some trace of the warm, moist spring air outside survives the filtering process. I'll go with the latter, since it's a more real connection to spring.

A good breakfast, a good morning of work, back on the IV for two hours (magnesium).

My dad brings in another lunch. Food Service is going to wonder if I'm on a hunger strike. More work.

I have a new attending today; they stay with a unit for about four weeks. He's not totally up to speed with all the details of my case, but he is able to answer some questions. So, I learn that, barring complications, I can travel by public transportation (bus, train, plane) by the middle of June. I can shave with a regular razor when my platelet count reaches 30 (thousand) for sure, and my supervising physician might even be OK with 20. When I get home,

I should try sleeping without any chemical aids for a few days before deciding whether I still need the help. (This was my plan anyway.)

"Can you tell me my counts?"
"Counts? They don't really matter anymore, now that you're past 4,000. I think it was 5,000 something... maybe 5,800..."

Counts don't matter?! I have a graph to update! As soon as he leaves, I request a copy of today's blood work results.

5,100! (But I guess the specific number no longer matters.) My platelets and hemoglobin are also slightly higher than yesterday, without the benefit of transfusions, so I'm creating the various types of blood.

Because I have reached the magic number (4,000), I no longer receive Neupogen shots. Going forward, this means I can expect my blood counts to drift down before they climb again. For example, the WBC might go as low as half of its Neupogen-induced peak. The doctor says this is normal.

A little more work, some blogging, a walk, dinner (grilled tuna steak on a salad, McClintock fig bar for dessert), a shower.

I am (almost certainly) going home on Saturday. Once I'm home, the pace of blogging is likely to slow down. There will be fewer changes from day to day, and I will have more responsibilities. But it's still a different-than-normal life, so I will post something every few days. If something interesting comes up, I'll post more often, but I'm hoping it's all pretty boring for months and months and months.

Posted by Joseph Seeley at 7:18 PM

Friday, March 18, 2011

D+14—Last Night!

The night passes reasonably well. Again, I forgot to ask for my recent sleeping meds. However, this time I don't need them, and I fall back to sleep after each interruption, eventually. Part of my difficulty returning to slumber is my growing excitement about walking out of here some time tomorrow. At one point, my eyes get teary—I'm not crying, but close.

Later, I have Earth, Wind & Fire songs running through my head—"Sing a Song," "September"—upbeat songs that are hard not to dance to. (Except that I'm in bed.) Not sure why those songs, this night, though my musical preferences are heavily influenced by the music I listened to in high school. Judging by the number of songs from the baby boomer high school years running in commercials these days, I assume I am not alone in my arrested musical development.

I have a now-typical morning of breakfast and some work, broken up by a return visit from the president of the medical center. She tells me she has been keeping up with this blog, tracking my progress, and getting useful information about what it's like to be a patient here. We talk about my next few months and her first few weeks ("like drinking from a fire hose"). It is clear, again, that she has a strong will to make it easier for the staff to provide a better patient experience. I have done what I could during my 9+ weeks. Thankfully, my time here is up. However, I am confident I am leaving the medical center in very good hands :-)

Respecting the wishes of my subconscious self, I put on Earth, Wind & Fire's greatest hits.

The attending and fellow drop by. WBC = 8,100 (but it doesn't matter). Platelets are up, hemoglobin slightly down.

Mara calls, to check in. She's very happy with the productivity of her stem cells, after concern over the slight shortage. "Quality over quantity," is her explanation. Works for me!

Dad brings macaroni and cheese from the Au Bon Pain. It is a completely different dish than the macaroni and cheese from Food Service. I can taste a few cheeses, and I want to eat the whole thing. Adrian, volunteer extraordinaire, stops by, and he and Dad engage in a freewheeling discussion of the history of mathematics, mathematical heroes, and more.

Dad heads to the train station, to arrive in Champaign this evening. He'll be back late morning tomorrow to break me out of this joint.

Listening now to Eric Clapton's *Unplugged* album. Probably going to Bonnie Raitt next.

In the late afternoon, a nap pounces on my eyelids. I am awakened by a call from a local pharmacy about a prescription I need to get filled up here since it can't be filled in Champaign. They will deliver it tomorrow, in the early afternoon. Depending on how early "early" is, we may be all packed up and ready to go, waiting on them.

Paul e-mails me a homecoming preview: (Thanks, Paul!)

I work on the race website with the UNC-LIU Brooklyn game on.

Last dinner from Food Service: frank and beans, fries, salad. (Papa Del's pizza is on the menu for tomorrow's dinner.) More basketball, including the Illinois-UNLV game. Looks like they brought back the Illinois team from the beginning of the season, the one that plays for 40 minutes. More work on the race site. A little packing. (!)

To bed.

Last night!

Posted by Joseph Seeley at 8:12 PM

The first signs of spring at home.

Saturday, March 19, 2011

Goodbye Room

In the sickly green room
There was a telephone
And a button red
And no view of—

Anything much outside my head

And there were transport staff who didn't care

And sleep in bursts and one bad nurse

And sweats and chills and countless pills

And a small TV and surgery

And fiber-free, oversalted food

And a secretary supremely rude

Goodbye room

(Not a moment too soon)

Goodbye space without leaf or bloom

Goodbye gown and goodbye pole

Goodbye oatmeal piping cold

Goodbye shower that doesn't wet

Goodbye pillow that makes me sweat

Goodbye oversalted food

And goodbye to the secretary supremely rude

Goodbye transport that doesn't care

Goodbye hospital, hello fresh air.

(Any similarity to the children's classic *Goodnight Moon* is entirely intentional.)

Posted by Joseph Seeley at 5:09 AM

Part 2

There's No Place Like Home

Spring and early summer marked a time of innocent optimism in our family's journey with Joe. He came home from the hospital following what appeared to have been a successful stem cell transplant. He enjoyed simple, everyday pleasures, like peeing into a toilet instead of a handheld urinal. In June, he began to map his training strategy for a 5K in the fall and dreamed of an ambitious day hike the following summer, in New Hampshire's White Mountains.

In early August, Joe, Jan, Jake, and Paul were able to make the annual summer trip for the extended family vacation in New Hampshire, something that had not looked likely earlier in the year. My pent-up desire to be useful in some way found its outlet in scrubbing the vacation house for my immunologically challenged and adored older brother. New Hampshire was his favorite place, and we wanted everything to be perfect.

In a bittersweet way, it was. Joe walked in the garden and admired the flowers in the late afternoon sun. He floated on his back in the pool while we stood around the edge and watched in gratitude and wonderment. We took a short walk through woods on a winding trail

(continued)

fragrant with dry pine needles to a cove on Squam Lake. While we swam, he crouched on the shaded shore, making graceful leaf boats, which he set adrift on the water.

By this point, there were hints of trouble ahead, and we all knew that another New Hampshire August was far from assured. I drove him to the Laconia hospital for blood work, and asked why he hadn't been more persistent in trying to reach his doctor to get the results from his last round of tests. "Why risk ruining a family vacation with what might be bad news?" he asked.

Sadly, there was bad news, and more treatments to try. In early October, I went to Champaign for a few days while Jan was out of town. I made Joe's favorite meals, curled up on the carpet outside his bedroom door while he slept, and watched movies in comfortable companionship. It's not the way I would have chosen to spend so much quality time with Joe, but I was grateful for it, grateful for his humor and grace.

—Lauren Seeley Aguirre, Joe's sister

Joe and Lauren: Newton, Massachusetts, circa 1969

There's No Place Like Home

Just a quick note, since I have some other things to do today. I'm now at home, feeling pretty healthy. It's great to be here.

Some future blog post topics: the excellent medical care I received, the things that can go wrong over the next few months (a short list), and the precautions I need to take to minimize the risk that things do go wrong (a long list).

Interesting fact brought to my attention by the man who delivered my medications today—today is St. Joseph's Day. (St. Joseph is the patron saint of people named Joseph.)

Posted by Joseph Seeley at 3:45 PM

Monday, March 21, 2011

Simple Pleasures

Highlights from my first 24 hours at home:

Our first walk at home, post transplant

▶ Papa Del's pizza

▶ A salad that is not predominantly iceberg lettuce

▶ Watching basketball with Paul

▶ A shower with a higher flow rate than a spray bottle

▶ A bath towel larger and more absorbent than a dish towel

▶ Peeing into a toilet instead of into a handheld plastic urinal

▶ A comfortable bed

▶ Sleeping with Jan

▶ A long morning walk outside with Jan

▶ Bread from Great Harvest

Bliss.

Posted by Joseph Seeley at 7:39 PM

D+17—Excellent Report Card

In the morning, I receive a visit from a local home care nurse. There is some paperwork, and then the plan is for the nurse to show me how to flush my lines. However, the supplies have not been delivered to my house, so she can't do it. It's not a medical problem, because I'm headed back to Chicago for my first outpatient appointment after release from the hospital today, and they can do the flushing there.

The nurse also notes that the supplies ordered for my flushes are missing a typical component, the syringes of saline. I add that to my list of questions for the doctor this afternoon.

At noon, my father and I drive back to Chicago, this time the outpatient clinic. While I head over for my blood draw, my dad heads back to the unit I just left, to see if he can retrieve the two items I left behind: the new foam pillow that Jan brought me, which was disguised as a regular pillow and so avoided the packing frenzy; and the marionberry preserves from Jeff, which were hiding in the refrigerator by the nurse's station. No pillow, but the preserves are still there, thank goodness.

I get my vitals taken, lines flushed, blood drawn, and dressing changed. The nurse notices that the whites of my eyes are slightly yellow—a topic to raise with my doctor.

I head over to the waiting area to see my doctor. It's a short wait. First, a nurse reviews how things are going and reviews my two lists of medicines, making notes for the doctor.

Shortly, my doctor comes in, with most blood test results already in hand. I'm doing about as well as one can do at this point. While the white blood cells have dived—expected after discontinuing the Neupogen—the leading indicator of successful engraftment, the platelets, are increasing at a good pace. My appetite and energy level are very good for D+17. She attributes at least part of this condition to my positive and cooperative attitude. (It had never occurred to me to be uncooperative with the doctors, due to my confidence that they knew what they were doing, but apparently I would be surprised at how often that happens.) She resolves the differences between my two medication lists, answers my long list of questions, and concludes with, "See you next Monday."

The last time we talked, by phone, she had said she expected to see me weekly. Subsequent interactions with other doctors and nurses had prepared me for the possibility of a return visit on Thursday, so "next Monday" was the cherry on the sundae for a very good Monday.

After she left, the fellow and the transplant nurse came in. The fellow had a serious face. "So, you've heard... you're being readmitted tonight." Since this was the same fellow who previously promised to increase the frequency of my nightly interruptions and told me on discharge day that discharge time was not midday but 7:00 p.m., I wasn't fooled. I just hope he reserves his kidding for patients he knows are on to him, because it could distress less prepared patients.

The nurse and I discussed a few things, and she got the information she needed to update my line flushing supplies.

Then my dad and I drove home, in a very good mood.

Posted by Joseph Seeley at 8:06 PM

D+19—No News Is Good News

There is nothing much to report from the last couple of days. Win!

Both mornings have started with an early morning walk, trying to beat the sun. (More on my need to have something approaching a vampire's fear of the sun in a later post.) Then breakfast, some work, a nap either before or after lunch, some more work, another nap, dinner.

Yesterday, I walked by myself. On the path around the pond in Mattis Park, as I was approaching the footbridge, I saw a hawk sitting on the railing. It kept peering down over the railing and then back at me, and it allowed me to get within 10 feet. I rued my failure to bring a camera. It finally lit out for a nearby tree. As I crossed the bridge, two squirrels bolted from under the bridge to a different tree, so I think I spoiled the hawk's breakfast plans. (Sorry, hawk!) (You're welcome, squirrels!)

Today, I walked with Jan. This is a great small pleasure, for both of us, though I do ask her to slow down occasionally. My exact words are, "Slow down, Sparky." This deprives her, she jokes, of the satisfaction of walking faster than a man recovering from treatment for leukemia. Those who know Jan know that she's usually multitasking and doing whatever she's doing at a quick pace—that's how she gets so much done. So it runs against form for her to stroll, even when we are walking somewhere in no particular hurry, and the current situation is not the first time I have tried to rein Sparky in while we're walking or when she drops something in the kitchen.

I have learned that I should take naps before they take me. Late in the afternoon yesterday, I headed upstairs to get something. Going up stairs dispels any illusion I may have that I'm back to normal. I have a muscle memory for how quickly I go upstairs, and I have had to unlearn that. First, I slowed the pace. That was not enough. Now, I climb them using the technique I learned when climbing Mt. Rainier with my dad, just out of high school—when the air gets especially thin, you take a few steps, rest; take a few steps, rest.

When I got upstairs and into the bedroom, whatever my mission was got deprioritized so that I could lie down for a brief rest. That was when the nap saw its chance and ambushed me, dragging me off into Sleepytime Woods for an apparently much-needed rest.

Today, enlightened, I took a brief nap after lunch and a longer one before dinner. So take that, naps. You're not the boss of me.

Around midday today, I had a return visit from the home care nurse, to show me how to flush the lines on my Hickman Triple Lumen. She was supposed to do that on Monday, but the supplies had not been delivered. Even if they had been, the lesson would not have been conducted, because the supply order from the hospital had been incomplete. When I was back at the clinic on Monday, the nurse said she would get the full order sent down. Yesterday morning, I received a box of supplies, but they were the original incomplete order. Late in the afternoon, I received a second box of supplies, containing the full order. So I now have everything I need, and twice as much as I need when it comes to heparin and alcohol wipes. Jeff tells me the alcohol wipes are useful for getting a fire started in the woods when it's wet, so that would be useful, except that's not a situation I have found myself in very often. I can't think of any use for extra heparin that wouldn't be criminal.

Anyway, supplies on hand, I had my lesson on line flushing. Wipe the nib vigorously for 30 seconds with the swab (and then don't let it touch anything until I'm done), take the cap off the 10cc saline syringe, push out the air bubble, attach the syringe, release the line clamp, squeeze in the saline, take the cap off the 5cc Heparin syringe, squeeze out the air bubble, detach the saline syringe, attach the heparin, squeeze it in, detach it, close the line clamp. Repeat for the other two lines. To keep track of which I have done, take advantage of the three different line end colors and go in this order: red, white, blue.

At the hospital, they used a different wipe, which one nurse said was better than the alcohol wipes. Every time I straightened up my room during my stay, I had another 3 or 6 or 8 of these stronger wipes lying around, which I stored in a plastic bag, which came home with me. So I have a good supply of them, although they are so good at cleaning that you need to wear gloves, which I don't have yet. Maybe I'll snag some on my next trip up.

As I push the plunger on the syringe, I can't help picturing a junkie, since that's the only image I have of people using a syringe. I have to do this every other day for at least a couple more weeks, so I'm sure I'll come to feel less like a junkie over time.

Fantastic dinner tonight, courtesy of our friend Mary, with a big assist from her dad on the roast beef. I had had the exact same combination once in the hospital: roast beef, mashed potatoes, gravy, broccoli, brownie. It was one of the better meal options there, but tonight's was a completely different experience, and only slightly because I was sitting at my own dining table. Flavorful roast beef, real mashed potatoes, a gravy that you had to mix because it separated, chewy brownies... Mmmmm....

= = =

Update (translation: I forgot something): Tuesday morning, I received a call from my doctor. "I need to talk to you about your Prograf levels." Hmm. Could be minor, such as I need to take a little more or a little less. Or, something else...

I get to see (hear) the medical sleuth at work.

"Are you sure you did not take your Prograf yesterday morning before coming to the clinic?" I am as certain as I can be, although that's only about 90% certain, since my short-term memory isn't great. The doctor says it's chemo brain—let's go with that.

"Where did you have your blood drawn?" There are two choices on my clinic's floor if you are having blood drawn. I had been directed to the apheresis lab, which I'm guessing is the more sophisticated of the two, and that is where I had gone.

"How did they draw your blood?" From one of my lines.
"For all of the blood?" Yes.

Eureka! (She didn't say that.) Prograf levels cannot be tested in blood drawn through the line—something about Prograf sticking to or being absorbed by the line over time and then being released from the line when you draw blood through it, greatly inflating the result. My doctor is not happy that the lab tech did not draw my blood correctly, but relieved that I'm not in danger. If I truly had the level reported by the test, my doctor tells me, I would be in kidney failure. Since I'm feeling well, and had my Prograf level tested shortly before discharge, she feels comfortable waiting until my Monday appointment.

Posted by Joseph Seeley at 6:59 PM

Saturday, March 26, 2011

D+22—One-Week Anniversary of Being Home

A decent night's sleep in my wonderful bed, with my wonderful wife. Even without the vitals checks, blood draws, and medication deliveries, I still wake more often than I used to during the night. I might still be adjusting. Last night I awoke three hours after going to sleep, lay awake for about an hour, awoke again after three more hours, and then got another hour or so of sleep. I'll take it.

It is quite cold this morning for my walk. 25 degrees and windy. The only skin that's going to be exposed is around my eyes and nose, so that is where I apply sunscreen. Overkill, in March, early in the morning? Maybe. But the Black Book keeps saying you can't be too careful, so I try to be more careful than I need to be. It's working so far.

It feels like winter, but it looks and sounds like spring: a lot of crocuses, a few daffodils, and many more bulbs in leaf but not yet in flower; chickadees, finches, titmice, cardinals, robins, a woodpecker.

I'm feeling (a little) stronger every day. Yesterday, I forgot to use the mountaineering approach to the stairs and didn't pay for it when I got to the top. I feel that I'm walking faster than a few days ago. I think I might even be able to jog a little, so I give it a try. I am disappointed, but not surprised, that jogging is too tiring. I *am* surprised that it only took 5 steps to determine that. Lovely day for a walk, isn't it? Especially a walk accompanied by castanets, which are actually the three nibs of my Hickman Triple Lumen, hanging from my chest and clacking against each other with every other step.

The day is uneventful. (Yay!) Breakfast; meds, temp (normal), and weight (steady, but 15 pounds less than when I entered the hospital); some race site work; lunch; a nap; more site work; some basketball (watching, not playing); dinner; U.S. v Argentina (1-1!); a little work on taxes (boo!); meds and temp (normal); bed (yay!).

Posted by Joseph Seeley at 6:48 PM

Tuesday, March 29, 2011

D+25—I Have a Drinking Problem

Lauren is in town for a couple of days, cooking up some great food—Norwegian rolls, Spanish chicken stew, fresh lemon-limeade, strawberry-blackberry pie—and driving up with me yesterday (Monday) for my second check-up back at the clinic.

I have not yet needed to be driven to Chicago, physically, but I do need to have a second driver in the car. It is a long enough drive, and I can get sick so quickly, that I could start a drive feeling fine and not be able to complete it. I do some of the driving, but I also take naps (while not driving).

On Monday, I was a little extra draggy—didn't go for a walk, got winded going up the stairs again, felt especially lightheaded when standing up. I predicted that my hemoglobin levels would be low when I got the blood test results in the afternoon.

My family and I are becoming very familiar with the stretch of I-57 between Champaign and Chicago. I think we're even seeing the same hawks sitting on the same fence posts on our various trips.

Whenever I have parked up at the clinic, I have had to go to the very top of the garage before finding a spot. My dad has always found a spot on or near the first deck. Lauren is currently in first place, after finding a spot about 8 cars in from the exit we take to walk across the street to the clinic.

I check in for my appointment and get sent over to Apheresis for my blood draw. Apheresis takes vitals and then sends me over to a different lab, because my doctor wants to make sure the Prograf level test is done on blood drawn from my arm. (My blood pressure is 100/60, which is low for me.) Then it's back to wait for my appointment.

I get called in at 3:00, half an hour before my appointment. Maybe we're going to get out of here sooner than expected. Some questions from a nurse, then waiting in the exam room.

I feel something on my tongue. Like a small piece of food, but I haven't eaten in hours. I pick it off my tongue and put it on a tissue. It's the size of a split pea, mostly yellowish, but with fine streaks of black or dark brown. Then I feel more, almost all smaller than the first. Some look like single short hairs, an eighth of an inch long. Some are just pale little yellow chunks. I gather them on a couple of small tissues to show the doctor, but I know what it is.

Ever since I had the Black Tongue, the flora of my mouth has been out of whack. Brushing my teeth and rinsing with mouthwash after every meal helps. Brushing the tongue is very helpful, but I can't brush all the way to the back of my tongue due to the gag reflex, and that is where things grow—on my tongue—during the day. For some reason, the party dies down at night. At times during the day, I can feel a bumper crop of crap back there, but I can't get rid of it.

Now, waiting for the doctor, my tongue is shedding. It's disgusting. But good!

The fellow comes in. I proudly show him my harvest of whatever it is that's coming off my tongue. He appreciates the visuals and gives me permission to throw them out. He has preliminary blood test results for me. Mostly reasonable, especially the hemoglobin, so my prediction was wrong. My creatinine level is higher than desired, an indication that I am dehydrated and that my kidneys are having some trouble. He floats the idea that I might get a rehydration IV before leaving and/or receive one at home in the next few days. He leaves. More waiting, more shedding.

Around 4:30, my doctor comes in. She wants to know how often I'm peeing. I think every four hours is pretty normal, but it's not enough. She wants me drinking enough that I'm peeing every one to two hours. Also, no tea, not even herbal, which has been a staple of my days. Even herbal teas can dehydrate you. So, I have really had *two* drinking problems: not drinking enough, and some of what I'm drinking being the wrong stuff.

My doctor's solution to the dehydration problem—drink more of the right stuff—illustrates one of the things I like about her. She seems to be firmly in the "first, do no harm" camp of medicine, where other doctors seem to think first what medical intervention will help—what pill, what procedure. My doctor, though not averse to prescribing procedures and pills, respects the body's ability to heal itself, given a little help.

After my appointment, I have to get some blood redrawn, because the sample that provided the preliminary good news about blood counts turned out to have clotted, rendering its results invalid. This means I leave the clinic not knowing my blood counts or my Prograf levels.

Today (Tuesday) is a day of heavy drinking and frequent trips to the bathroom. I check in with my doctor at the end of the day, having not heard anything. As I assumed, no news is good news. The second blood draw yielded valid and solid blood counts. My Prograf level is a little higher than desired, which probably explains the elevated creatinine counts. She adjusts my dosage.

I'm headed back on Friday for a pulmonary function test and the first bone marrow biopsy since my transplant.

But right now, I have to go pee.

Posted by Joseph Seeley at 6:55 PM

Saturday, April 2, 2011

D+28—Blood, Breath, and Bone

Lauren left Wednesday morning, and my mom came in Wednesday evening, the final leg of the Seeley Family Relay—dad, Lauren, mom, each coming in from the Boston area.

On Friday, my mom and I drove up for a bunch of tests: blood work, pulmonary function, and a bone marrow biopsy.

I check in at the clinic, and they send me to Apheresis for my blood work. When I get there, they say I have to go to Phlebotomy. (Apheresis draws from my lines, Phlebotomy from my arm.) The first clinic blood draw was faulty, because they drew from my line and got invalid Prograf levels. The second time I had blood drawn, I was sent to Apheresis and then (correctly) redirected to Phlebotomy. The Prograf level was measured fine, but they had to redraw for some other tests because a sample clotted. Anyway, I go off to Phlebotomy without a fuss. Maybe the third time will be the charm.

When I arrive at Phlebotomy, the clerk tells me I need to have my blood drawn at Apheresis. I tell her I'm sure I am supposed to have the blood drawn from my arm, and she accepts that. (There's no downside to the arm stick, except the arm stick, whereas drawing from the line can distort test results.)

Once I'm in the Phlebotomy bloodletting room, I start reading the appointment sheet I was handed when I checked in. There's a note saying, "Blood must be drawn at Apheresis!", so I start to doubt my decision to insist on Phlebotomy. I page my doctor, who (as always) calls back within minutes. I tell her there is some confusion about where I should have my blood drawn. She is not surprised. Despite the note directing me to Apheresis, she wants the blood drawn at Phlebotomy, because one of the tests is a Prograf level. Uh oh.

I don't recall hearing we were testing my Prograf level, so I took my Prograf in the morning, which invalidates the results. My doctor tells me it no longer matters where they draw my blood, so I have it drawn where I am. I will get a Prograf level when I return on Monday.

Then I'm off to the Pulmonary Function Test. I had one of these during my hospitalization, pre-transplant, as a benchmark, and the goal is to compare then to now. I sit in a cylindrical booth while the tech explains what's going to happen. There are several different tests, repeated a few times. I clamp my mouth around a breathing tube and obey instructions. For a couple of the tests, the booth is sealed around me—combined with the tube in my mouth, I feel slightly claustrophobic. It's a good thing the booth has transparent sides.

The first time I took this battery of tests, the tech used a drill sergeant approach. She would tell me to breathe in deeply and then breathe out as hard and as long as I can. Then she would start yelling, "Keep going! More! More! More!", even as I was sure I had breathed out every whiff and maybe a wisp of lung. Then we would do it again. Each time, I felt like I had let her down because I stopped breathing out before she stopped yelling at me. (It's not a mean yell, and I have heard from others that this is a common technique for getting people to maximize their scores on these tests.)

Today's tech has a much more relaxed style. He tells me what we are going to do and then calmly directs me through each test. He has the monitor turned so that I can see my own data being recorded, and I see that even when I think I can squeeze no more from my lungs, the numbers are still climbing. So I keep exhaling. The biofeedback approach, intentional or not, suits me better than being yelled at.

I have no idea how today's numbers compare to my earlier numbers, but I feel like my lungs are fully functional. On my way back out to the waiting room, I hear the tech from my first test battery, behind closed doors, barking, "More! More! Keep going!"

Off for the biopsy, my fourth in 2011. Sadly for my insurance company, there is no "every fourth one free" policy. I'm fairly relaxed, because these biopsies have not been too uncomfortable. The woman doing the drilling this time has little trouble getting through for the marrow pull. In the past, there have been a couple of short painful pulls. This first pull is surprisingly painful and feels like it is drawing marrow from my hip, my thigh, my shin, and my ankle. I know this is not physically the case, since even though the hip bone is connected to the thigh bone, and so on, their marrows are not connected. The second pull is less painful. And each of the next four—I had previously consented to supply marrow for research, so they're collecting much more than usual—is less painful than the one before.

Then it's on to extracting a core sample of bone, in the same numbed spot. She spends some time finding just the right place and angle, but once she settles on one, she has pulled out a sample—extra large, again for research— before I realize that she's done.

I'm feeling good. On Monday, all these test results will let me know if I'm doing as well as I think I am.

Posted by Joseph Seeley at 2:38 PM

Monday, April 4, 2011

D+31—"Our Most Boring Patient"

My mom and I drive up for my regular Monday appointment. Mom takes the lead in the parking spot contest, finding a space two spots from the exit we take to reach the clinic. And one of those spots is reserved for the handicapped, so it's going to be hard to do better.

On the elevator ride up to the appointment, two young men get on, wearing doctor's jackets. I hesitate to say they are doctors, because they appear, to my mom and me, to be in high school. That makes me feel old.

I get my blood drawn at Phlebotomy, as it should be. I get my dressing and caps changed at Apheresis. The fellow declares me their "most boring patient." Fantastic!

The doctor tells me I'm doing great—all the counts are reasonable. Why am I doing so well? At least in part, because I was admitted in good shape, and because I'm "so young." (Thank you, Doctor! I needed that.)

We won't know the bone marrow results until tomorrow (hoping for lots of blood cells), later in the week (hoping for entirely Mara's cells), and later next week (hoping for no signs of leukemia). But the doctor thinks it likely there will be good numbers all around.

To go with the probable good news, I get some certain good news:

▶ I don't need to go back for two weeks.

▶ I can drink alcohol, in moderation. (Since I get light-headed on a full glass of beer, this will not be a hardship.)

I'll drink to that!

Posted by Joseph Seeley at 8:33 PM

Saturday, April 9, 2011

D+36—What Could Possibly Go Wrong? (Part 1)

The two main risks for a stem cell transplant patient, after transplant, are infections and graft-vs.-host disease (GVHD). The latter is when the new immune system (the graft) starts to attack one or more organs of the old body (the host). More on GVHD later, and I hope it's not from personal experience.

To minimize the chances of GVHD, I take a medication that suppresses the activity of my new immune system, which isn't yet fully functional anyway. My white blood cell counts are lower than normal, which *is* normal at this point. The combination of low counts and medication makes me exceptionally vulnerable to infection. A bacterium, fungal spore, or virus that a healthy person would typically dispatch without breaking a sweat—without even noticing—can now easily and quickly make me sweat. And spew. And squirt. (Feel free to take this as a warning to proceed at your own risk.)

A couple of weeks ago, I had a mild sore throat. Neither Jan nor Paul were sick. Based on the symptoms, my doctor felt it was likely a virus and, as long as I didn't develop a fever, it was safe to ride it out. It went away after a few days.

This past Wednesday, after a really good Tuesday, I wake up anticipating another really good day. It starts well enough. I get up, have a bowl of cereal (first breakfast), do a little work. My belly is slightly gurgly, and I am a little queasy.

As I am taking my morning medications, I choke on one of the pills. The choking leads to gagging, which leads to my first post-transplant upchuck. It feels more like a gag reflex than something more serious, but it's reason enough to call my doctor. (The rule for transplant patients is, everything is reason enough to call the doctor—a splinter, a small cough, a tiny rash, a reddish eye, a mild earache...)

Is anyone else in the family sick? No? She tells me to keep hydrated and watch for fever. If I can't stay hydrated, or if I develop a fever, she wants me back up at the clinic, and possibly readmitted. I'm not really in the mood for eating, but I can drink, and I do. I tell Jan what's going on, and she asks for regular updates.

Meanwhile, my body is doing its best to dehydrate me. It is the Day of Diarrhea. I do not spend the whole day on the toilet, but there are quite a few increasingly fluid trips. Between trips, my intestines are occasionally at peace and sometimes amusingly noisy—gurgles, gloops, rumbles, blips. And sometimes it feels like miniature dolphins are playing tag inside Joe's Intestinal Fun House. And that's usually when it's time to make another trip to the bathroom. I also keep a bucket with me.

Lunch is a piece of toast. Then I take a nap, during which Jan can't reach me, so she comes home to work and keep an eye on me.

In the afternoon, I'm feeling that the worst is over. The diarrhea seems to have played itself out—could there be any more in there? My parents call, knowing that I was ill earlier in the day, wanting some peace of mind before they go out to a play. I reassure them, honestly.

As soon as I hang up, the dolphins start chasing each other again, but they're headed the other way. And my bucket's in the other room! Paul, home from school, runs into the living room (my "office") with the bucket and gets out as fast as he can.

This episode is more convincing than the morning's, which I could pass off as a gag reflex. This one is more productive, more gripping, longer lasting—everything a vomiting episode would want to be, really.

I'm feeling a little better, as one often does post-purge. I don't have a fever. Still, I'm clearly not well. Jan has some race commitments at the end of the day, and it turns out Paul has a movie to watch for school at roughly the same time. We put out a couple of calls for a "sitter," and quickly find a willing tandem: Robert, when he's done with soccer practice, and Cathy in case Robert is late.

After Robert arrives, I make some white rice. I have been drinking all day, but the only food I've had is cereal (temporarily) and toast (also temporarily). I sit down to some plain rice, while Robert gets a can of Guinness for dinner.

After two bites of rice, the dolphins are at play again. I'm off to the bathroom, with my bucket. Which is a good thing, because I'm already retching before I reach the bathroom. Then I'm on the toilet, forcefully emptying my digestive tract from both ends, simultaneously. (Why is that even possible? Wouldn't that create a vacuum in the middle?) All the drinking has its effect, so I'm peeing at the same time, and the retching is so powerful that my eyes are watering. I'm dehydrating through four types of orifice at once! I dub this accomplishment, The Quad. Rarely attempted, never enjoyed.

(Maybe if I had drunk more heavily in college, this experience would have been less novel. No regrets there.)

The Quad marks the high/low point of this infection. The rest of Robert's visit is uneventful, even pleasant. (Thanks, Robert!) During the night, I run a low fever but not above the call-the-doctor threshold. The next day, I'm still queasy but everything stays down. Friday is a good day, Saturday better.

Time to get back to boring.

Posted by Joseph Seeley at 2:30 PM

Thursday, April 14, 2011

I Am Woman

The first half of this week featured a sequel to last week's intestinal distress. Like most sequels, it didn't live up to the original, at least in intensity. Also, it was too long. Instead of all the symptoms combining on a single day, this time each symptom got its own day: Diarrhea Monday, Upchuck Tuesday, Nausea Wednesday. Di and Chuck just mailed it in, if you ask me. In Act Three, however, Nausea, merely a supporting player in the original, stole the show. I was so impressed, I had to go to bed around 6:00 p.m. and not get up until this morning.

I checked in with my doctor on Tuesday. As long as these symptoms come and go, without fever, and not too often, we (I) will just ride them out. If the symptoms persist, I'll get scoped. Colonoscopy, sigmoidoscopy... I don't know. Seems viral for now, but it could be a manifestation of graft-vs.-host disease.

My doctor also had the second round of results from my bone marrow biopsy. Round One was that I have strong numbers of all the right kinds of blood cells in my marrow. Round Two is that the blood cells are more than 99% female—XX, not XY. (Or, as Sen. John "Not Meant To Be Factual" Kyl of Arizona would put it, my blood cells are more than 99% male.)

Since my donor was my sister, this is excellent news. The less host (XY) blood there is, the more successful the transplant has been, and the less chance there is for any leukemia to have made it through the treatment.

The final result we're waiting for is whether there are any cells with "deletion 7": chromosome 7 missing some genetic material. My leukemic cells had this marker, so they will be relatively easy to find if any have made it. I should find out Monday.

Until then, I'm very happy that my blood is (almost) all woman. Hear me roar.

Posted by Joseph Seeley at 3:30 PM

Friday, April 15, 2011

This Doesn't Always End Well

Around the time we were preparing for me to leave the hospital, we learned that someone in town was following a somewhat parallel path. Her son was a teammate of Paul's on the high school soccer team, so we knew each other from the sidelines. She was diagnosed a week before I was. Like me, she was being treated in Chicago. If we had been in the same hospital, we would have been on the same corridor.

We spoke once by phone, after I was home and a few weeks before she was going to receive her own cells back again. Her treatments had been hard on her—multiple rounds of chemo and radiation. The week after her transplant, we learned from her husband she was doing OK but was tired and had a fever. A couple of weeks ago, she was doing better.

She died earlier this week. Wake and mass tomorrow.

Posted by Joseph Seeley at 5:26 PM

Failing to be Boring

Since being pronounced the "most boring patient" just under two weeks ago, I have had three separate bouts of nausea + vomiting + diarrhea. Last night, after a really good day, during which I even mixed a little jogging into my morning walk, was the most draining (literally and figuratively) of the three. Around 2:00 a.m., I started having a new additional symptom—shakes and chills—so we called my doctor.

We discussed going to the local ER vs. driving up to Chicago. My past experiences with ERs is that you often wait a very long time to be seen, unless you're bleeding heavily. I thought the odds were good that I could get to Chicago in less time than it would take to be seen locally, and then I would still need to be transported to Chicago. The doctor called the ER in Chicago so that they were expecting me. Jan called our friend Bonnie to ride up with us, and the two of them split the driving.

We checked into the ER in Chicago around 5:00 a.m. Initially we were given the impression that they would start some treatments in the ER (like IV drips to rehydrate me and provide additional antibiotics) and that I would shortly be admitted back to the sixth floor. As the morning dragged on, we learned that there was not currently an available bed up on the floor I would be heading to. The ER nurse recounted a cautionary tale of a patient warehoused in the ER for five days while waiting for a room.

Around 7:00, the blood cancer fellow comes by doing his rounds. He tells me there will be a bunch of tests to look for infection, but I might also get scoped, from both ends. And don't eat anything for now, because the GI doc may decide now is a good time to take a peek (I'm already empty). The fellow has blood test results from blood taken shortly after my arrival. Good counts! My platelets are at 130, which is higher than they have been since I was diagnosed with aplastic anemia six-plus years ago. My white counts are also very good, with hemoglobin lagging but still good enough.

There's less privacy in the ER than there is on the blood cancer floor, where each patient gets his or her own room. The ER is more similar to a cube farm. Each "room" is a (fairly large) curtained space, which means you hear what's happening on nearby beds. There's the woman from Puerto Rico who can't breathe or communicate in English. (Fortunately, at least one of the doctors speaks passable Spanish.) There's the man with some excruciating pain, leading to over an hour of "ohhh... ohhh... ohhh... OHHH... ohhh... oh, God... ohhh... ohhh... ohhh... ohhh... Jesus!... ohhh... ohhh...." It could be the soundtrack for a particularly unimaginative porn flick. After an hour, he receives some pain relief, and a few hours later, I see him walking out a much happier man.

The attending comes down to visit. As he puts it: the number one suspect for my symptoms is an infection, the number two suspect is an infection, and the number three suspect is an infection. So they will initially focus their attention on getting some cultures (blood, stool) to look for infection. There are several types of infection, not based in the intestines, that can cause the on-again off-again pattern I have been experiencing. Or, it could be something intestinal. He does not think it is graft-vs.-host disease, because of the pattern.

I get cleared to eat, since the attending does not think any scoping is in order at this time. I start thinking about what I would order off the menu that I have memorized from my previous stay, but it turns out to be a waste of time. In the ER, they decide what you want to eat and when. For a patient in the hospital because of nausea and vomiting, this seems like an approach sure to fail to supply adequate nutrition. Of the lunch that is delivered, the only food I feel like eating is the tomato soup and the crackers. I supplement later with more crackers and some ginger ale.

Back to privacy: I have an 8-foot curtain at the front of my space. Unfortunately, the front opening is 10 feet wide, leaving me 20% exposed when peeing into a handheld urinal. Oh, well.

I take a nap. The mattress is nice and firm, but there are no pillows in the ER. They earlier brought me some extra blankets, folded up to form a "pillow" slightly softer than a log.

At 5:30, my dinner arrives! They have decided I would like roast turkey, dressing, french fries, cooked carrots, salad, applesauce, milk, and decaf coffee. I hope they're right... but they're mostly wrong. I have a little turkey, a little dressing, a few fries, a little applesauce. Then I hear I've got a room to move into, so I stop eating, figuring I can order what I want when I get up there.

At 7:00 p.m., I get transported to my old stomping grounds. It's one of the medium-sized rooms—not palatial like my last one, not claustrophobic like one I spent a few weeks in. It will be fine for what I hope is a stay lasting only several days.

My nurse and NSA (nursing student aide) remember me from my earlier nine-week stay. Around 7:30, I place an order for some bland food: baked fish, plain noodles, canned pears, ginger ale. A mere 2 hours later, my order arrives. I pass on the fish, since I don't know that it hasn't been floating around the hospital for two hours. At least the noodles with parmesan hit the spot.

And then, after an intake interview with nurse and my nighttime meds, it's time for bed.

Posted by Joseph Seeley at 8:42 PM

Tuesday, April 19, 2011

Brief Update

I came back from the hospital yesterday (Monday). We found two explanations for my recurring intestinal insurrections: an intestinal infection called *Clostridium difficile* ("c diff") and something (infection?) going on with my gallbladder. Either one could explain the symptoms I have been having. Maybe they have been taking turns!

I now have medications for each condition, and a follow-up appointment on Thursday to discuss the fate of my gallbladder.

Nice surprise from my stay: My room had a fully functioning shower—hot water *and* water pressure.

No surprise: Spent 50 minutes waiting for transport after my ultrasound. Probably would have been longer had one of the techs not made a phone call after 40.

More later. Feeling pretty good now.

Posted by Joseph Seeley at 10:02 AM

Sunday, April 24, 2011

Galling

On Saturday, April 16, I went to sleep back on the sixth floor of the hospital. Someone had written "Welcome back!" on the whiteboard. Thanks, I guess. I do appreciate the welcome and, if I have to be in the hospital, I'm glad it's with familiar and highly competent staff.

On Sunday, we learn that I have *c diff*—very common among hospital patients and others taking heavy antibiotics—and I start some new antibiotic. A sharp pain under my right lung suggested that I might also have a gallbladder problem, which could also explain at least some of the recurring nausea and vomiting. During Saturday and Sunday night, the pain was constant and caused me to ask for relief. During the day, it only hurt when I breathed deeply.

My attending physician tells me I have an ultrasound scheduled for some time on Monday, and I should not eat for six hours before the exam. What time is the exam? Can't say, so don't eat after midnight, to play it safe. Well, I'm not usually eating after 8:00 p.m., so this should be fine.

Sunday night into Monday is a second straight bad night of sleep. They're pumping me full of saline solution, even though I am no longer dehydrated, so I have to get up every 1 to 2 hours to pee and/or have vitals checked and/or have blood drawn. "Welcome back!" (The Thursday night before I got readmitted to the hospital was the very first post-hospital night that I had slept all the way through.)

Monday morning comes. No breakfast, because eating or drinking would interfere with the ultrasound. Which is when, again? They can't say. Late in the morning I learn that my exam is scheduled for 2:00, which means I am going to go from 7:00 p.m. Sunday to 3:00 p.m. Monday (if I'm lucky)—20 hours—without eating or drinking, because they couldn't give me any idea of when my exam would be. I express my unhappiness, but what can they do? There are 15 people ahead of me. The cable guy and the appliance repair guy can at least pin it down to morning or afternoon, which allows a little planning. And you can eat while you're waiting.

Transport shows up to take me to the ultrasound exam (early!), and my mom and I head down. I get rolled into one of two outpatient ultrasound rooms, as the other outpatient room and an inpatient room seem to be occupied. The exam takes about 15 minutes. At the end, the tech tells us she called Transport about 10 minutes ago, because they've been running late today and she wanted to get a head start on the waiting. (They're running late *today*?)

Forty minutes later, my mom wanders back to where the tech headed when she was done with the exam. Several techs are sitting there, at least a couple of them waiting for Transport to clear patients out of their rooms so that they can get another patient down for an exam. It is clear that they, like the other techs and the nurses, are consistently frustrated by how long it takes Transport to get patients where they belong. In this case, transportation may explain why it takes so long to get through 15 patients—the exams are quick, but it takes a long time to get the patients out of the exam rooms.

Back in my room, I finally get to eat and drink. A little later, the report: I do have something going on with my gallbladder, though I'm not clear what—stones, infection, maybe both. Another drug,

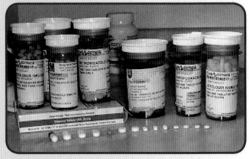

Every morning, I take these pills, plus a multivitamin. Same in the evening, minus the multivitamin and the four small pills on the right. The number of medications doubled in the past week.

and a follow-up appointment on Thursday. Then we're on the way home.

Back up on Thursday. Blood work. The phlebotomist is excellent—a pain-less stick, pride in her work. A meeting with a surgeon, whose initial inclination upon hearing my symptoms was, "This is a no brainer." (Take out the gallbladder.) Now, examining me, he rethinks. The pain went away after two days, and I'm having no other symptoms. I do have gallstones, and they could bring the pain and illness back at any time, but there's no rush. With yet another new medication, and some dietary adjustments, I might be able to shrink the stones and avoid surgery, at least for now when I have a lot of other things going on medically. A dye scan will provide more information.

I ask the resident (the surgeon is gone) whether the gallstones are related to the rest of the recent assault on my body. He doesn't think so, which makes them just a cruel coincidence, like my medical plate isn't already full enough. How galling!

At my next appointment on Thursday, with a transplant nurse practitioner, I learn that my blood counts are really good. My platelets are higher than they have been since before I was diagnosed with aplastic anemia, six-plus years ago, and are now fully in the normal range. Hemoglobin is also better than it has been since chemo started in January. I ask about the gallstones. Her experience, contrary to the opinion of the resident, is that stem cell transplant patients have more gallbladder issues than the average patient. There's chemo, immunosuppression, changes in diet, rapid weight loss—a lot of reasons for the body to get out of balance. This makes me feel slightly less aggrieved.

Since Monday, I've been feeling pretty good. I've been adding short jogs (about a minute for every four minutes of walking) to my morning outings, and my appetite has been good. I have been enjoying the birds and flowers, both while out on my jog/walks and through our windows.

I head back up to meet with my doctor this Monday (April 25), and I have a radioactive dye scan scheduled locally later this week to have a closer look at my gallbladder, to make a more informed surgery decision. If there's no surgery, I'll be able to have the Hickman Triple Lumen removed from my chest, which would be a nice treat. No more line flushing, no more plastic-bag-and-tape jobs before every shower—it would be another step toward normal.

(Thanks to Jan for the title.)

Posted by Joseph Seeley at 7:55 PM

Sunday, May 1, 2011

May Day

The scan we did earlier this week of my gallbladder came back negative, which is positive news. There were no signs of blockage or wall thickening or sludge or anything that indicates it should be taken out. It's not even clear, given the new evidence, that the pain and nausea from a couple of weeks ago was due to a gallbladder problem. Maybe it was, and the problem has passed, or maybe it was a red herring. I do have gallstones, but so do lots of other people without any negative impact.

So, I get to keep my gallbladder, which means there is no more reason to keep the Hickman Triple Lumen in my chest. It is coming out next Monday morning (May 9), before my now-biweekly Monday afternoon checkup. No visit this coming Monday.

Occasional running partner and local TV sportscaster Aaron Matas interviewed me as part of a story on charity runners and the Illinois Marathon. He boiled 45 minutes or so of ums and ers, and some pithy observations, down to a small gem. This broadcast marked the start of a 12-hour Seeley media trifecta: I was on TV (cameo from Jan), Jan was on the radio, and Paul was on the cover of the local newspaper sports section, by virtue of finishing right next to the winning woman in the Friday night 5K. (Paul wants all to know that even though the picture shows him slightly behind the women's winner, he did kick past her before the actual finish.) If he ever stops loathing to run, he's going to be really fast.

Yesterday was the third running of the Christie Clinic Illinois Marathon. Since Jan is a co-race director, it's been crazy hectic in the Seeley household for the last week—even more than it has been for the last several weeks. So far, it looks like Jan got enough sleep, food, and liquid during the week to stay out of the emergency room on the day after, an improvement over last year.

The race went off extremely well. I missed being as fully, physically involved as I have been the last two years. It's draining, but it's also a kind of high, with great camaraderie, reminiscent of working on a theater production (only bigger). This year, I was confined to the house, both to protect me from exposure to infection and to conserve my energy. I have to keep reminding myself that I am still recovering.

I kept the website updated as we transformed the home page from come-to-our-race to the-race-is-almost-here to the-race-is-here to it's-done! The last couple of days, I answered one of the race hotlines, and I also pretended to be Jan as I processed a backlog of her email. (If you got a reply from Jan that seemed unusually terse, that's why. It's so hard to find good help.)

In general, I have felt quite good since my second discharge from the hospital. Some new medications for confirmed and potential infections probably help, and my mom has been in town since then as well. She says she's like the umbrella you take with you so it won't rain—I am fine when she's here. She is leaving on Tuesday, and we hope it doesn't start "raining" when she leaves. Besides exercising her maternal medical magic, she has done a lot of cooking and yard work and bringing-of-tea and general errand-running—a big help.

Looking forward to an excellent May.

Posted by Joseph Seeley at 11:11 AM

Sunday, May 8, 2011

Mother's Day (D+65)

Nice day today. We took in a couple of soccer games, as Paul's team won its semifinal and championship games in his club's hometown tournament. Paul took a hard fall in the second of yesterday's games and missed this morning's game with back spasms, but he recovered enough to play some good minutes in the championship game.

I have to protect myself from sunlight. Some sources say it's because sunlight can trigger graft-vs.-host disease, and my doctor says it's because I will burn easily. This is why I go for my walk/jog early in the morning or in the evening. Youth soccer games are typically very sunny affairs with no shade to be found. Luckily for me, the boys played on a field with trees on the east and north sides, and an official's tent on the west side, which meant I was always able to find a place to sit out of the sun and take in the game. For two of the weekend's four games, this meant being at the opposite end of the field from most of the action, but it was still a lot of fun to be out watching Paul and his teammates play some beautiful soccer.

Other precautions I need to take, besides avoiding sunlight, all to minimize the risk of catching something:

▶ Avoid small children (or, as they are known in the transplant world, "disease vectors")

▶ Avoid people who work with or have small children

▶ Avoid people who are sick

▶ Avoid crowds (because you never know who in the crowd might be sick)

▶ Avoid shaking hands

▶ Avoid salad bars (because you don't know who preceded you through the line, touching the serving utensils, maybe sneezing on the food...)

▶ Avoid meat and cheese sliced at a deli (less risky than a salad bar, but still...)

▶ Avoid yard work, gardening, dusting, and vacuuming (because it kicks up fungi and bacteria)

▶ Wash and/or sanitize hands frequently (because even with all of the above precautions, you're still touching things—money, handles—that are also loaded with microorganisms that a fully functioning immune system can usually handle

As long as I am taking the anti-rejection medication, my immune system is suppressed. So I take a bunch of anti-bacterial, -viral, and -fungal medications, and I take the precautions above.

Tomorrow, Jan and I head back to Chicago for my now-bi-weekly appointment. The highlight is that I'm also having my Hickman Triple Lumen taken out, another sign of progress ("you won't be needing transfusions") and another step closer to normal existence (no more line flushing and extra shower precautions). Jan will also get to meet my doctor in person for the first time.

As for Mother's Day, it was pretty low key. In addition to the soccer games, Jan also got in a couple of naps. I made dinner—baked chicken, roasted white and sweet potatoes, asparagus, salad (spinach from our garden, clementines, glazed walnuts, peppers, mushrooms). We got some flowers, but they have to stay outside—cut flowers, or more precisely the vases of stagnant water in which they sit, are another infection risk we need to avoid. Instead, we got a mass of potted lilies that are sitting on a table on our patio and that Paul can plant soon.

Happy Mother's Day to all you moms out there!

Posted by Joseph Seeley at 5:23 PM

Sunday, May 22, 2011

Only When I Breathe (Day+79)

It has been a while since I checked in. Not much was going on. We went to Rockford last weekend for the State Cup soccer tournament. Paul's team won their Saturday game, which earned them a quarterfinal match against the defending state champs. The game was 1-1 at halftime, with both teams having missed some good chances. In the second half, the other team pulled away, but it was a good overall effort. Every year, his team closes the gap on the top teams in the state.

On Saturday night, I started having some pain in my left calf. I have had varicose veins there for a few years, but never any associated pain. Now, the veins themselves were tender to the touch, and standing shot pain from my ankle to my knee. One possibility was a blood clot in my leg. We checked in with my doctor, who gave me a few things to look for—redness, swelling, pain moving to other places.

Over the next few days, the pain got slightly worse, but it did not change in the ways I was supposed to be alarmed about. The worst pain was when standing after sitting or lying down. It was fine when I walked or jogged, and fine when sitting or sleeping. But if I got up to make a sandwich after sitting for a while, it hurt enough that I made some of my lunches and snacks while pacing around the kitchen.

By Thursday morning, my leg felt a little better when I got up. I could stand still without discomfort. Around the middle of the afternoon, I noticed a slight stabbing under my lower right ribs, and up into my right shoulder. It reminded me of last month's (possible) gallstone attack, though the location was a little lower and more to the side. It got more intense until, around 5:00, in consultation with my doctor, we decided it was time to seek medical attention. My doctor suspected a renewed gallbladder problem. All I knew was that every time I breathed, it felt like someone was twisting a knife under my ribs.

At the E.R. of our local hospital, I get to use my "go to the head of the line" card—a transplant patient with a suppressed immune system does not spend time in the waiting room, so I am fairly quickly taken into my own room. Jan is there to support me, and our friend Bonnie is there to support Jan.

Getting out of the waiting room quickly does not mean that the rest of the night moved quickly. Since I am not bleeding or having a heart attack, the testing proceeds at a leisurely pace. (I'm not complaining.)

First, blood and urine tests. Given the nature and location of the pain and the recent gallbladder history, they are looking for signs that the gallbladder or liver are malfunctioning. After about an hour, those tests come back negative.

The pain continues to mount. I get some morphine through an IV they stuck in my arm, but it doesn't seem to do anything. They ask where the pain is on a scale of 1 to 10. I have a hard time answering this question. If I don't breathe, it doesn't hurt at all. If I try to take a normal breath, the pain quickly reaches a *no más* point. Is that 10? I can use my yoga breath training to use only the top third of my lungs, and that is a tolerable pain. I assume I have never felt pain at level 10. That might be reserved for prolonged and painful labor or having your testicles caught in an escalator. Since I'm still (except for my blood) a guy, and I don't bodysurf escalators naked, I don't anticipate having either of those experiences.

So, what is my pain? I can't push through it to breathe, but it isn't the worst pain imaginable. Is 9 too high? Is it even a linear scale? For most of the night, I go with 8, plus or minus 1. But only when I breathe. Looking back, that seems high. But maybe a given pain always hurts less in the past than it does in the present.

Next, ultrasound of my abdomen, again looking at liver and gallbladder, but also pancreas and kidney. Another hour or so, and more negative (good) results. Not only do all of the suspect organs look fine, but there is no sign of gallstones.

Next, x-rays of my chest. The protocol involves taking and holding a big breath, but that really is not an option, so I don't know that they get good pictures. The results are generally negative, but do show something that looks like pneumonia. I don't have the other symptoms of pneumonia—fever, phlegm—so it might be scar tissue from the pneumonia I had in February.

Next, a CT scan of my chest. Positive test results! Wait, that's bad. I have a pulmonary embolism, a blood clot in my lungs. I need to be hospitalized and started on blood thinners immediately. I don't know anything about pulmonary embolisms at this point, but it sounds scary.

One likely scenario is that a clot had formed in my leg, causing the pain earlier in the week. It, or some of it, broke loose on Thursday, relieving the leg pain but migrating through the circulatory system until getting lodged in my right lung. If I remember my high school biology correctly, this makes sense. On the way to the heart from the legs, the veins get larger and larger, so a dislodged clot has clear sailing. From the heart, the blood gets pumped to the lungs through an increasingly finer network of blood vessels, and a clot stands a good chance of getting hung up there.

The morphine still isn't doing anything, but my yoga breathing works. Or maybe the morphine *is* working, and if I didn't have it in my system, I would know what an 8 or 9 on the pain scale really feels like.

I get admitted to a hospital room around 3:00 a.m. I get a morphine pump, which means that every 10 minutes I can press a button and get a small dose. I can't detect any benefit, but whenever I take too deep a breath and remind myself why I'm in the hospital, I press the button. There is a timer built into the pump, so that if you press the button before 10 minutes has elapsed, it just chirps at you.

Not much happens on Friday. We keep adjusting the pain medication higher, to no obvious effect. I take some naps, since I didn't get much sleep the night before. Jan comes to keep me company starting in the mid-morning. My lunch is, against expectations, excellent: grilled salmon, brown rice pilaf with cranberries, broccoli. Dinner is a picnic courtesy of our friends the Morgans. After dinner, I take a walk in the corridors, with my IV pole. Just like old times. At this point, I have heard that I could be going home as soon as Sunday or as late as Tuesday. After my walk, the pain begins to ease.

After breakfast on Saturday, I get a full ultrasound scan of both legs, from ankles to groin. Having identified a blood clot in my lungs, we're searching for any more that might be hiding. The results are positive: I have a clot in the leg that had been hurting, and another in the other leg. Since I have already started the treatment for clots, there isn't much to do with the news. And they have decided that I don't have pneumonia, so I might as well go home.

The diagnosis means more medications: I am currently on an injectable blood thinner and a blood thinner in tablet form (Coumadin). When my blood reaches the desired level of unclottiness, I'll just be on the tablet form, but I will then be on that medication for months.

The lung pain is mostly gone, at the moment (Sunday night). Today, it only seems to occur if I have been lying down, and it's never as bad as it was on Friday.

Tomorrow we go back up to Chicago for the regular blood tests and check-in with the doctor. And there are some additional test results to get from my weekend visit to the local hospital, to try to identify a cause for the clots. Having cancer (though usually not leukemia) is another factor leading to clots, as is being sedentary. I go for daily walk/jogs, and I move around the house during the day to prepare food or take medications, but maybe I need to take more frequent and purposeful activity breaks.

There are also genetic causes. My brother has had blood clots in his legs. Maybe I have a genetic predisposition to clots that was masked by my low platelet counts during the years I had aplastic anemia and now has a chance to shine. Bodies are very complicated!

Posted by Joseph Seeley at 8:11 PM

Wednesday, May 25, 2011

Number and Adjustments (D+82)

Went up to Chicago on Monday, and got some good numbers:

▶ The genetic test looking for deletion-7 (which would indicate a trace of leukemia) came back negative. This doesn't mean there's nothing there, but it's as clean a bill of health as I can get.

▶ My blood counts are still looking good, and are better than they were over the weekend (while the blood clot was keeping them down).

I also got a couple of adjustments to the plan settled on over the weekend:

▶ Because I have a bone marrow biopsy coming up in mid-June, I should not currently be ramping up my Coumadin levels. You can't be on blood thinners during a bone marrow biopsy. The injectable blood thinner I am on clears the system within 12 hours, so I will stay on that alone until the biopsy and *then* make the transition to Coumadin, which builds up in the system over time and stays in the system for a long time.

▶ My local hospital is testing my blood for a genetic predisposition to clotting. Except, they aren't! When the test results come back, we will know whether Mara has such a predisposition but we won't know anything about me. The Chicago hospital will run the same test, using some genetic material they already have. If I have it, we'll want to check our sons.

(The fact that I bleed my sister's blood creates an interesting criminal scenario.)

Lying down seems to provoke the pulmonary embolism, so I have been sleeping the last couple of nights in a sitting position. It's better once I get up and start moving around.

Posted by Joseph Seeley at 8:04 PM

Wednesday, June 1, 2011

Be Careful What You Wish For (D+89)

I don't believe in making New Year's resolutions. I figure that if you have a change that's worth making, why wait until January 1 of next year to start? Of course, I rarely make resolutions at other times of the year either, so I'm really just undemanding of myself year-round.

However, I did sort of have a goal for the year—lose 10 pounds. Over the course of a year, for a guy weighing nearly 200 pounds, that's not very ambitious, and it seemed attainable through only minor adjustments to eating (a little less) and exercise (a little more). I had lost about 10 pounds the previous year, and I figured I could do it again.

And now, only five months into the year: goal achieved! I currently weigh roughly 15 pounds less than I did at the beginning of the year. It's amazing what a few rounds of chemotherapy, hospital food, a stem cell transplant, and an intestinal uprising can do. However, I still think my original plan was better.

Unfortunately, it looks and feels like most of the loss was muscle. My belly button is still more of an inny than it was in my super-fit college track days, so I don't think I lost much fat there. I don't know how much of the muscle loss is atrophy due to disuse and how much is loss due to energies being directed elsewhere. I had been lifting regularly for much of last year, which had not changed my weight much but had traded some fat for muscle. Now, my chest, legs, and arms are noticeably thinner than they were in December. My clothes are baggier. Fortunately, we all know I don't care much how well my clothes fit (or that they match) (or that they are not inside out).

Where I most notice the loss of muscle is on my morning walk/jogs. In April, I started adding a minute of jogging every five minutes or so. It felt hard. In May, I worked up to a 2:30 jog/2:30 walk pattern. Still hard. Today, the first day of June, I moved to 3:00 jog/2:00 walk. The jogging is slower than 11:00/mile, according to my running gadget.

My gadget also tells me that 11:00/mile pushes my heart rate to 155 pretty quickly, which explains why that "speed" feels hard. I don't feel like I could run much faster if I tried. My legs ain't got no giddy-up! I know the speed will come back (mostly), as I keep jogging a little longer and a little faster, and as I add some strength training.

Eventually, I'll make the transition from jogging to running—I don't know what the official distinction is, but I know it when I'm doing it. For me, jogging is like walking, only faster, while running is like flying, only slower.

My mid-term goal is to run (not jog) a 5K this fall. It will be the slowest race I have ever run, and it's going to be great.

Posted by Joseph Seeley at 1:40 PM

Saturday, June 4, 2011

Hivectomy (D+92)

Medically speaking, all is well. I had a doctor's appointment yesterday, and my blood counts are great. My follow-up appointment is a month from now, preceded by a bone marrow biopsy on June 20.

Perhaps sensing the lack of drama, our house came down with an infection of its own. It started on a Tuesday evening 11 days ago, when Jan noticed a lot of bees outside one of our living room windows. Around the same time, we noticed a few bees inside the house, apparently entering through light fixtures. Once we started paying attention, we could hear bees banging against the first floor ceiling from the spaces between the floor joists.

I called an exterminator that night and made an appointment for the next day.

The exterminator looked around, outside and inside. The bees were entering the walls of the house at the northeast corner, at the gap between the brick covering the first floor and the wood siding of the second floor. Again, we could hear them banging around in the spaces between joists. He was getting ready to describe the extermination program when I showed him one of the bees that we had killed inside the house. Hmmm. Might be a honeybee. He took it out to his truck for more careful analysis.

When he came back in, he told me he could not solve our insect problem. The commercial exterminators are not allowed to kill honeybees. He gave me the number of a local honeybee guy.

Talking to the local bee guy, I learned that I could, if I wanted, kill the bees as a homeowner. However, there are several reasons not to do this:

▶ Honeybees are valuable, pollinating local crops. I'm a big fan of bees. But not in the house.

▶ Killing a large colony leaves pounds of dead bees in your house, where they will rot and smell.

▶ Once the bees are dead, they no longer keep the hive cool by fanning their wings, and the wax of the honeycomb melts.

▶ The melted wax can stain walls and ceilings.

▶ The honey, now released from the comb and no longer protected by the bees, attracts ants and rodents.

So, the preferred approach is to move the hive. When the hive is in a tree or under eaves, this is fairly easy. When the hive is inside a house's walls, it can be a major project. If the hive is beyond reach behind the bricks, you would have several unhappy choices: remove the brick (costly); remove the hive from the inside of the house (costly, and you get a lot of unhappy bees in your house for a while); exterminate the bees (bad, as explained above).

Bee Guy 1 couldn't come to the house in the next several days, so he referred me to Bee Guy 2. Bee Guy 2 came out on Friday and confirmed what the exterminator had told me: The bees are building a hive within the walls.

We hope it's behind the wood of the second floor and not the brick of the first floor. He thinks he can come out over the weekend to pull back wood siding and see what's up.

But he doesn't make it over Memorial Day weekend, having forgotten about other plans. He is not able to make it until Thursday—beekeeping is a relatively recent hobby for him, and he has a full-time job. In the meantime, the bees are making themselves at home. Fortunately, they are happy with their chosen spot within the walls and are no longer scouting out the rest of the house.

This past Thursday, Bee Guy 2 comes over with some scaffolding, his bee suit, empty bee boxes and comb frames. He admits he's a little nervous, and he's only done this once before. Yikes! Fortunately, Bee Guy 1 soon comes to join him. Bee Guy 1, who I call the Bee Whisperer, is the one who doesn't wear gloves and only sometimes wears headgear.

In the end, this worked out as well as it could have. They were behind the wood and not behind the brick, the hive was all within arm's reach, the queen and her colony were relocated to a box, and The Rookie got a new hive. Everybody is happy, except possibly the wife of The Rookie.

The eventual new home for the hive.

The Bee Whisperer and The Rookie start to pry off the wood siding.

The smoke calms the bees down, for some reason. It seems to bother the Bee Guys, though.

They dump the first load of bees into the box.

You can tell the hive is new because the comb is so white.

The Bee Whisperer pulls out sheets of honeycomb (with his bare hands), and The Rookie puts them into the box. They keep checking each comb for the queen, because if you don't get her, your efforts are wasted. The colony will just rebuild where the queen is.

Once the queen is in the box, along with much of the comb, the box becomes the colony's new home.

Posted by Joseph Seeley at 4:52 PM

Sunday, June 12, 2011

Milestone and Goal (D+100)

Milestone: I am 100 days into my post-transplant life.

According to the protocol I am following, D+100 is when you have another bone marrow biopsy. Mine is scheduled for Monday, eight days from now. There is no reason to expect anything but good news, given how well I have been doing since the transplant.

On the other hand, I am approaching it with slightly more dread than the previous ones. I don't know whether this is because the last one was painful in unexpected ways or because I am simply becoming less brave about pain.

I have also noticed declining bravery regarding my twice-daily injections to treat my pulmonary embolism. They don't hurt any more than they did when I started, no worse than a brief pinch. But instead of it getting easier and easier to do, I find myself hesitating more, and using breathing techniques to ready myself, before the tiny stab. Maybe with everything else going so smoothly, I'm less sanguine about even brief and mild discomfort.

Goals: I am going to run a 5K this fall.

Before my diagnosis, I had been planning to concentrate on the 5K this year, though with actual time goals. I felt that with a little speed training on top of my existing distance base, I could break 20:00 early in the year, and then I would go from there. Under the circumstances, my new goal is simply to run a 5K.

It seems premature to worry about speed, based on my current walk/jogs. I have been gradually adding jogging intervals, and I am up to 20 or so minutes (total) out of a 50-minute outing. A couple times this week, I finished a few of the jogging intervals with 30-second runs. When I try to run fast, I feel like a marionette controlled by an unskilled puppeteer. I know my knees and heels are supposed to come up, and they do a little, but not as fast as I am telling them to and without much grace. These "sprints" are at about a 10:00/mile pace, and they push my heart rate to 160.

Fortunately, "this fall" gives me a big window in which to run a 5K, especially if I combine the common definition that starts with September and the astronomical definition that ends December 21.

Next year, I'm looking at a Presidential Traverse. This is an ambitious day hike covering the length of the Presidential Range in New Hampshire's White Mountains. 19.2 miles, nearly 9,000 ft of elevation gain. It is roughly 14 hours of hiking, but my vision of it involves a lot of running. (If you have seen the Lord of the Rings movies, and you remember Aragorn, Gimli, and Legolas running tirelessly along dramatic mountain ridges, then you have seen my vision.)

Posted by Joseph Seeley at 7:04 PM

Lost in Translation (D+107) (M+25y)

Tomorrow (Monday) Jan and I drive up for regularly scheduled testing: pulmonary function test, bone marrow biopsy, and the usual blood work.

Assuming all is well, and I do, the next milestone is D+120, when I start going off the drug that suppresses my immune system.

This past Tuesday was our 25th anniversary. When it comes to "in sickness and in health," Jan has kindly left the physical "in sickness" part to me and reserved the supportive spouse role for herself. It works for us.

I didn't get Jan flowers on our anniversary. One restriction imposed on a patient with a suppressed immune system is no cut flowers. The flowers themselves aren't that bad, but the water they sit in is a breeding ground for mold, and mold is bad. For Mother's Day, we went with potted lilies that we kept on the patio and later planted, but it's not quite the same.

Clever boy that I am, I took advantage of Jan's first business trip since my diagnosis. (I'm not counting the one she was on, outside Las Vegas, on the day I was diagnosed. The conversation that night started like this: "Are you sitting down? No, really. You have to be sitting down.")

After arranging for a lineup of friends to be on call for 24-hour shifts in case of emergency, Jan and her magazine business partner Rich drove to Duluth for the Grandma's Marathon, an annual four-day trek for Jan.

Although we can't have flowers at home, there's no reason Jan can't have flowers at her hotel room. So I called a local florist and arranged to have flowers delivered. The florist was very helpful, working with me to make adjustments to the bouquet when they did not have the white lilies I wanted to go with the roses.

I had worked out a short poem during my morning outing. I was very pleased with myself.

> It's clear I am the smarter of us two
> 'Cause you married me, and I married you

When I talked to Jan that evening, she didn't mention the flowers. I called the hotel and confirmed that they had been delivered, so they must have arrived after Jan checked in but before she returned from dinner. The next morning, I saw I had a text from her from later the previous night, loving the flowers.

When Jan got home today, after being home for a few hours, she somewhat sheepishly came over with the card that came with the flowers. She said she had been trying to figure out what it meant, but she really couldn't. The card read:

It's clear I am the martyr of us two
'Cause you married me, and I married you

Good grief! It's the perfect sentiment for the Dysfunctional Marriage Anniversary section of the card rack, right next to "25? It feels like 50!"

Well, here's to another 25 years of martyrdom, sweetie! So far, so good.

P.S. No need to bring the "in sickness" account into balance.

Posted by Joseph Seeley at 6:47 PM

Wednesday, June 29, 2011

Can You Strain a Muscle in Slow Motion? (D+117)

Two weekends ago, Jan and I did a hill workout. In Champaign! (Park Haven Drive, which runs into Kirby Avenue from the south at Hessel Park, is a great training hill.)

We did my usual walk for 10 minutes, followed by intervals of jogging and walking, until we got to the base of the hill. Then we jogged up the hill and walked down a few times. On the third up, I completely ran out of gas about three-fourths of the way up and had to stop, but I think I was going too fast —in my case, that means something faster than 11 minutes per mile. We did a couple more, with me running more cautiously, and then we headed home.

The next couple of days, I couldn't jog. I'm pretty sure I strained a calf muscle. I didn't think that was possible, at 11 minutes per mile, but apparently it is! The rest of the week I gradually added a little more jogging each day to my walks as I recovered from my overuse injury. By this past weekend, I was jogging pain-free.

This past Saturday, Jan and I did a "long run." The jog-(walk) intervals were 1-(1)-2-(1)-3-(1)-4-(3)-5-(3)-4-(1)-3-(1)-2-(1)-1, followed by 4 1-(1)s, for a total of 29 minutes of jogging. PTPR! (Post-transplant personal record.) With the warm-up and interval and cool-down walking, the total was 5 miles. At the end of the longer jogs, still around 11 min/mile pace, my heart rate gets close to 160. During the rests, it gets into the 120s.

I'm getting out almost every day, usually a mix of jogging and walking. Some days are just walking. One of these days, I'll remember how to run.

Posted by Joseph Seeley at 5:43 PM

Saturday, July 2, 2011

Unleash the Hounds! (D+120)

According to the protocol I'm following, patients start tapering their im-munosuppressant drug 120 days after transplant. This drug has kept my new immune system from being fully functional, until now. A fully functional but grafted immune system, while useful for fending off bacteria, viruses, and fungi, could also mistake the host's liver or intestinal lining or skin as an en-emy, leading to graft-vs.-host disease. So far, luckily, I have had no GVHD symptoms.

I don't know what's different after 120 days. Maybe everyone has had enough time to get to know each other, or at least not go around picking un-necessary intercellular fights.

I am not quite following the protocol.

I had my D+100 biopsy on D+109. The initial results were as good as they could be. "Zillions and zillions of cells," to use my doctor's technical term. My next biopsy would be in several months (D+180). Having had the bi-opsy, I was able to start the transition from an injectable blood thinner to an oral one. (I have been on the injectable thinner since my pulmonary embo-lism, because it has a short half-life and clears the system in a day. Blood thinners and bone marrow biopsies do not go together, and Coumadin takes about a week to clear the system.)

On D+118, my doctor called with more bone marrow biopsy results, based on chromosomal analysis, and they are not as good as they can be. We would like to see none of my cells in the marrow, but 1% are mine, which we know because they have the XY chromosome. Worse, 2% of that 1% (0.02%) are leukemic. It's not enough to cause mischief, but it's the first evidence that we didn't get it all.

Fortunately, I now have a powerful weapon in this battle that I did not have in January: an immune system that should treat the native 1% as hostile threats. (Historically speaking, the 99% are the newcomers, but now they act like they own the place. This behavior should be familiar to students of U.S. history.) Starting two days ago, I am no longer taking the drug that kept my new immune system from attacking enemy cells. Over the next few weeks, the recently unleashed cells carrying the XX flag should be hunting down every blood cell foolish enough to wave the XY flag. While graft-vs.-host disease is a problem, the related graft-vs.-leukemia effect is beneficial.

Later this month, I'll have another biopsy to see how well the extermination campaign is going. Sadly, there is no special reward for filling my biopsy punch card. The last time, Jan bought me a pastry.

Posted by Joseph Seeley at 3:05 PM

Monday, July 11, 2011

And No Snoopy Bandage :-(

Today is my first doctor visit since going off my immunosuppressant drug. I haven't had any symptoms such as rashes or intestinal distress that would indicate that my new and now unfettered immune system is attacking anything it shouldn't, so that's good. Meanwhile, I hope Immunity 2.0 is quietly and thoroughly tracking down the lingering traces of leukemia, but we won't get that report until after a bone marrow biopsy in a couple of weeks.

At tomorrow's appointment, I begin my re-inoculation. My new immune system has not been exposed to those childhood diseases I either had as a kid or was vaccinated against: measles, mumps, chicken pox, and a few other reasons we got to stay home from school for a few days. I'm not sure what the schedule is, but it's a lot of shots over the next several months. Some have to be repeated. And, at my age, they don't put a cute bandage on your owwie or offer a lollipop.

Jan and I went on another "long run" yesterday. After the usual 10-minute warm-up walk, the jog-(walk) intervals were: 1 (1) 1 (1) 2 (1) 2 (1) 3 (1) 3

(1) 3 (3) 3 (1) 3 (2) 3 (1) 2 (1) 2 (1) 1 (1) 1 (some). A total of 30 minutes of jogging, a new PTPR.

I hadn't been planning to have a 2-minute break after the fifth 3-minute jog, but I needed it. On a couple of the longer intervals, I achieved muscle failure in my lower legs. Most marathoners have experienced this feeling in a race or two, when they start doing the "death march." The foot can no longer push off, and the thighs can barely lift, so even though you are willing your legs forward, you are just lifting your feet and then putting them down again a few inches ahead of where they left the ground. You tell yourself that you're still running, but you're not. You're doddering. You could walk faster, but you're too proud to walk, so you keep taking these tiny steps on append-ages that look like legs but feel like loaves of french bread. Stale loaves.

I am familiar with this sensation, from a few marathons, but also from some shorter races, and even from some workouts. Some call it rigor mortis, or carrying the piano. It's a common sight at track meets.

I got some satisfaction running into it in workouts, like repeat 200s. It meant I was running as fast as I possibly could at that point in time, and even though my legs were failing me at the moment, I knew they would take the hint and be a little stronger in a few days.

Being familiar with dead legs on a run does not mean I'm happy about it. Intellectually, I know I'm doing the same thing I did 30 years ago—I'm running up to my limit, recovering, repeating. And, like 30 years ago, I take rest days between hard workouts. Except now a rest day means just walking, instead of an easy 5-mile run.

It's still hard to fully accept that I can reach muscle failure while moving as slowly as I am.

I also wish I were seeing more of a training effect. A few weeks ago, I did a pyramid workout with a 5-minute jog in the middle, and that was hard but possible. But I have had trouble making it to 4 minutes ever since. And I'm pretty sure I'm not running any faster, based on my GPS gadget.

On the positive side, I did modify a training plan last week (when I could not finish a 4-minute jog interval) to include a set of 1-minute "sprints," and those felt great. I was actually, finally, running.

Posted by Joseph Seeley at 3:52 AM

Remedial Math

I'm afraid I need to correct my earlier calculation of how much leukemia my most recent biopsy turned up. I had said that one test found 1% XY chromosomes, and another test had found 2% leukemia. Those were the test results, but my assumption that it was 2% of the 1% (which would be .02%) was incorrect.

The real story is that one test counted 3 cells with XY chromosomes out of 400 counted, which rounded up to 1%. The other test counted 6 cells (also out of 400) with the deletion-7 genetic marker that my leukemia cells have been helpful enough to wear. So that's 1.5%, rounded up to 2%. If they counted another 400, they might find 5, or 3, or 7. It means that, at the time of my biopsy, there were a few of my own cells still in the mix, and they appear to be all leukemic.

The corrected calculation doesn't change anything. I had more leukemia left than I thought, but it's still a small amount and not out of the ordinary. The rest of my blood counts are solid, indicating that what leukemia is still there isn't causing any trouble. "It's nothing to lose sleep over," says my doctor. Of course, leukemia has a way of getting out of hand, so it's also nothing to ignore.

Another biopsy this Friday will tell us whether going off of the immunosuppressant medication has had the desired effect of routing the remaining XY cells, and with them the remaining leukemia. If not, there are other treatments to try.

I assume the current treatment will do the job, even though I know it's not guaranteed. There's no benefit to fretting about what might go wrong, if you can't do anything about it. People who dwell on possible future suffering suffer more than they need to—guaranteed anguish before anything happens, and then again if it does happen. Once is enough, if it comes to that.

I also believe it's medically harmful to worry about all the things that could go wrong, and medically helpful to believe in your treatment. Hope is good medicine. It won't beat leukemia on its own, but it helps.

Posted by Joseph Seeley at 7:25 PM

Training

My basic training pattern these days is a day of walking mixed with jogging, followed by a day or two of only walking. That's my version of alternating hard days with easy days.

A little over a month ago, I did a workout of increasingly longer jogging intervals, up to 5 minutes, and then back down, for a total of 29 minutes of jogging. That was very encouraging.

Shortly after that, my endurance began to wane. I could barely get to 3 minutes on my jogging days, then barely to 2, then 1... I was prepared for training plateaus, but this was a definite step back.

A few Sundays ago (July 17), Jan and I did 31 one-minute jogging intervals. It was a PTPR in terms of total jogging time, total workout time, and total mileage. But if I didn't start getting my endurance back, I wouldn't be running a 5K any time soon.

What was going on? I don't know. My doctor was not very interested, either. A stem cell transplant patient who is walking and jogging about an hour a day is in better shape than the rest of her patients, almost all of her colleagues, and herself, so it's hard for her to be concerned about it.

My diminished endurance coincided with going off my immunosuppressant drug and letting my new immune system go to work hunting down the traces of leukemia found in my previous biopsy. My theory is that a lot of internal work was going on and sapping energy, similar to how you sometimes feel lethargic before the other symptoms of an immune system in battle mode —fever, aches, congestion—manifest themselves. I never had those other symptoms, but there's plenty of reason to think my immune system was busy. We certainly hope that's been going on.

A couple of days after my discouraging accomplishment of 31-minutes-of-jogging-in-1-minute-intervals workout, I bounced back with a pyramid of jogging (and walking) that had a 4-minute jog in the middle: 1 2 2 2 3 2 4 3 3 2 2 2 1. A couple of days later, I did a "speed" workout of 10 one-minute runs. It felt great, but resulted in my third strained calf of my recovery, so I had to take quite a few days of walking only. Lesson (finally) learned—no hills, no fast running.

This past Sunday (July 31), Jan and I jogged some 1-, 2-, and 3-minute intervals, for a total of 32 minutes of jogging. Another PTPR!

We're still waiting on the results of my July 22 biopsy, to see if my new immune system tracks down the lingering leukemia. I feel good, for what that's worth.

Posted by Joseph Seeley at 5:04 PM

Sunday, August 14, 2011

Not a Fairy Tale

Since the beginning of the year, I've been living the fairy tale version of fighting leukemia. A scary monster appears, things look grim for a while, but, with grit and cleverness and magic potions, the monster is vanquished. True, there was more than the usual amount of vomit and shit than in your typical fairy tale, but it was still the (relatively) short story with the happy ending.

It looks like my story is going to be more like a novel, and we're only a few chapters into it. Maybe a short novel, maybe a long novel, but not a fairy tale.

Until June, I was following the shortest and best possible story arc: I tolerated chemo better than most, I tolerated the stem cell transplant better than most, my first post-transplant biopsy found no leukemia.

Then a biopsy in June turned up a little bit of leukemia, but I could still stay on the same arc by going off the immunosuppressant drug and having my new immune system clean up the rogue leukemia cells. It was possible I would need no additional treatment, just recovery time. That's the fairy tale version. It happens for some people.

But that is not my story.

I don't have exact cell counts from my most recent biopsy yet, but there are other numbers indicating that there is still a little leukemia. The number of blasts is slightly higher than normal (6.6% versus 5%). The number of platelets is declining (from 136 to 88 over the last month), and falling platelet numbers are an early warning sign of leukemia. No eyewitness testimony of leukemia, but strong circumstantial evidence.

The falling platelets, combined with the blood thinner I'm taking after my pulmonary embolism, make me bleed very easily. I have scabs on my hands and wrist from wounds I don't remember getting. There is another on the back of my ankle that I do remember getting. We have carpeted stairs, and the back of my leg grazed the front of a step on the way down to the next step. For most people, that's at worst a tiny rug burn. For me, it's a wound bleeding into my sock.

Back to the root problem, the chemo didn't eliminate the leukemia, and the gradually strengthening new immune system hasn't done so, either. What's next?

Most likely, I will start another course of chemo next Monday (August 22). Might be a five-day course or a seven-day course, probably done as an outpatient here in Champaign-Urbana.

This chemo treatment is, according to my doctor, much less potent than what I had in the hospital. The goal then was to wipe out all cells in the marrow, both to eliminate the leukemia (which it almost did but not quite) and to prepare the marrow for the stem cell transplant (which it did). The goal now is to knock down my blood counts enough that my new stem cells go into overdrive and churn out an oversupply of lymphocytes. Then we will watch blood counts carefully for the next several weeks to see, we hope, stabilized or improving platelet counts. If we see that, I'll do another round of chemo, and then a biopsy to see where I am. If not, then we're onto another treatment and another chapter.

I'm not sure why more lymphocytes will be better at finding rogue cells than are the nearly normal number of such cells I have now. My understanding is that lymphocytes either do or do not recognize other cells as being unwelcome, in which case numbers wouldn't matter, but I must not understand what's going to happen. I'll see what I can learn about that.

I do know that flooding the system with lymphocytes, no longer held in check by immunosuppressant drugs, increases the risk of graft-vs.-host disease. So we'll need to keep careful watch on my skin, eyes, liver, and intestines. I may already be exhibiting a little GVHD already, as my scalp and to a lesser extent my face are kind of itchy and flaky.

Meanwhile, I had my best run of the year today: Ladders of decreasing length, for a total of 35 minutes jogging. Even on the longest interval, I didn't reach muscle failure, and my heart rate fell pretty quickly back to around 120 during the walk breaks. In other words, some training effect! Finally!

$$1 \,_1 2 \,_1 3 \,_1 4 \,_1 5$$

$$^2 1 \,_1 2 \,_1 3 \,_1 4$$

$$^2 1 \,_1 2 \,_1 3$$

$$^2 1 \,_1 2 \,_1 1$$

At the 5K mark, I noted the time: 40:50. That's for a mix of jogging and walking, and it gives me a benchmark measure of training intensity.

Posted by Joseph Seeley at 7:10 PM

Tuesday, August 16, 2011

More Good Training

Beautiful weather this morning, again. 60 degrees, clear. Since I'm out the door at 6:00, it's not yet sunny. Chemo makes me extremely sensitive to sunlight, so I have to train early or late in the day.

Today, 10 2-minute jogs, with 1-minute walks in between.
29:00 workout time. (There's also 10 minutes of walking to warm up and more walking after.)

2.37 miles covered.
29:00/2.37 = 12:16/mile

Heart rate around 160 at the end of each jog, and between 120 and 130 at the end of each walk. Slightly higher than that for the last couple of intervals.

Posted by Joseph Seeley at 5:22 AM

Sunday, August 28, 2011

Chemo Week

This past week, I started each day (after exercise and breakfast) with a visit to a local cancer center for chemotherapy. The current plan is a week of chemo, three weeks off, another week of chemo, another three weeks off, and then a biopsy to see what's going on. I'll need to monitor my blood counts, and I may need transfusions of platelets and/or red blood.

I had thought the point of the chemo was to create an oversupply of white blood cells on the rebound, making it easier for my immune system to overwhelm the remaining leukemia. My new understanding is that the point of the chemo is to attack the leukemia, because leukemic cells are more susceptible to the chemo than are other cells. So all fast-dividing cells will suffer, but the hope is that the leukemic cells suffer disproportionately more, making it easier for my immune system to overwhelm the remaining leukemia. Same goal, different mechanism.

The Infusion Suite is very nice. It is a large, airy room with lots of comfortable chairs and a friendly set of nurses. I picked a chair looking out the enormous window. There are other patients using the room, some for chemo and some for blood. There are also private rooms, if that is your preference.

The infusion itself takes a little over an hour—plastic bag, hung on a pole, with a line running from the bag and into me. Over the course of the week, the nurses spread out the "sticks" across both arms.

The side effects have been as advertised. I had an evening of productive nausea, and I have needed a couple of naps a day. I also have a non-itchy rash on my face, but that might be graft-vs.-host disease. (Which would be good.) It's a good thing I am not looking for a date, because I'm sure there's not much demand for guys over 50 with bad skin who have trouble staying awake and might throw up on your shoes. Sorry ladies, I'm taken!

= = =

I got in some good workouts before the chemo started wearing me down.

Last weekend, I did the following jog/walk sequence:

$$2\ _1\ 4\ _1\ 6\ _1\ 4\ _1\ 2$$
$$_2$$
$$2\ _1\ 4\ _1\ 6\ _1\ 4\ _1\ 2$$

I passed the 5K mark at 40:40 (a PTPR), and I averaged 13:07/mile for the entire workout (jogging plus walking).

On Monday, before my first chemo visit, I did 8 3-minute jogs with 1-minute walk breaks. I averaged 12:34/mile for the workout. (Speed work!)

On Wednesday, after two days of chemo, I did two ladders:

1 $_1$ 2 $_1$ 3 $_1$ 4

2

1 $_1$ 2 $_1$ 3 $_1$ 4

12:12/mile average!

On Friday, which would have been a jogging day, I walked. And I took Saturday off. And took a lot of naps.

On Saturday morning, I stopped by Jan's office to pick up some papers. The elevator was out. *No problem, I'll just walk up to the fourth floor.* I have walked up those stairs many times, and sometimes even run them. (We don't have many hills here in Champaign.) This was the first time I had to stop partway up and catch my breath.

Today, Jan and I repeated Wednesday's workout, sort of. That is, we jogged and walked for the same time intervals, but we covered less ground than I did on Wednesday and averaged 13:33/mile for the workout. Thanks, chemo! I hope you're accomplishing something good in there, because you're interfering with my training.

Posted by Joseph Seeley at 1:28 PM

Sunday, September 4, 2011

The Joy of Sets

This post is about interval training, in which you run sets of something (200m, 2min) with a specific rest interval between each effort. So, it really should be called *The Joy of Intervals*, but where's the pun in that?

Recovering from my stem cell transplant has forced me to break my jogging into small pieces. To keep it interesting, I come up with different patterns:

► repeats (e.g., 12 x 2)
► ladders (e.g., [1 2 3 4] x 3)
► pyramids (e.g., [2 4 6 4 2] x 2)

While I wish I could jog longer without rest, I am happy to reacquaint my-self with interval training. I had forgotten how much I like it! It was a staple of my training as a college 800m runner, and for a few years after that as a competitive road racer.

But I have been a recreational runner for a long time, and just about all of my running for many, many years has had the following pattern:

▶ run some distance at some pace

The run might be 3 miles or 14, fast or slow, but it was almost always just a run.

One thing I like about intervals is that they add variety to the run. I need to avoid sunlight, so I stick to a route that is well shaded in the early morning. But it's pretty boring traveling the same route every day, even if I sometimes get to travel it with Jan. Having an interval pattern to follow shifts my focus from the route to how I'm feeling during the tiny jog and rest pieces.

Another reason I like interval training is the way it breaks up the run into bite-sized chunks. Even in my current state, I can jog for a minute, or some-times even for six minutes.

I am surprised at how similar my current interval training feels like my train-ing 30 years ago, given the difference in speed.

How slow am I going? During my last interval session (12 x 2), there was a man about my age and build out for a walk, a few dozen yards ahead of me. I was jogging for two minutes and walking for one, and the man ahead of me kept increasing his lead. *Sure, you can take me now. Just wait until I get some red blood cells.*

Aside from training at one-third the speed of 30 years ago, the effort and psychology feel familiar. My heart rate is getting up around 160 at the end of a jog, and down to 130-140 by the time I start the next jog. And I enjoy pass-ing milestones: halfway done, only 3 to go, this is the last hard one... There are a lot of little victories along the way.

When I progress to being able to really run, I need to remember to stick with the intervals.

Posted by Joseph Seeley at 10:10 AM

Neutropenic Fever

Saturday morning, I woke up feeling a little listless and a little achy. Jan and I headed out for our morning walk. I had been hoping to jog, and I thought that the blood transfusion I received on Friday would make the jog faster than my previous one, when I was left in the dust by a walker. But after twenty minutes of easy walking, I was ready to stop.

I took my temperature when we got home: 100.6. Half an hour later: 101.8. I called my doctor, and we discussed whether I should go to the local hospital or make the two-and-a-half-hour drive to Chicago. We decided to stay local, both for convenience and to avoid the risk of getting seriously ill somewhere between Kankakee and Peotone.

Until yesterday, I have never been in an empty emergency room. I guess Saturday morning isn't a popular time to have an emergency, at least compared to Saturday night. So I got right in, had some blood drawn and x-rays taken, took Tylenol to bring down the fever (102.8), started an intravenous antibiotic drip, and got admitted to the hospital.

Neutropenic fever is a common occurrence after chemotherapy. The chemo drops all the blood counts, which is why I received platelets and blood late last week. But that still leaves the white cells wherever they have dropped to, which means chemo patients are especially vulnerable to infection. Of the white cells, the neutrophil cells are the most measure of infection resistance.

My neutrophil count reached zero today, and it was nearly zero yesterday. People with low (or no) neutrophil counts are neutropenic, and neutropenic patients often have high and unexplained neutropenic fevers.

That describes my case. The labs here have checked my blood, urine, and lungs without finding any infection. I slept most of Saturday and Saturday night, and today I feel pretty good. I have a low-grade fever instead of the sheet-soaking heat of yesterday.

I will stay in the hospital until my neutrophil count reaches 1,000. That will probably be about a week.

While I'm not happy about being back in a hospital, I'm very happy with the care. I have a large room, the staff are very good, the food is good (really), and they brought me an exercise bike.

Posted by Joseph Seeley at 2:19 PM

Stuck

When I was admitted a week ago with a neutropenic fever, the expectation was that my blood counts would recover over the course of the week and I would go home.

The most important number is the absolute neutrophil count (ANC). The low end of normal is 1,600, 1,000 is pretty good, and even 500 is often enough for doctors to release you to a safe environment. But below 500, you have to be in the hospital, because infections can get out of control very quickly. That's why I'm in a room with an airlock and positive air pressure (to keep airborne microbes out) and specially filtered water.

Here are my numbers:

9/3:   20 OK, this is what chemo does
9/4:   0 nowhere to go but up!
9/5:   20 here we go... once they start climbing, they usually climb exponentially
9/6:   10 um...
9/7:   0 huh...
9/8:   10 yeah, yeah... we'll see what happens tomorrow
9/9:   30 this looks promising
9/10: 20 oh, come on!
9/11: 10 good grief

According to the doctor making the rounds this weekend, about 20% of patients take longer than a week to start recovering. It looks like I'm one of those.

I seem to be creating new red blood cells, so my stem cells are doing something. They may be creating neutrophils, too, but something else might be destroying them.

I feel fine. My appetite and energy are normal. I'm just stuck here in the hospital until my neutrophils come back.

Posted by Joseph Seeley at 10:21 AM

Still Stuck, But Home

The original thinking, upon entering the hospital with a neutropenic fever two weeks ago, was that we would wait for the neutrophil count to get back to normal (1,500), which the local doctors thought might take a week, and then I would go home.

As the first week went on with no real movement in the neutrophil count, the threshold for going home dropped to 1,000, and then 500. And the counts kept wiggling along between 0 and 30.

For training, I was back to walking the corridors with my IV pole or riding the exercise bike they brought to my room. At first I was partial to the bike, because I could work harder, but the highest setting of the seat was still a little too low for me, making it uncomfortable.

Into the second week with no real movement in the counts, the expectations and the plan changed again. The plan became to finish my two-week course of intravenous antibiotics and go home as long as I felt fine, no matter what the neutrophil count. With the double burden of recent chemotherapy and an infection, it could take a long time for the neutrophils to come back even to 500, and I might as well do that recovery at home.

So I came home yesterday, with a neutrophil count of 50, and I'm back to the extra precautions in force when I was discharged after the transplant: check my temperature regularly, avoid people. My legs felt pretty dead this morning, despite all my walking and biking during my incarceration. I think it's just not the same. Also, I'm pretty low on hemoglobin.

But I'm home!

Posted by Joseph Seeley at 6:44 PM

Still Stuck, But Home, the Sequel

In case anyone was wondering, being home is far better than being in the hospital.

It took most of a week, but my sleep has returned to normal. The food in the hospital was pretty good, but the food at home is better. My appetite has not returned to normal, but I usually get in three meals a day.

I still don't have much energy or muscle strength. I added a few 30-second jogs to one of my morning walks a few days ago. Exhausting. My hemoglobin levels are still low, but not low enough to require transfusion, thankfully.

I have a large unexplained bruise on my arm, and my legs are covered with petechiae, which look like red freckles but are actually tiny superficial hemorrhages caused by low platelet counts. But not low enough to require transfusion, thankfully.

The critical blood count, the absolute neutrophil count, continues to tease me. I left the hospital at 50. It was 50 again on Monday. It was back to 0 on Thursday, which means I have no internal protection against infection. I test again this Monday. Can't get worse!

My doctor in Chicago reminds me to be patient, because it still might take another couple of weeks to see the neutrophils come back. I can be patient. I used to coach seven-year-olds in soccer.

Posted by Joseph Seeley at 8:04 PM

Sunday, October 2, 2011

In Limbo

Another week, another couple of blood tests showing no increase in neutrophils. Fortunately, platelets are climbing, and red blood cells are holding, so I don't need transfusions.

I have a biopsy scheduled for October 10, in case this week shows no improvement. Blood counts can only suggest what is or isn't happening in the marrow. To really know, you have to get a piece of the marrow.

I guess it's not really Limbo. When you're in Limbo, you don't know when or if you're getting out. With the biopsy on my calendar, I do have an end in sight for what has been weeks of waiting for the neutrophils to get off the floor. In a week from tomorrow, either they will have started to climb or I'll be getting a biopsy.

In more definitive news, the Red Sox granted its younger fans full citizenship to Red Sox Nation, adding 2011 to the pantheon of exquisitely painful season-ending games: 2003, 1986, 1978, 1975... Now the kids get it.

Posted by Joseph Seeley at 6:55 PM

Nine-Month Anniversary

Nine months ago today, on January 10, I received my diagnosis of acute my-eloid leukemia.

To celebrate the anniversary, I was back in the same office, having a bone marrow biopsy and then a consultation with my doctor.

We won't have a clear direction until later this week (Wednesday or Thurs-day), when my biopsy results are in and various teams have met to discuss them. My doctor suspects, based on blood tests, that I still have leukemia, and that the chemo treatment I had six weeks ago was not sufficiently poi-sonous. The biopsy will provide a lot of useful information: how healthy is my marrow, how well is the graft doing, how aggressive is the remaining leukemia.

One scenario is that I go back to Chicago soon (maybe Friday) for a differ-ent kind of chemo, possibly followed by a second transplant. (Sometimes it takes several transplants to put leukemia into remission.) A variation of that scenario is that we do the chemo, it (finally) knocks out the leukemia, and my counts recover on their own, without a transplant. Or the biopsy might send us in another direction entirely.

So, I don't know exactly what's next, but I'm mentally prepared to reopen my satellite office in Chicago. If I do have to go back, I'll be better prepared this time—I know what food to bring, and my iPad and Kindle are loaded.

Happy anniversary!

Posted by Joseph Seeley at 5:52 PM

Part 3

Good News, Bad News: The Sequel

When I left Chicago in February 2011, after the first stem cell donation, I never imagined that I would be back for a second stem cell donation. Rather, I was very hopeful, thinking that Joe had all the cards on his side for a successful recovery. It seemed to me that the leukemia had been caught relatively early, when he was still asymptomatic. He was in extremely good health and had weathered the initial chemotherapy treatment without being too much the worse for wear. I also took it as a good sign that the blasts didn't seem to be repopulating his bone marrow after the initial chemotherapy. My interpretation was that the blasts had been pretty well eradicated. So I assumed we just had to hope that the stem cell transplant was successful—that my stem cells would establish themselves in Joe's bone marrow without causing unmanageable graft-vs.-host disease. If the transplant was successful, I thought that eventually life for Joe might return to a reasonable semblance of normal. With the second stem cell donation, I knew that this disease was far more complicated than my rudimentary understanding of cancer—and leukemia in particular—would have led me to believe.

(continued)

I arrived in Chicago for the second stem cell donation, feeling both hopeful and disappointed. On one hand, I knew that the stem cell transplant could actually work. But I also knew that even if it was successful, life for Joe might never return to the reasonable semblance of normal we had wished for the first time around. Still, when I visited with Joe, I could easily forget that he was in the hospital being treated for a serious illness. He acted so healthy and full of energy, and to me he looked like the high school athlete that he used to be.

When I left Joe on my last evening in Chicago to have dinner with my cousins, the doctors were coming in to check out an infection in his nose; we were told it was probably nothing to worry about. As it turned out, while I was enjoying dinner with my cousins, Joe was having emergency surgery to remove the infection. Seeing how miserable and defeated Joe looked the next day, in such stark contrast to the previous days, was a harsh and painful reminder of just how precarious his health was. As Joe recounts in the next section, the infection did turn out to be something very serious.

—Mara Seeley, Joe's sister

Joe and Mara: Amsterdam, Holland, 1962

Good News, Bad News: The Sequel

The good news is, I know how to do this.
The bad news is, once was enough.
The worse news is, once was not enough.

The good news is, I'm back under the direct daily care of one of the best AML teams in the country.

The bad news is, I need to be back under the direct daily care of one of the best AML teams in the country.

The good news is, the menu has a new insert including everything I asked for during my previous stay.

The bad news is, making fun of the food was one of favorite pastimes.

The good news is, I know how to do this.
(Also, there's a treadmill.)

= = =

We don't have final results from the biopsy yet, but we have enough information to know that, without a change of plan, the leukemia would eventually win. Unlike the initial diagnosis, this was not a complete shock. We knew this was a possible, maybe even probable, explanation for the behavior of my blood counts. It is still hard news to hear.

Anyway, I am back in Chicago for a different mix of chemo drugs than we used before. As was the case nine months ago, the first goal is to knock down the leukemia. Depending on how that goes, there are several possible paths: another round of chemo, another stem cell transplant, a donor lymphocyte infusion...

With so many possible paths, I don't have a handle on how long I'm going to be here. I know the plan for tomorrow—start the chemo. Four days later, end the chemo. Then some waiting.

There is a lot that is familiar, which isn't surprising considering I spent nine weeks here at the beginning of the year. Coincidentally, my first nurse this time was my first nurse the last time. I remember many of the other nurses and staff on the floor. As before, a good night's sleep is a fantasy.

- ▶ 12:00 a.m. Admitting doctor makes final decisions about evening medications.

- ▶ 1:15 a.m. I get stuck for a blood draw.

- ▶ 1:20 a.m. I ask the nurse about progress on the evening medications. I get one of them.

- ▶ 3:20 a.m. Another medication.

- ▶ 4:15 a.m. Vitals.

- ▶ 5:25 a.m. I get stuck for another blood draw. Luckily, my nurse is passing by the room and persuades the phlebotomist in my room to perform an additional draw scheduled for 6:00 a.m., saving me another stick within the hour.

- ▶ 7:00 a.m. More meds.

In addition to the familiar aspects, good and bad, there are some welcome changes.

The first difference I noticed after getting admitted last night was the menu. There is the same menu I ordered from at the beginning of the year, but stapled into it is a full-page *Health & Wellness* menu. (The original menu is, I guess, for people who are hospitalized but unconcerned with health and wellness.)

For me, the highlights of this new page are whole wheat pancakes, whole wheat waffles, fruit toppings for both; hummus and veggies; black bean soup; black bean burger; chicken, turkey, or tofu wraps; grilled portabella mushroom; whole wheat pasta; veggie or tofu stir fry; whole wheat pizza; veggie quesadillas on whole wheat tortillas; black beans, brown rice, sweet potato fries.

I brought some supplemental food based on my experience last winter, but I'm not going to have to rely on it that much. Tonight I had the hummus and veggie appetizer, whole wheat pasta with marinara sauce and grilled chicken, and sweet potato fries. It was all good.

Today I also had several transportations. No long waits, no getting left alone in halls. What am I going to write about?

Posted by Joseph Seeley at 8:09 PM

The Same, But Different

Since I'm back in the same hospital being treated for the same disease as I was nine months ago, a lot is obviously the same. The IV pole, the quiet grunting and occasional chirping of the pump, the semi-regular interruptions for vitals or blood or medications or consultation, Rectal Swab Tuesdays, the expected but unpredictable fevers and chills and sweats.

Not surprisingly, there are a lot of the same staff. Their usual greeting is something like, "It is so nice to see you again." I know what they mean, and I'm glad they're taking care of me because they are really good, but I can't help thinking, you know what would be even nicer? If I weren't here!

There are also a lot of differences. I have already mentioned the improved food service, where the changes are so large they deserve their own post.

The treatment plan is different. Last time, I got a cocktail of three drugs over seven days. This time, I got two drugs on day one, three days off, with a repeat yesterday. One of the drugs is the same as last time, but at a much higher dose. The new one is bright blue, and it's pretty disturbing to see something that color running into your body. It is also disturbing to have your pee turn blue, but I was prepared for that.

Another different side effect, and I'm not sure which chemical is responsible, is the onset of rigors about an hour after the infusions are done. In the span of 10 minutes, I go from having a slight chill to mild shivering to intense full-body shaking. The first time it happened, I was pretty freaked out, but it stopped as soon as they gave me some Tylenol. Last night, I could tell it was coming. Since I was already taking Tylenol, they gave me Demerol, which stopped the shaking in about 20 minutes.

My fitness level is different. In January I had recently run a half marathon and had been lifting weights regularly, so I was in very good shape for someone my age. While I was able to build up my running over the summer and had started some strength work, I was still a long way from getting back to my January fitness level. And with the late August round of chemo, I was reduced to walking. So, I come in to this round less fit than I was the first time, though still relatively fit compared to the population at large.

My marrow is different. My understanding is that in January, 50% of the blood cells in my marrow were blasts. That's a lot of leukemia. This time,

20% of the blood cells in my marrow are blasts, and half of the marrow cells carry the XX chromosome, which means they came from my sister. 50% blasts versus 20% works in my favor, because there is less leukemia to kill than before. I thought that having half of the cells from my sister would also be helpful, but it doesn't matter. Before the transplant, we kill them all and start from a clean slate.

My perspective is different. The first time through, it didn't really occur to me that there might be a second time through. Kill the leukemia, do the transplant, recover—sure, there could be (and were) some painful or uncomfortable bumps along the road, but it was still a story with a relatively simple arc. This time, I am aware that this is the second of X attempts to beat the leukemia. I'm hoping that when we get through all the wrangling, we find out that X=2. But I know it might be 3. Or more. For now, 2 is my new favorite number.

Posted by Joseph Seeley at 7:20 AM

Sunday, October 23, 2011

Come for the Chemo, Stay for the Food

OK, it's not *that* good. But the improvement in the food offerings since I was here last winter are remarkable.

There is a full-page add-on to the menu—the Health and Wellness page—loaded with whole grains, legumes, baked fish, and other healthy additions to the previous menu.

There is an after-hours menu, in recognition that patients don't always get to, or want to, order food between 7 a.m. and 8 p.m. We sometimes have procedures that take us away from our rooms at inconvenient times, or we might feel nauseous in the early evening.

And there are Food Service ambassadors who stop by every room at least once a day to ask about the food and how you're eating.

A few days into my stay, after hearing that I had little appetite, my Food Service visitor told me about an off-menu item that a lot of patients enjoy: homemade ginger ale, which is a small bottle of Perrier and a cup of homemade ginger syrup, so you can mix it to the strength you want. Ginger is a traditional appetite aid. The syrup is heavy on the ginger and light on the sugar, so it makes a great drink if you love ginger (which I always do) and if sugar turns you off (which it currently does). The chef also makes homemade candied ginger, which is OK but not as good as the Reed's Crystallized Ginger that my brother, Karl, brought me.

It is a shame that I can't really enjoy much of the new menu, since it contains so much that I was craving when I was here before. For now, there is very little that appeals to me from either the new or the old menu. The only items I actually enjoy are Cream of Wheat and grits, with a little bit of brown sugar. I force myself to eat other things—baked fish, fruit, hard-boiled eggs, hummus with veggies—because I know I need to eat a variety of foods for my own good.

The hospital does offer a couple of nutrition drinks for people who can't bring themselves to eat. One is Ensure, a protein and calorie shake available in chocolate and vanilla. The other is a Gatorade-like drink, also loaded with protein and calories. Both are very sweet, perhaps acceptably so under normal circumstances but nauseatingly so for me right now. So I had better keep putting away the bland proteins and calories I can tolerate, because I can't imagine keeping either of those drinks down.

Most of the Food Service improvements started a little over a month ago, when the hospital hired a new chef. What excellent timing on my part, waiting for the Food Service to turn around before I returned.

Posted by Joseph Seeley at 12:06 PM

Friday, October 28, 2011

Full Speed Ahead

On Tuesday, I had my Day 12 bone marrow biopsy. (Twelve days from the start of chemo.) On Wednesday, we had the preliminary results we wanted—an empty marrow. On Thursday, we got insurance approval to move ahead with the transplant. My sister will fly out on Sunday and start the health screening process on Monday.

This timetable is shorter than the one I followed this winter. I think one reason is that I have so far avoided the opportunistic infections that added so much excitement the last time: conjunctivitis, sinus infection, pneumonia, fungal gum infection...

Posted by Joseph Seeley at 8:49 AM

What's Going On

Not a question; an update.

Not much is going on with me, which is ideal. Last night was the first really bad night of sleep I've had since the first night. In general, the interruptions have been minimized and consolidated to midnight and 4:00 a.m. Last night, my nose was so congested I had to breathe through my mouth, which in the very dry hospital air leads to a parched mouth in about 15 minutes. So, every 15 minutes, if I had fallen asleep, I would wake up with a parched mouth and need to drink a little water.

I asked for some relief around 2:00 a.m. and was brought a nasal spray that the nurse said would work wonders. I suppose it might be helpful before your nasal passages become solidly blocked, but once that happens, the spray doesn't actually go anywhere useful.

At 3:30, I asked for a sleeping aid. At 4:00, the nurse told me she was waiting for a response from the doctor. At 4:30, the nurse told me the doctor had denied my request, because if I got a sleeping pill in the early morning I would sleep for much of the day. I said I didn't see the problem with that, since I was probably going to sleep much of the day anyway, having not yet had any sleep. At 5:00, the nurse brought me a sleeping pill.

During the day, my sinuses have been unplugged, and I have been using the nasal spray to try to keep them that way. I also will be getting a decongestant and a sleeping pill tonight.

My sister Mara came to town Sunday evening, in advance of tests on Monday. Tomorrow (Thursday), she will donate lymphocytes, which I may or may not use in the future. Then she will start taking her Neupogen to stimulate stem cell growth. She will be getting a higher dose this time, so she may feel more uncomfortable. She'll head down to Champaign on Friday and come back Sunday to begin stem cell collection on Monday.

Last time, the harvest did not yield the ideal number of cells. Among the possible reasons are the difference between our weights and some difficulty with her veins. My doctor does not think the lower-than-optimal number is related to my relapse, because for a while after the transplant all the numbers looked as good as they could look. However, it doesn't hurt to have more.

The higher dose is one part of the effort to collect more stem cells this time. They will probably also use a femoral vein rather than a brachial vein, and if that's not doing the job, they may even put in a temporary central line on Tuesday. After the harvest, Mara can go home.

Meanwhile, my instructions are to cool my heels until November 15 while we wait to see my mid-term response to the most recent chemo. The early results are what they should be: my blood counts, and especially my white counts, are very low. I haven't lost my hair, though I did see more strands than usual on the washcloth during my last shower.

When we get to November 15, there are several paths we could go down. If there is no real blood count recovery, we will probably wipe everything out with another round of chemo and proceed to a transplant. Given my chemo response history, this seems like the most likely option.

If there is a solid recovery, and if a bone marrow biopsy shows that all or nearly all of the new marrow cells are offspring of Mara's cells from the previous transplant, then it might not make sense to wipe everything out and do another transplant. Instead, I might get a donor lymphocyte infusion (DLI). The idea would be to supercharge my immune response, hoping to find the right balance between killing any remaining leukemia cells and not doing too much harm to various organs (graft-vs.-host disease).

A third path, and I think the least likely, is that the blood counts look so good that we just let me recover without further intervention, closely monitoring the counts. Sometimes patients go into remission after this round of chemo.

= = =

In sports news, our sons' teams had historic soccer seasons this fall. Paul's high school team lost only twice all season and made it to the state quarterfinals, going several rounds farther than any soccer team had gone previously in school history. The core of the team is juniors, including Paul, so they have a good shot at success next year as well. I got to watch quite a few games before entering the hospital, and then several more on video thanks to a team parent.

Jake's Haverford team lost their first 4 conference games but won the remaining 5, making the conference tournament for the first time in the conference's 11-year history. (Fun trivia: Haverford is the oldest college soccer program in the country.) Tonight they won their first-round game, putting them into the semifinals on Friday. It's been a steady climb for Jake and the other seniors, who as freshmen joined a team that had not won a conference game in years. I have been able to watch a few of Jake's games this fall, through poor quality live video feeds.

As for me, I'm walking 30 to 60 minutes a day, up and down the hall. There is a treadmill, but until I'm up to running, I'd rather really walk. It's hot enough in the double gown I have to wear, and when I walk the hall I get a slight cooling effect from moving through the air, and I don't have to wear gloves as I do on the treadmill.

Given my current training, I have amended my goal of actually running a 5K this fall. Instead, my goal is to complete a 5K, walking the whole way if that's what it takes. As long as I continue to be able to walk for 60 minutes straight, this seems realistic.

Posted by Joseph Seeley at 7:32 PM

Tuesday, November 8, 2011

Things That Go Bump in the Night

I had been running a mild fever in the evening for a few days, but not high enough to warrant any action. On Sunday evening, my fever reaches the magic threshold—38 Centigrade.

This means tests, throughout the night. They don't take any chances with fevers.

Around 1:00 a.m., Transport arrives to take me down for chest x-rays, to look for pneumonia. He wheels me to the elevator, down to the scanning floor, through a maze of turns and doors to the x-ray waiting area, which is empty. I am feeling pretty weak, and I am just about to get out of my chair and lie down on a couch when the tech comes in for me. As we're rolling down the hall, I feel a little flushed.

He takes me into the x-ray room and has me stand up with my chest against whatever it is they shoot us against. I'm tired. He aligns me and the background the way he wants, and steps out of the room into the control room. A voice tells me to breathe in and hold it, and then to breathe normally. I'm feeling lightheaded. I say out loud, "I'm feeling lightheaded."

The next thing I know, I am regaining consciousness in the wheelchair. I'm sweating and disoriented. The x-ray tech is next to me and tells me I was out for two minutes. (None of the doctors or nurses I later tell this to believe the two-minute estimate, chalking it up to the natural tendency to overestimate the duration of scary or unpleasant events.) The tech brings me a wet hand towel to cool me off, and somebody calls for the nurse from my corridor to come down.

By the time the nurse arrives, I feel fine. She gets into protective garb—why am I not in protective garb?—and stands next to me while we take the x-ray. And then she wheels me back to my room.

There's no obvious explanation for me passing out. My blood pressure is OK. I have only a light fever. I do sometimes get lightheaded when I stand up after sitting for a while, but in this case I had been standing for a while before all the blood suddenly rushed away from my brain. I had a nearly identical experience my first day back, during a CT scan of my head. (Sorry, I forgot to blog about that.) In that case, I was dehydrated. Maybe this time was a psychosomatic replay—back in the same corridors, standing up, getting aligned with the machine. Next time I'm doing one of these tests, I'll know to warn the tech.

After I get another hour or so of sleep, they're collecting blood for blood cultures. They also leave a kit for collecting a urine sample. The collection protocol is far too complicated and too time-consuming for me to comply with at 4:00 a.m.—I really have to go. At 6:00 a.m., I am able to follow the rules. Disturbingly, what initially comes out is blood instead of urine. Just a little, but still. The only amount of blood that is OK in these circumstances is none. I would have been even more disturbed if the same thing hadn't happened about a week ago. It doesn't hurt, there is no sign of infection, and I do have really low platelets. It's still just wrong. If it happens again, say my doctors, we'll consult a urologist.

Now, each time I pee only pee is a small victory. Every few hours, another win...

Posted by Joseph Seeley at 7:15 PM

First Harvest—1.1 Million

Monday is Mara's first collection day.

There had been talk of using a femoral vein instead of her arm, since there is some thought we didn't get the optimal number of stem cells in the winter because her veins were not cooperative. However, they went with the arm again today. They had no problem getting the volume of blood they wanted, but there were not as many stem cells as they hoped for.

They collected 1.1 million today. I thought this was pretty good, since I remember 2 million being the target in the winter. We only got 1.7 million back then, but the doctors decided to proceed anyway. It turns out 2 million is the minimal amount they like to transplant. The real target is 5 million.

Mara came over to my room around dinnertime, bringing with her some excellent coffee ice cream. I'm gradually adding foods to what I feel like eating, and coffee ice cream is definitely on the list.

Posted by Joseph Seeley at 7:28 PM

Saturday, November 12, 2011

Second Harvest

Tuesday is the second day of collection. We don't really know what to expect.

A doctor comes in and tells me they collected 2.6 million cells today! That gives us a total of 3.7 million, which is well on the way to 5 million. Very exciting. Wednesday's collection seems likely to top us off at 5 million.

Also exciting is the first citing of a neutrophil. Note the use of the singular form. This corresponds to an absolute neutrophil count (ANC) of 10. I don't actually get that excited, since I remember my ANC bouncing between 0 and 50 during my hospital stay in September. But 10 is definitely not zero, and maybe tomorrow we'll see more growth.

On Wednesday morning, Mara calls me with two pieces of news. They didn't get 3.7 million cells after all, they only have 3 million. (There is a preliminary count, which was too high, and a final count.) The second piece of news is that they aren't going to collect any more. Mara's platelets have dropped by half each time, leaving her in the 40s on Wednesday morning. So they decide to stop collecting. Three million is enough, and they don't want to harm her.

So, three million it is.

Posted by Joseph Seeley at 6:56 PM

More to Say Than Energy to Say it

Wednesday was great until late in the afternoon. Then it all turned very dark very quickly.

In an extremely uncreative reprise of the original movie, the ENT (ears nose throat) people made increasingly concerned and invasive and painful visits to my room until they were wheeling me down for emergency surgery at 10 at night. It was sinus surgery this time instead of oral surgery, but otherwise completely derivative.

I've been recovering since, which involves listening to the radio and dozing off in 20- and 30-minute intervals. My sinuses are packed with gauze, and they are still bleeding, which makes it nearly impossible to sleep. Today we have figured out a way to breathe more humid air that has made it slightly easier to sleep.

Had a bone marrow biopsy Friday. Results Monday or Tuesday.

Jan's visiting this weekend. My dad is coming later this week.

More later when I perk up.

Posted by Joseph Seeley at 7:09 PM

Tuesday, November 15, 2011

I Know an Old Lady Who Swallowed a Fly

To treat the fungus they rooted out of my nose as last Wednesday turned into Thursday, I am taking a couple of antifungal medications. At least one of them works by poking holes in the fungal cell walls.

Unfortunately, a side effect is that it also does the same thing to some cells in the kidney, causing me to shed potassium.

To treat the loss of potassium, I am taking a lot of intravenous potassium and also a diuretic that helps the body hang on to potassium.

Unfortunately, a potential side effect of the diuretic is that it could cause me to develop breasts.

I'm not sure what they'll give me to treat that side effect, but I'm sure it will have its own interesting side effects.

On the other hand, having breasts would open up some new career options: bearded lady, drag queen.

I am now in my sixth day of having my nose packed with stuff, which means sleep remains difficult to come by. Sunday night, I got an Ambien, and that helped. I still had to wake up every hour to pee, because I'm having drugs dripped into me all the time, plus liquids to make me pee. My nose is still bleeding, and I'm still hacking up bloody mucus, both of which are disgusting, but still better than peeing blood, which I have not done for a while. Hooray for small victories!

Last night, I was ready for my Ambien again. However, I had a fever, which meant more tests, including a chest x-ray, so they didn't want to give me a sleeping pill until after the x-ray. Which didn't happen until 4:00 a.m., due to emergencies that took priority. While it was disappointing to have my night ruined even more than usual, I'd rather be the non-emergency patient.

I did not pass out during the x-ray—another small victory. Sort of. I cheated by taking the x-ray while sitting on a stool.

Later today I should get a lot of information: biopsy results and a treatment plan. Until then, I just try to catch up on sleep.

Posted by Joseph Seeley at 9:01 AM

A Narrowing Path

The biopsy results are in, and the leukemia survives. Ideally, we would start treating the leukemia immediately with something new.

In the less-than-ideal world I'm living in, we can't do that. Complicating matters is the fungal infection that the surgeons think they were able to cut out of my sinuses six days ago. The thing about infections is that they are hard to totally remove physically, which is why I am still being flooded with antifungals.

This means we are trying to pick our way through a tricky and narrowing path.

Even though I barely have an immune system, I do have a trace of one, and it is presumably fighting any infection I might have, including any residual fungal infection. If there is any infection lurking, attacking the leukemia would wipe out what little immune system I have and unleash infections.

So, we will be monitoring me for signs of infection, beginning tomorrow when the ENT surgeons revisit my sinuses. In keeping with the tone of the day, I learned about this plan in a less-than-ideal way. Someone from anesthesiology stopped by my room early in the afternoon to talk about her role in the upcoming surgery that nobody had yet discussed with me.

Ideally—and I feel like I'm due some news from the ideal column—they don't see anything bad and they are able to remove the packing and other stuff that has been stuffed up there for the last six days. Then the oncology team and the infectious disease team weigh the confidence in there being no infection against the risk of leukemia getting out of hand. At some point, and this is what passes for ideal these days, I get another round of chemotherapy, I think in preparation for transplant.

The negative result is that they see more fungus and have to do more surgery, which means I'm further from being able to treat the leukemia, which would give the leukemia more time to grow and cause trouble.

My doctor was pretty somber when delivering the news. It felt like a transition from the odds being with me to the odds being against me. For all I know, that transition happened a while ago, but this is the first time I felt it.

Odds are about populations and probabilities. My case is about me. I feel healthy and hopeful, taking the next step, and then the one after that.

Posted by Joseph Seeley at 4:43 PM

Thursday, November 17, 2011

Looks Like Clear Sailing Through the Sinus Passages

The return trip to my sinus passages yesterday has so far yielded positive results in the most important ways. I went down at 3:00 p.m. for my 2:00 p.m. procedure, which started around 5:00 p.m. A kind secretary brought me a phone so that I could call Jan and let her know about the delay, so that she didn't get concerned that my procedure had turned into something much more involved than we were anticipating.

The surgeons did not see any more fungus. They took additional samples, to make sure. The initial tests on those samples came back negative. They still need to wait a few days for a final verdict, but so far, so good. I think the packing stays in for that same period of time.

Because they took more samples, my nose is still packed with internal splints and other stuff. There is less packing than before, and there is less drainage both out my nostrils and down the back of my throat. (More small victories.) I still have to breathe through my mouth, which quickly gets intensely dry. Last night, each time I woke up, my mouth and lips were so dry that I could not close my lips around a straw or the lip of a cup. I had to open my mouth, pour a little water in, and then swish it around to moisten the tissues enough that my mouth would actually function.

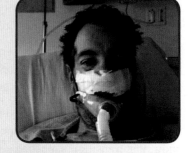

I have a breathing mask that supposedly provides more humid air. I have been using it for the last several days, and it seemed to be helpful. For some reason, it isn't helping with the current mouth dryness. Sipping water does help, but that technique is incompatible with sleep.

Some time today, I am going to get a new line for medications and transfusions. The one going into my chest is infected and needs to come out. So far, based on tests and the relative lack of fevers, that infection appears to be contained on the surface of my skin.

Never a dull moment! I want some dull moments.

Posted by Joseph Seeley at 9:27 AM

Step by Step

I am successfully navigating the current path, getting infections under control before the leukemia gets out of control.

I have been running low-grade fevers every few days, which the infectious disease team has decided are not important. The ID team also suspected a surface infection of my Hickman Triple Lumen (the port into my chest for putting in stuff and taking out blood samples) as the source of the fevers.

Yesterday, I got a PICC (peripherally inserted central catheter) line into my arm, which allowed the removal of the Hickman. So far, no fevers since the Hickman came out.

The fungus is no longer considered an issue. Fungal infections take a long time to be completely eradicated, especially with a weak immune system. But there is no sign of an active infection.

This morning, ENT removed splints and packing from my nose. It sounded worse than it turned out to be. I still can't breathe through my nose, because the nasal passages are blocked with clotted blood and some stuff they put in there to encourage clotting, but I'm getting closer. I still wear a gauze mustache to catch bloody drainage out the front. Several times a day, I now spray saline solution into my nostrils to help break up the crud in there. I also got a great tip from the ENT folks, which is going to save me a small amount of grief as long as I'm wearing the gauze mustache. Instead of taping the gauze under my nose —which leads to repeated removal of tape from my face, which hurts—the ENT folks just use a folded face mask that hooks over the ears. I wish they had passed that tip along nine days ago, but better late than never.

Here is the current treatment plan, subject to change (as always):

1. Continue to have a quiet (infection-free) weekend, and maybe Monday and Tuesday, too.

2. Start another round of chemotherapy, using a different class of chemicals than we have tried before. Instead of induction chemotherapy, which is what we did in October, this will be a bridge chemotherapy, used to buy time after one chemo treatment in preparation for transplant.

3. Twelve days after that chemo starts, do a biopsy. Again, we need to see barely any leukemia at that point.

4. If we don't see any leukemia, do a conditioning round of chemotherapy (to clear out the marrow) and then do a transplant.

My dad was visiting the last couple of days. He is down in Champaign now, doing a few home maintenance tasks and providing an adult presence while Jan is up visiting me for the weekend.

Posted by Joseph Seeley at 12:26 PM

Onward!

I had my first shower in a few days, including my first shampoo since my initial sinus surgery. Showers are currently quite tricky. I have to find a window of time when I am not receiving something through my lines. We have to wrap the PICC line in plastic and cover the site from which the Hickman was removed. (I can't see it, but everyone who looks at the infected Hickman site says it looks terrible.) And I have a mustache of gauze under my nose. I was so preoccupied with keeping various dressings dry and keeping the gauze mustache in place with one hand while dispensing and applying shampoo with the other hand that I was halfway through my shower before I realized I still had my glasses on.

I just heard that my chemo (clofarabine) is starting today. That's good! This means I have navigated not only the infection challenge but also the scheduling challenge of aligning treatment dates with biopsy dates, transplant dates, and the schedules of other transplant patients. I'm not the only patient preparing for a transplant, some key staff do not work on weekends, and there are limits to how many patients can be processed on a given day. Anyway, it's working out.

So, starting today, five days of chemo, seven days of recovery, biopsy... then, with the right biopsy results, more chemo, and then a transplant. Last Tuesday, when we learned that the leukemia had survived the October chemo treatment, was a rough day. Since then, everything has broken the right way.

Perhaps this turn of fortune is due to the flood of support coming my way. Cards and emails (often with humorous links—gotta keep laughing) and positive thoughts and prayers from all over, a complete set of *Frasier* episodes, work parties and meals at my house...

The most unexpected support, and almost certainly the largest in terms of the number of prayers, comes from the Swat Valley in Pakistan. If that location sounds familiar to you, it's most likely because the Swat Valley is the site of frequent U.S. drone attacks against suspected Taliban. It's also the home of a woman who is part of an English conversation group that my mother hosts for immigrants. So, five times a day, this woman's very large extended family prays to Allah for my health. (This gives me prayer coverage in all three Abrahamic religions.)

As a friend from high school commented recently, even a narrow path can get you where you need to go. Onward!

Posted by Joseph Seeley at 1:37 PM

Coolest Mani/Pedi Ever

I have finished three of the five days of chemo treatment. Each dose takes two hours.

The first time someone talked to me about the side effects of clofarabine, I was told there usually weren't any.

A few hours before my first dose, I receive the standard patient information sheet, which lists the same side effects I have seen on all the other chemo info sheets: chance of infection, feeling dizzy, feeling tired or week, nausea or vomiting, loose stools, skin irritation, headache, mouth irritation, anemia. I think these are all symptoms brought on by the severe drop in blood counts, not direct side effects of the medication, which is why they appear on every info sheet. Anyway, I'm feeling pretty comfortable about the whole thing, because I have tolerated the chemo treatments before relatively well, except for infections, and I'm already as vulnerable to infection as I can get.

Shortly before my first dose, the nurse comes in and asks, "So, did they tell you about the cold packs?"

No, they did not.

An until-now unmentioned side effect of this medication is Foot and Hand Disorder, in which the chemical wreaks havoc on the soles of the feet and the palms of the hand, causing massive blisters. Some studies have indicated that keeping these areas very cold while administering the chemo reduces the incidence of this problem by reducing circulation. Massive blisters on my palms and soles would definitely cramp my style, so I'm up for the cryotherapy.

On the first night of this round of chemo (Monday), the nurse wraps my feet (tops and bottoms) with chemical cold packs, and hands me two more, one for each hand. My job is to let the nurse know when they aren't cold anymore, so we can switch for new packs. I'm a little concerned, because I no longer have full feeling in my feet—a result of past chemo—and I wonder whether I will be able to tell if the packs are too cold. It turns out I can still feel cold just fine.

Anyway, the first round goes pretty well. About every half hour I decide the cold packs aren't cold enough, and two to ten minutes later the nurse comes in and replaces them. (One of the delays was because they didn't have enough cold packs on the floor.) With my feet bound in cold packs, I get to use a handheld urinal while sitting in bed. Tricky, but I've had practice.

On Tuesday, I have a different nurse. She asks how it went the first time, and I tell her it wasn't bad at all, and she starts gathering supplies: cold packs, gauze wrap to fasten packs to my feet. She gives me a couple of activated cold packs to hold while she leaves to get something else. She comes back with six small bags of ice.

"Those cold packs just are not very cold. I was talking to some of the other nurses, and I think we should try ice bags. Or, to make your hands colder, we could get a tub of ice and you could bury your hands in it."

"For two hours?"

"Yes."

"Ice bags will be fine."

So, my nurse straps an ice bag to each sole, and hands me two ice bags to hold.

"See? These are much colder."

Yes, they are.

I have a DVD of *Frasier* loaded up, so I'm ready to go. The ice bags are colder, but I get through the two hours with help from the episodes; a call from my niece Isabel; and another call from my parents, brother Karl, sister-in-law Kate, and their sons Ben and Garrett. Kate and Karl are visiting my parents from upstate New York for Thanksgiving. Jan and the boys are coming up Wednesday into Thursday for our own version of Thanksgiving.

My feet hurt as they warm up, and my palms are bright pink, as I suspect my soles are. It's been a very special spa treatment, as designed by the White Witch of Narnia.

Day three of chemo is Wednesday. We have been moving the time up two hours each day, since 8:00 p.m. is not a great time to start chemo. By today, we're starting at 4:00; it ends up being 4:10 before the pump actually starts. I'm pretty locked in to being done at 6:10.

At 5:10, I text Jan that I have an hour to go. A little later, I request new ice bags, since the ones in my hands are more water than ice. "You call this cold? Bring me more ice!" I'm hoping I don't need to change the ones on my feet, since they're feeling OK, but no such luck. One of the pumps starts beeping, and my nurse spends some time getting it to shut up. I'm watching *Frasier*.

At 5:40, I text Jan that I have half an hour to go. She is picking up Jake at the Bloomington airport and then driving up here with the boys.

5:55, 15 minutes to go.

6:05, 5 minutes to go.

6:10,... no pump alarm.

6:15,... no pump alarm. I call for my nurse. "Can he bring you anything?" "No, I just have a question."

I ask my nurse how much time I have left. "About 15 more minutes... that trouble with the pump slowed things down."

Aargh. I can do 15 more.

Fifteen minutes later, my nurse comes in to do a flush. "Can I take off the ice bags now?"

No. My nurse wants to wait until the flush is done, another 5 minutes.

Lucky me. A bonus 25 minutes of the spa treatment, at no extra charge, thanks to the merciless minion of the White Witch, who is pretending to be my nurse. If I had known, I could have watched one more episode.

Checking in with Jan and the boys, I learn that Jake has a runny nose. This means he cannot visit—a big disappointment, since visiting was the main reason he flew out from Philadelphia for the holiday.

I need to pee. I don't see my urinal, so I assume my nurse took it away when he released me from my ice bags. I head to my bathroom on numbed soles, which feels really weird, like somebody taped blocks of wood to the bottoms of my feet. On my way back to bed, I see my bedside urinal is still there. Oh well. I get into bed and take a nap.

On the bright side: three down, two to go.

Also, first day without the gauze mustache, because my sinuses have (mostly) stopped draining bloody mucus. I am enjoying immensely something I do not recommend to anyone: breathing through one's nose for the first time in three weeks.

Posted by Joseph Seeley at 1:56 PM

A 21st Century Thanksgiving Dinner

Jan, Jake, and Paul came up to Chicago Wednesday evening, staying over for Thanksgiving. Jake flew in from Philadelphia. As noted earlier, Jake got off the plane with a runny nose and a cough, putting him on the corridor's Do Not Enter list. But we made the best of it.

Staff from Food Service, who stop by for a quality check at least once a day and sometimes three times a day, had highly recommended the dining service's macaroni and cheese and the sweet potato pie, special for Thanksgiving. I was skeptical about the macaroni and cheese, since I had ordered it before, but she assured me that they made it the real way for Thanksgiving. So, I ordered the mac and cheese (take that, Pat Robertson) and the sweet potato pie, to supplement what my family was bringing from Boston Market. The dining hall had the mac and cheese, but they were out of pie.

The dining hall mac and cheese arrived shortly before Jan with the Boston Market bag. I couldn't tell the difference between the special Thanksgiving version and the usual awful stuff. Then again, not much tastes very good to me these days, so I'm not the best judge.

By 4:00, when Jan got to Boston Market, most of the sides we wanted were gone. The remainders were OK, but I really missed the cranberry-walnut relish we had seen on the menu.

We had our meal, chatted with Jake in exile, and later in the evening they all headed down to Champaign for the weekend. Jan is coming back up on Sunday for the day, after taking Jake to the airport.

Jake in exile in the Au Bon Pain
five floors below.

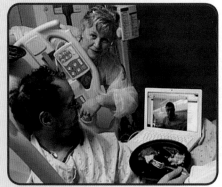

Chatting with Jake, in exile at the
hospital restaurant, via Skype.

A little later, my night nurse came in with good news—the nurses had a few extra pieces of sweet potato pie and were offering them to patients. Sure, I'd love one.

It was awful.

But the Thanksgiving dinner was basically as good as it could be, under the circumstances.

Posted by Joseph Seeley at 7:17 AM

My Black Friday Tale of Very Mild Woe

I had been both dreading and looking forward to the last day of this round of chemo. The cold hand and foot treatment is no fun, but Friday would be the last one.

I was all set. I had the next *Frasier* DVD in the player. I was mentally prepared for the two hours of chilling. Once I'm iced-in, I'm stuck in bed with my DVD controller and my little handheld urinal.

As soon as the drip started, I knew something was wrong. On Thursday, I had been watching disc 1 of season 2 of *Frasier*, and Niles was barely repressing his infatuation with Daphne. Suddenly, they appeared to be a couple, with Daphne pregnant. Was it a dream sequence?

Then it came to me. When Jan and I had earlier been looking through the DVDs, we noticed that one of the box sets had two Disc 2s, and one of the extras was a different color. Possessing between us only two Ivy League bachelor's degrees and two University of Illinois master's degrees, we just figured it was a mystery. If only we had had a kindergartner with us to suggest that the red disc belonged in the red box.

So, I was stuck many seasons in the future from where I had left off the day before. And since that was the worst thing that happened to me all day, it was a pretty good day.

Posted by Joseph Seeley at 6:33 AM

My Campaign for Quiche

I have mentioned before that the improvement in the food service has been tremendous: many new healthy choices, an after-hours menu, and daily inquiries about me and my food orders. Patients can also order from the staff cafeteria menu for lunch and dinner on weekdays, further adding to the variety available.

And I have found the food service open to modifications. One common modification for me lately: the hummus appetizer with cucumbers, carrots, and pita chips, substituting extra cucumbers for the carrots and pita chips.

There are two women with responsibility for two floors, and I think they stop by each room at least once a day to check in with the patients. I think one may be responsible for recording information about each patient, while the other one is focused on helping patients find items that may appeal to them, but they seem to ask similar questions and make similar suggestions. And there is an occasional phone call asking for my overall feedback on the service.

My feedback: I am very impressed with how thoroughly the hospital system has embraced the idea that eating well is a critical part of the patient experience.

(Ironically, as I write this, I have experienced my first delivery delay. We pretty consistently receive our order within 45 minutes, and tonight's dinner took 90 minutes to get here. Given the length of my current stay, that's still very good performance overall.)

On Sunday, Jan visited with some leftovers from the Champaign Thanksgiving dinner she and the boys had made on Friday. (I had joined via Skype, from a laptop sitting on a counter overlooking the dining room table.) These leftovers were much better than the Boston Market offerings we had shared on Thursday. My favorites were a cranberry chutney that Jan made, pumpkin cheesecake that Paul made, and a ham and gouda quiche that Jake made.

While enjoying my leftovers, I had a revelation: there was no quiche on the menu, and there should be. For many chemo (and other) patients, it is hard to get enough nutrition. People have low appetites, taste buds have gone haywire, mouths have sores in them. In general, eating is a chore. The typical solution is to offer these patients a liquid nutritional supplement such as Ensure or Boost, which packs a lot of carbs, protein, and fat into a small drinkable package. My personal experience, and I know this is true for others, is that these drinks are nauseatingly sweet. I can't drink them, especially with chemo mouth.

But cold quiche, on the other hand... loaded with carbs, protein, and fat; smooth and creamy; not sweet... perfect.

The next time my regular Food Service visitors stopped by, I pitched quiche as a menu addition. A nutritionist also stopped by—a weekly occurrence, I think—and I made the case for quiche to her, too. They all agreed it would be a good idea and said they would pass it on. One of my daily Food Service visitors also told me quiche is available in the staff cafeteria two mornings a week. Patients cannot order from the cafeteria in the morning, but she promised to bring me some personally. Which she did. (It was not as creamy as I think a quiche should be, but it was decent.)

Operation Quiche is not as significant as my previous Patients Need Better Food Campaign, but that's a great thing. When you are suggesting a single addition to the menu instead of arguing for a total overhaul, you're in a pretty good place.

Posted by Joseph Seeley at 6:00 AM

A Widening Path

My blood counts and I have been doing what we should this past week. No white blood cells. No fevers. Clear lungs. No indication, either from test results or symptoms, that the fungal infection in my sinuses is active. Daily walks (about 30 minutes). Eating well.

My reward is that I have a bone marrow biopsy scheduled (originally Friday, now moved to today for staffing reasons) and a tentative chemo + transplant schedule starting next week.

Yesterday, I had a lot of doctor visits. I had been requesting a visit from the ENT folks, to confirm that the crud I still have in my nose is an expected part of the recovery. I got one visit, got my confirmation after a little viewing with a pen light, and thanked the doctor for reassuring me. I told her that was all I needed—just a figurative (but informed) pat on the hand telling me I'm doing fine. Later in the afternoon, a larger ENT team showed up, somehow under the impression that I was increasingly concerned about my sinuses.

For them to really tell me all is well, they would need to run a scope up my sinuses. This is mildly uncomfortable, but the bigger problem is that it carries risks. With my blood counts as low as they are, sticking anything into my sinuses could, despite sterilization precautions, introduce some infectious agent that I can't fight, or could restart the bleeding that finally stopped after three weeks. In the absence of clinical evidence of an infection, it's not worth the risk. Which is fine with me.

I also had a couple of visits from the Infectious Disease team. The first informed me that they were running some tests on the vulnerability of my particular fungal antagonist to one of the antifungal meds I was receiving. The second informed me that they had just learned that that particular antifungal appeared to be quite ineffective, so they were switching me to something else. Yikes! I'm glad they did the legwork and figured this out before anything bad happened, but it's still unnerving.

Posted by Joseph Seeley at 6:23 AM

Monday, December 5, 2011

The Good News Is...

My biopsy results indicate that I am ready to proceed to the transplant phase. (!)

Since the failure of the October chemo, and the sinus infection, the plan has been to avoid infection, try a different chemo, do a biopsy, and—if the biopsy results were as desired—head into the transplant phase.

Left unspoken has always been, what if the biopsy results weren't good? Fortunately, we can skip right over that possibility now.

Posted by Joseph Seeley at 12:13 PM

Thursday, December 8, 2011

All Aboard for Transplant Station

My chemo started Tuesday morning. 4:00 in the morning. Lots of bags and pre-meds and blood draws. I didn't care. No noticeable side effects. On the first day, it's Fludara and Campath.

Repeat Wednesday morning, with the addition of Busulfex. Still not seeing any side effects, including the one that would alarm me most: changes in menstrual cycle. Sleep is constantly disrupted, as is the day time, but I don't care. I had blood drawn in the morning to test my response to a dose of platelets which I would receive several hours later. They're going to be disappointed in the results, and I'm going to get stuck again later so they can get real results. Doesn't bother me.

Proof that cranial cooling is happening, and it's caused by man.

I decided it was time to shave my head, since I was not fond of the retreating glacier model of hair loss.

Speaking of fungi, the ENT team is still nosing around my sinuses like pigs after truffles, trying to decide whether to start digging again. A recent CT scan showed "some stuff" where ideally there wouldn't be anything, but where there often is stuff even in perfectly healthy people. It seems like still an open question for the

This is my "kick leukemia's butt" look.

ENT team, but I get the sense they are leaning toward watchful waiting in the absence of symptoms.

Two more days of chemo (Friday, Saturday), two days of rest (Sunday, Monday)... Transplant on Tuesday!

Posted by Joseph Seeley at 9:25 AM

Saturday, December 10, 2011

Deck the Halls

Because we have always visited family in the Boston area over the holidays, we have never decorated our house. With my upcoming travel restrictions, the Seeleys will be spending their first Christmas in Champaign since Jan and I moved out here in 1987.

On Saturday, a team from Human Kinetics visited to give the Seeley home an uncharacteristic holiday makeover. Our neighbors are going to wonder who is living at the house and what they have done with the Seeleys.

Keri wonders what she has gotten herself into.

Joanne and Keri before working their magic on the tree.

Doug untangles lights under the guidance of Steve's kids.

Kim, Dalene, and Jill prepare exterior decorations.

Looking good at night, too,

Wow!

The Seeleys, real-tree people since childhood, have made the transition to a ... reusable tree. This was our wonderful work crew, minus the Ruhlig family that had to leave earlier.

Enjoying some well-deserved refreshments.

Posted by Joseph Seeley at 2:48 PM

Sunday, December 11, 2011

Yard Work

I usually handle most of the yard work at our house. I don't resent it; I enjoy it. I like the smells, the colors, the sounds, the effort, the results... Unfortunately, one aspect in particular, the smells, is inextricably linked to the molds and fungi that keep trying to establish colonies in my head and/or lungs, with potentially deadly results. So, no yard work, even when I was home in the spring and summer.

Since my medical team did not approve my leaving the hospital to take care of the end-of-fall yard work, we were blessed with a work crew.

Bob goes the solo route.

Mary, Janna, and Mandy
take a team approach.

Lisa, Mara, and Ellen

Paul likes letting machines do
some of the work.

Fred and Mark round out the crew.

Posted by Joseph Seeley at 2:46 PM

Minor Monday Becomes Major

I didn't think Monday was going to be as important as I have now learned that it is.

I *thought* it would just be the last day before my stem cell transplant, and the day I got a new line. For several days, my attending physician has talked about how we were just counting down the days to transplant, and that Monday would be a little busy because we would be putting in a temporary line for the transplant. (After two infected central lines, my team has decided to avoid long-term ports for me.)

Over the last few days, the ID folks would occasionally stop by to say everything seemed fine, which also suggested a clear path to Tuesday's transplant.

I had not seen the ENT staff since Wednesday, when some ambiguous imagery on a CT scan encouraged them to take a look with some bedside tools. They could not see as far in as they would have liked, but in the absence of symptoms—pain, vision problems, fever—they also didn't seem too concerned. Without hearing any more from them, and with my attending's repeated description of minimal action on Monday, I *thought* I knew what Monday would be like.

Then, for not the first time in this round of treatment, I get a visit from anesthesiology about an upcoming sinus surgery that I am not expecting. This throws me off balance. I feel like the various teams of doctors looking after me aren't communicating with each other, because I feel like I'm getting different messages from different teams. I let various doctors and nurses know how I feel about this.

At one point, I'm wondering whether the sinus surgery can actually prevent the transplant from happening. (It cannot.) The surgery does not sound too bad—mostly a looking around—but I still dread it, for multiple reasons.

If I'm lucky, they clean out some crud left over from earlier visits, they don't find anything new and alarming, and they pack my nose full of crap for another week and a half. Transplant on Tuesday.

If I'm less lucky, everything is the same as above, except that they find more active fungal infection hiding underneath the crud, which they (again) do their best to remove. Then there's a complicated couple of weeks as the fungus tries to exploit the missing immune system, the doctors battle the fungus with medications, and the new immune system boots up after the transplant.

So, I'm not happy about my upcoming surgery. I'm not happy that it was a surprise, I'm not happy that I'm going to get my nose packed again. I'm especially not happy that my illusion that I was past worrying about the fungal infection has been broken.

But, on the other hand, it needs to happen, so I'm glad it's happening. We need to know what we're dealing with.

Posted by Joseph Seeley at 8:00 PM

They Missed an Option... Thank Goodness!

Last night, when ENT was describing the two outcomes of today's sinus surgery, there was the *lucky* outcome (no fungus, can't breathe through my nose for a week or more) and the *unlucky* outcome (fungus, can't breathe through my nose for a week or more, and I'm in a precarious battle after the transplant).

For some reason, they missed what turned out to be the *actual* outcome, which was even better than the lucky one: no fungus, I should be able to breathe through my nose in a day, and they removed a clown car's worth of mucus, blood, crud, old packing, and other mysteries from my sinuses, left over from their earlier expeditions. I think of this as a delayed version of Carry In, Carry Out.

They did see something suspicious, but it's already checked out.

Tomorrow is Transplant Day.

Posted by Joseph Seeley at 6:08 PM

Wednesday, December 14, 2011

Transplant Day

Tuesday was transplant day. A little after 10 a.m., I got four bags of my sister's stem cells.

The rest of the day I was very tired. Then I started running a fever, which continued all night. The nursing assistant kept taking my temperature, and the temperature kept rising: 38.5, 39.3, 39.7, 39.9. Normal is 37.0 (98.6); 38.0 is when they start calling it a fever. 38.5? If I weren't feverish, I could do the conversion. Instead, I page the nursing station and ask for the conversion so that I could text Jan a number she could understand. (39.9 = 103.8)

Wednesday... still feverish, with occasional breaks.

More later...

Posted by Joseph Seeley at 1:42 PM

Thursday, December 15, 2011

D+2—Fever Gone

No fever at all today. It might be the round-the-clock Tylenol, or it might be, if I do have an infection, that one of the powerful antifungal/viral/bacterial medications I am on is keeping that infection in check.

The cause of the sustained high fever remains a mystery. (Solving the mystery is now a matter of curiosity rather than urgency.) Here are the suspects:

▶ An infection stirred up by the sinus surgery the day before my transplant (I did have a low fever before the transplant)

▶ Reaction to the transplant

▶ Some other infection

Although I am on Tylenol now, that was not an option during the fever. The key pre-transplant chemo drug, Busulfan, is hard on the liver, and Tylenol accentuates the effect.

Instead of Tylenol, I got a special pad for my bed. It's a thin plastic pad with a honeycomb of channels that fill with water, connected to a machine that keeps the water at whatever temperature you want. Even though it did not decrease my temperature, at least for the first day, it did increase my comfort. Or maybe it kept my fever from getting even higher.

I'm now rid of the fever and the pad. My complaint of the day is a strong metallic taste in my mouth. It makes everything taste terrible. I hear it's a common post-chemo experience.

It will pass.

And then something else will be my complaint of the day.

And as long as I have a complaint of the day, it means I have another day. Under the current circumstances, that's a victory.

Posted by Joseph Seeley at 7:54 PM

Monday, December 19, 2011

D+6—Could Be Worse

I am now six days beyond the transplant. Everything is going as expected: blood counts extremely low, no appetite (probably because all food tastes bad), and mucositis.

Mucositis is the inflammation of the mucus membranes lining the digestive tract, from the mouth to the anus. These cells, like leukemic cells, divide rapidly, and Busulfan (the key drug in my most recent chemo) attacks both with ferocity. Symptoms are mouth sores, painful swallowing, and diarrhea, which are all the result of the mucus membrane dying and shedding.

My mucositis started a couple of days ago, with a slightly sore throat. Since then, swallowing has been a little painful, but it has not reached the point that I can't bear to eat. It can get that bad, and that could still happen for me. But it might not. Currently, my appetite and the way food tastes are greater obstacles to eating than the pain of swallowing.

Mucositis usually lasts five or six days, and I am into my third day. Every day it's not horrible is one more day I'm avoiding the most severe symptoms. Or, as I tell myself many times every day, about many things, it could be worse. (And it's going to get better.)

= = =

The next big event to look forward to is the appearance of white blood cells in my daily blood tests. The white blood cell count has been negligible for a while now. Sometime around D+10, give or take a day, there will be enough white blood cells to count. Their numbers then typically grow very rapidly, and they are the primary factor in being able to leave the hospital.

In my case, they could start showing up as early as D+8, because I am receiving Neupogen shots. This is the same drug my sister Mara injected herself with before having her stem cells harvested. In my case, the idea is to speed up stem cell production so that I get my white counts up a little sooner than I would otherwise, because then I can help fight my current infection(s).

Posted by Joseph Seeley at 10:26 AM

D+7—I Knew It Could Be Worse

My typical night is not a good night of sleep. In addition to the external interruptions of vitals checks and medication changes and blood draws—sometimes from a line and sometimes from a needle in the arm—I also get up every hour to pee.

Last night, shortly after getting into bed, I got a back spasm at my tailbone. I have had back spasms before, but usually with an obvious cause like a sneeze or a poorly executed lift of something heavy. This one was just out of nowhere. And it was bad.

It took a while for a nurse to come in and talk to me. She wanted me to rate the pain on a scale of 1 to 10. I always have trouble with this question. After all, no matter how much something hurts, it could hurt more. Can you ever reach 10? In this case, I decided that writhing and moaning was equal to 8, which was high enough for my nurse to make an inquiry. Of course, that takes time, during which I'm still writhing and moaning on the bed. The first drug they tried didn't help, and then they switched to morphine. Not very much morphine, but it did the trick. So, two hours after the start of the spasm, I started my typical sleep in 60-minute pieces.

But that's not all! The mucositis has gotten worse over the course of today. No mouth sores or diarrhea, but the pain of swallowing has reached the point of me not being willing to eat. Since this afternoon, we have been trying to find the level of pain medication (currently morphine) that will allow me to swallow. So far, we haven't found the dosage, but I'm sure we will.

So, not a very good day. But I am one day closer to being through this un-comfortable phase. In a couple of days, we should see the start of countable white blood cells.

Almost there.

Posted by Joseph Seeley at 8:12 PM

Friday, December 23, 2011

D+10—Counts!

At this point, it's all about the counts.

My white blood cell count (WBC) has been essentially zero since my last round of chemo, as expected. The WBC is normally between 4,000 and 10,000, and I need those white blood cells to fight infections. On D+8, they went from zero—listed as <0.1, because WBC is measured in thousands—to 0.1 (100). Yesterday, D+9, the counts were 0.2, and today, 0.6. They increase exponentially for a while, so they should reach the normal range in a few days.

In addition to the WBC, the other noteworthy number is ANC (absolute neutrophil count). Neutrophils are a subset of WBC. In this case, we're looking for 500, the minimum value for being able to fight infection on my own. Above 1,500 is normal. We haven't been measuring this yet, since there haven't been enough white blood cells to take a subset. I bet we measure ANC from now on.

Posted by Joseph Seeley at 9:19 PM

Sunday, December 25, 2011

Dilaudid Daze

Note: This timeline may or may not be accurate. I don't really know. I know the events below happened, and most likely in the order below. I am less confident in the specific days. The problem is that, until Christmas Eve, I have found it very difficult to write while getting enough pain medication to be able to swallow.

(D+9, Thursday?)

The morphine did its job for my back spasm. However, the next day, my throat was increasingly red and sore, and I was increasingly reluctant to swallow. Different nurses had different approaches to this problem, as the problem gets worse:

▶ I just have to do this. (For a few rounds of medication, I am able to force myself to swallow tablets and capsules. Then I start gagging upon swallowing anything without a smooth texture.)

- We can crush tablets and mix with applesauce, which I might be more capable of swallowing. (For a few more rounds, I am able to do this. Then I start gagging on the presence of any grains of anything.)

- We can open the capsules and mix the contents with applesauce. (But eventually, I can't swallow even water or applesauce.)

At some point, we switch from morphine to Dilaudid. One nurse says Dilaudid is more effective, while the doctor says the two are essentially the same, but you use smaller doses of Dilaudid to achieve the same effect. The main side effect of either one is confusion and sleepiness.

I often find myself waiting longer than expected to get my dose. First, there is a wait for the task of resolving my pain to rise to the top of the nurse's pile. Then, if we are changing the dose, there is a wait for getting through to the doctor on call and waiting for the dose inquiry to rise to the top of the doctor's pile.

Or at least, I think that's what's going on. I am not always competent to judge my nurses. One time, I asked for a dose of Dilaudid around 6 in the evening. Around 8, I was talking to Jan and complaining that I had not received a dose for hours. My night nurse, who had just checked my records, overheard me and corrected me—I had been given a dose at 6:18 and either forgot or slept through it.

There were definitely other times that I was not fully in charge of my faculties, such as when I would fall asleep while eating or it would take me an hour to write a paragraph that, upon later reflection, was pretty incoherent and often full of repetition. In these cases, I was probably getting more than I should, even though it was not sufficiently managing the pain.

In a discussion with the nurse practitioner on my case, we decide it's time to switch to a pump.

A few hours later, I request my next dose of Dilaudid, because my throat pain is no longer tolerable. My nurse tells me I can no longer request Dilaudid, because my order has been switched to the pump.

Patient: Can we set up the pump, then?

Nurse: No. We don't have one on the floor. But we have put in a call to transport.

Patient: (Uh oh...)

About every half hour, a different nurse pokes her head into my room to tell me that the pump is coming. I become increasingly skeptical and agitated. I make the point that it isn't a good policy to cancel one medical treatment in favor of its replacement until that replacement is actually in hand.

A couple of hours into waiting for the pump, a nurse observes that I can get a one-time dose of Dilaudid. That would have been good to know a couple of hours ago, but I am relieved to finally get some pain medication.

I get a visit from a transportation manager, apologizing for the mix-up. Then I get a visit from the nursing manager. From the two visits, I gather the following:

▶ Our floor did not have a pain pump. Each floor is supposed to have one.

▶ The initial request for a pain pump got lost.

▶ My nurse was fairly new to the floor, which may explain why she didn't think of the one-time dose.

The pump supplies a continuous flow of 1 mg of Dilaudid per hour, and I have a button I can press every 10 minutes to get an additional 0.3 mg. The idea is that if I ever pump myself into unconsciousness, I won't be alert enough to keep pressing the button.

On Saturday, I wake up with a tolerable sore throat. The pain pump is set to ensure that I receive at least 1 mg per hour, and I had added a few extra shots when I woke up during the night to pee. This tells me that even a fairly low dose does a fair job of managing the pain, which means the unmanaged pain wouldn't be so bad. Good news!

We lower the background dose on Sunday, which is Christmas, and I don't press the button all day. I can swallow without pain, so I'm back to my only eating-related problem being the fact that all food tastes terrible.

Posted by Joseph Seeley at 7:46 PM

D+12—A White (Blood Cell) Christmas

(with thanks to several commenters for suggesting the title for this post)

WBC

0.1 D+8
0.2 D+9

0.6 D+10
0.8 D+11
1.7 D+12

The doctors are not bothering to look at the ANC because, at this point in the recovery from a stem cell transplant, such a high proportion of the white blood cells are neutrophils that it is extremely unlikely that my ANC isn't high enough.

At this rate of exponential growth, my WBC will be sufficient for going home in a couple of days.

In addition to getting the WBC where it needs to be, we also need to figure out how to adjust my meds to the reality of being at home instead of in a hospital, and also how to monitor blood counts and deal with shortfalls as needed.

Not home yet, but I can see it from here.

Especially with a little help from my extended family in Boston.

Posted by Joseph Seeley at 8:16 PM

Tuesday, December 27, 2011

D+14—Trying to Eat

First, the WBC:

0.1 D+8
0.2 D+9
0.6 D+10

0.8 D+11
1.7 D+12
2.6 D+13
3.1 D+14

The WBC is no longer doubling, but it's still growing fast enough that the doctor wants to send me home on Thursday (D+16). Thursday allows me to come back Friday and report right away on how things are going at home. If I were to go home Friday, I wouldn't be able to come back until Tuesday because of the weekend and the holiday, and that's too long a gap for the first return appointment.

In order for me to go home with the fewest complications, I should be creating my own platelets consistently, and I should be taking medications only by mouth. Otherwise, I would have to go home with an IV pole, or stay in the hospital over the weekend.

One of the medicines the Infectious Disease team wants me to take performs best when taken with a fatty meal. Normally, this would not be a problem, but my current appetite makes it hard to eat anything and especially rebels at fatty foods. This evening, just the smell of a fried fish sandwich and fries caused me to retch up some juice I had managed to get down a couple of hours earlier.

Fortunately, my nurse suggested I give Ensure another try. I had found it repulsive weeks ago, but this time I was able to drink an entire bottle. So, if I can't eat regular food, I can at least drink Ensure. I sure hope my taste recovers soon.

Posted by Joseph Seeley at 8:22 PM

Thursday, December 29, 2011

D+16—What Was the Plan, Again?

(Midday, Thursday)

The only things that seem certain right now are (1) that I am having two procedures today, one to put in a PICC line (a line going in just above my elbow) and one to remove my current jugular line, and (2) that the doctors are aiming to discharge me today.

I have heard "getting discharged" and "going home" used interchangeably, and given my experience the first time around, we were operating under the assumption that, in our case, they both meant returning to Champaign. Yesterday, my doctor made it clear that his definition was, leaving the hospital but staying fairly close. Since we live two-and-a-half hours away, "going home" excludes Champaign in my attending doctor's definition.

For round one, in the winter, my main doctor (not my current attending) was willing to make an exception because I was very stable and, despite all I went through, I had come through fairly strong.

Anyway, we were completely unprepared for this development, so we have been scrambling to find an acceptable place nearby. There are not many options.

On the other hand, we are more comfortable with staying near the hospital for a week or so than with going back to Champaign. I'm not as strong as I was upon discharge in the winter, and sticking close offers some comfort.

We have a reservation at a Hampton Inn 24 miles from the hospital (mostly highway).

We have a lead on a furnished apartment available for short-term lease only a couple of miles from the hospital. Not sure about wi-fi, which would be essential for Jan and very useful for me.

We won't know if the Magnificent Mile condo that some friends have let Jan use in the past is available this weekend until this afternoon, but we suspect it is not.

We don't know if staying in the hospital into the weekend is an option.

(Mid-afternoon, Thursday)

The social worker has given us a lead on an apartment within two miles of the hospital. It looks fantastic. We also checked out a couple of extended stay hotels about 20 miles away.

Jan has rented a car, so that Jake and Paul can have a car, and is heading up to Chicago. Unfortunately for her, it is heavily perfumed to cover the smell of smoking. So, she is driving with the windows open, cold and nauseated.

I now have a PICC line in my left arm.

(Late afternoon, Thursday)

I get a very apologetic call from the nurse practitioner in charge of discharging. She and others who would be involved in the paperwork needed for my discharge have not been able to do what they need to do for me, due to an emergency on the floor for most of the afternoon. So the new plan is to stay one more night and have my jugular line removed tomorrow morning.

I'm OK with this development, though it's too bad that Jan had to rush up here this afternoon when it turns out she could have come up tomorrow morning.

As the nurse continues to apologize, I interrupt her. First, I understand that I am not the only patient. Second, I'm grateful the emergency wasn't me. Third, I think this actually works well for me. It allows me to have a night unconnected to the IV pole but still with nursing attention as needed. It's like a dry run for being out of the hospital.

(Early evening, Thursday)

The apartment is physically very nice, reports Jan, but it has a serious and probably disqualifying flaw. Like the car, it is redolent with what is sold as "air freshener" but which instead recreates the experience of being stuck in a broken elevator with someone who wears way too much cologne or perfume. All night. It nauseates Jan, and there is no way she can sleep there. Jan wonders if I would be able to sleep there either.

Right now, we're hoping the apartment complex has another apartment that hasn't been stink-bombed, but we suspect the air fresheners may be policy rather than an anomaly.

(Later in the evening)

The air freshener is apartment complex policy. Somebody in charge thinks it is better than the miscellaneous foreign smells (Chinese food, curry) left behind by some of the guests. We are working with one of the owners (who is out of town) and with the caretaker to see if an extended period of airing out will help. Give us curry anytime.

Jan may stay in the hospital tonight, choosing the nightly interruptions over the air freshener. And we may have to find another place to stay.

Posted by Joseph Seeley at 6:30 PM

D+18—"Home" Sweet Home

The apartment with the sickeningly "fresh" air is going to work out after all, and Jan and I spent our first night in it. I will be here for an unknown number of weeks.

Jan talked to one of the owners of the apartment complex, and he was very sympathetic. The caretaker and other staff put in extra time airing out the apartment and washing the wooden floors (again) while Jan was at the hospital. By the time we got here Friday evening, the air was still slightly perfumed but easily tolerable.

The apartment is very nice. There is a main living/kitchen/dining area, off of which are a bathroom with shower, a bedroom, and a master bedroom that has a Jacuzzi in its bathroom.

I slept better than usual, though I still woke up four times to pee. That's several times less than a typical night in the hospital, and each time brought the small thrill of not having to pee into a small plastic urinal so that the nurses could track my output and the larger thrill of waking up and not being in the hospital.

Today (Saturday), I get a visit from a home health care nurse who hooks me up to my own IV pole for four hours of saline fluid. She also collects two-plus hours of information about medications, medical history, current state... A lot of the questions, especially ones like when did I start taking a specific medication, seem like they would be better answered by the hospital. I don't remember very clearly when a specific medication started, especially since several medication changes happened during my Dilaudid daze.

In the morning, Jan and I took a walk on the balcony that runs outside the door along the length of the third floor. Coincidentally, the balcony is about the same length as the corridor I have been walking since mid-October.

During the day, we have been trying different foods that appeal to me. The best find so far has been whole milk, which meets my need to consume fat with one of my medications.

All in all, the last day of 2011 was pretty good, compared to most of the first and last three months. Here's to a better 2012.

Posted by Joseph Seeley at 5:54 PM

D+20—Settling In

We're finishing our third day in the apartment. It's going about as well as it can.

Yesterday, I went to the hospital for blood tests and possible transfusions, as ordered by the person in charge of discharging me. Surprisingly, to us, the hospital was not expecting me, and we had to wait about 40 minutes in Admitting for a doctor to put in an order. The woman in the admitting office who was serving us told us that what we *should* have done was call ahead to find out if there was a room available and to set in motion the process of getting an order. This would have been useful information to have upon discharge. We were not alone in our circumstances, as two other patients showed up while we waited in Admitting and found themselves in the same unexpected position.

Luckily, I didn't need any platelets or red blood cells, which is good both because we got to leave within an hour of the blood draw and because it means the marrow is producing enough of those cells to keep me above the danger line for those two types of cells. The WBC has been drifting down since its high of 3.1 (3,100), but nobody medical seems concerned as long as there are enough neutrophils to fight infection, and there's still a good cushion there.

Our friend Mary drove up from Champaign for a very brief visit while we were at the hospital and also brought a few household supplies from our house: cutting board, lemon squeezer, drying rack... items you don't always find in a "fully furnished" apartment. We keep discovering more things that are lacking, some of which really should be provided—pot holders, lids for pots—and others that we just would like to have—space heater, baking sheet.

After the hospital visit, my home care nurse came and gave me a magnesium infusion.

Today, I went for a couple of 15-minute walks... inside the apartment. It was a little slippery outside, and very cold.

My doctor, back from her two-week vacation, called to see how I was doing (on a holiday—she's really good). Mostly, I feel like I am 90 years old. I walk very slowly, and I am often tired. She was not surprised, given all that has happened to me since the leukemia returned.

One useful piece of information we learned from her was that, while it could be less or it could be more, I should plan to be in Chicago for a couple of months. This is going to take some planning, since Jan cannot be up here the whole time. We are lucky that my parents are retired and able to come out for lengthy caretaking trips.

Posted by Joseph Seeley at 6:47 PM

Thursday, January 5, 2012

D+23—Milestones

I have reached a few milestones in the last several days.

▶ Yesterday, I got out of the tub unassisted. It might have been better technique, or a little more strength, or some of each.

▶ Yesterday, I was finally able to break my large pills in half. Again, not sure about the mix of technique and strength involved, but it makes me feel good to be able to do it myself.

▶ Yesterday, I had my first squares of chocolate (Trader Joe's Bittersweet Chocolate with Almonds) in a long time. It has been a while since chocolate in this form appealed to me, and chocolate is one of my favorite food groups, so this is a big step. Chocolate, especially with nuts, is also a great and compact source of fat and calories, which I am currently trying to maximize.

▶ Today, I walked in the neighborhood for the first time, for 25 minutes. My dad and I discovered several interesting takeout options.

Tomorrow, I have lab tests and an appointment with a nurse practitioner for a check-up. In roughly a week, I have my next bone marrow biopsy.

Posted by Joseph Seeley at 6:27 PM

Monday, January 9, 2012

D+27—Quick Update

It was kind of a lost day, with about 5 hours of tests and appointments to start off the day, followed by some serious napping.

My blood tests show a small but not necessarily meaningful uptick in most numbers. The numbers had been drifting down, but not enough to alarm the doctors.

The big issue yesterday was that my infusion line was blocked. We think my dad and I failed to flush the line the day before, leaving some blood to clog things up. Fortunately, an IV therapist was able to open up the line today.

The big issue of today was a sharp stabbing pain at the bottom of my right rib cage, reminding me of both my gallstones and my pulmonary embolism. We still don't know what the cause is, but some over-the-counter pain relief (doctor's recommendation until she figures out what the problem is) has helped.

Next week, I have a bone marrow biopsy and an appointment with the ENT folks to check on my sinuses. As of now, those are my next visits to the clinic.

Jan was here yesterday and today, visiting me and giving my dad a break. It was a win-win-win. My dad got a break from 24/7 caregiving and went to the Blue Man Group. I got to see my amazing wife. And Jan got to help bathe her now scrawny husband, and also shepherd me through a five-hour clinic visit and watch me nap.

Posted by Joseph Seeley at 8:29 PM

Sunday, January 15, 2012

D+31—It Only Hurts When I...

(I note with nostalgia that my previous D+31 posting, after the first transplant, had the title "Our Most Boring Patient." It's odd to think of that period of time as the good old days...)

So, on Monday I had the sharp stabbing pain that felt like the gallbladder problem (minus the vomiting) and also like the pulmonary embolism. At times it was debilitating. I used the modified breathing technique that only uses the top third of my chest to avoid pain, but a laugh or burp or cough or sneeze, or even just turning the "wrong" way, would twist the knife hard, and even a normal breath was quite painful.

Before I saw the doctor on Monday, I saw a nurse who went over my medications and asked about any pain. I explained what was going on. She asked the "on a scale of 1 to 10" question. I tried to explain that it was constantly changing, ranging from 4 if I didn't breathe too deeply to 8 or so when I did. Apparently, her computer form had room for only one number. "What's the number right now?" In the interest of honesty, I said, "four," which she dutifully typed in, mostly hiding how much pain I was in. Maybe I should have averaged the high and low.

The doppler imaging they did on my line and the chest x-ray were both negative for blood clots, so it was left as a mystery.

On Tuesday, the pain had shifted to the left side. Since an embolism can't jump from one lung to the other, this shift pretty conclusively ruled out a PE. It also ruled out various organ-related issues, most of which had already been ruled out by my normal blood chemistry. It hurt a little less than it had the day before, perhaps because of the acetaminophen I was taking. Later that day, it appeared on both sides. I began to suspect it was nothing as dramatic as a pulmonary embolism or a gallstone.

What could it be? On Monday, during my appointment with my doctor, she had asked in passing if I was constipated. I said I wasn't, because I was having small, normal bowel movements a couple of times a day. Over several days, however, small bowel movements are not that different from constipation, so I started taking something for that.

By Wednesday, the pain just below my rib cage, which continued to migrate from one side to the other, had generally subsided to the point that I could move around freely with only occasional stabs from an especially deep breath. It was a sunny day and very warm for January in Chicago—above 50 degrees—so my dad and I drove to the nearby lakefront and walked to Promontory Point, which offers a beautiful view of downtown Chicago to the north. The outing included about 45 minutes of walking, the most for me in 2012. PR!

On Thursday, the upper abdominal pain was mostly gone. I could make it hurt if I tried, and at times it came back briefly to previous levels, but I could go hours without noticing anything.

In the afternoon, I took a nap. When I woke up, I did what I had done for most of the week: see how deep a breath I could take before I felt pain. The answer was, pretty deep! Excellent. I headed to the bathroom to pee.

Whoa! *That* hurts.

And what's this tiny bloody thing in the toilet bowl? It's not exactly a drop of blood, which would have dispersed. It's like a tiny bright red jellyfish, about the size of a fingernail. And it came out of my... This is not right!

And why do I still feel like I need to pee, even though I just did?

I called my doctor. It's probably some kind of infection. Instructions: Keep an eye on it.

At night, I get up every hour to go to the bathroom. Sometimes it burns a little, and sometimes it feels like I'm peeing tabasco sauce. Sometimes there's a little blood, and sometimes there's none that I can see, and sometimes there are what I assume are small pieces of the lining of the urinary tract.

Not much has changed in the morning. I call my doctor. "Would you like to submit a urine sample?" Hmmm. I was not expecting her to leave it up to me, but starting down the path of finding out what the problem was seemed preferable to sticking with the status quo, so she put in an order for the lab work and my dad and I headed to the clinic.

At this point, the urge to go was constant, even though my bladder was nearly empty each time. I didn't feel like I could hold out as I waited in one waiting room for lab paperwork, and then in the lab waiting room, even though I knew my bladder was close to empty since I had gone just before we left for the clinic.

= = =

[I am posting this now, Sunday, even though it's incomplete, because the infection I have been describing has made sitting uncomfortable, and it's hard to write lying down, and even lying down I am very uncomfortable, so I'm focused on just getting through the day, which is why I haven't worked on this post since Friday. The infection is most likely a virus, in which case there's nothing to do anyway except wait it out. I did get some encouraging blood counts on Friday: platelets went to 37 after drifting in the teens for a few weeks, WBC went to 2.5 after drifting around 1.5 for a while, and ANC went to 1.48, which is essentially normal. I get more counts tomorrow.]

Posted by Joseph Seeley at 8:36 PM

Saturday, January 21, 2012

Another Quick Update

I know I have left people hanging by not posting more regularly, and that creates concern. You can relax.

I'll have more to say about my bladder infection and its treatment in a future (and I hope not too distant) post. It won't be for the squeamish, which might be why I'm putting off writing about it. The family-friendly summary is that I went back into the hospital on Monday, and I have progressed from almost always uncomfortable and frequently in great pain to occasionally uncomfortable and rarely in pain, and that pain is not as bad as before.

Unlike the infections I have fought through before transplant, this infection does not interfere with the overall treatment/recovery plan.

As for the recovery from transplant, that is going well. The preliminary biopsy results show no leukemia and typical quantities of various cell types at this point after a transplant, but we won't know for sure until the more accurate test results are in, either late this week or sometime the week after.

Posted by Joseph Seeley at 8:20 PM

Thursday, January 26, 2012

It Only Hurts When I ... (cont.)

[This is a continuation of an earlier post. I have been out of the hospital, without any infection, since Tuesday afternoon.]

Over the course of a week, I moved from it-only-hurts-when-I-breathe to it-only-hurts-when-I-laugh/sneeze/cough to it-only-hurts-when-I-pee to it-only-hurts-when-I-pee-and-I-have-to-pee-all-the-time-and-why-is-there-blood.

So, I ended up back in the hospital to treat a strongly suspected (and then confirmed) viral bladder infection. It is called the BK virus, and I now have a visceral aversion to all things BK. Sorry, Burger King.

My doctor's initial preference was to ride out the virus, saying, "The treatment is often worse than the condition." When the condition became intolerable, she raised the prospect of returning to the hospital for treatment. She left it up to me, but she was clearly leaning toward readmission, and I agreed. So, following my regular appointment on Monday (1/16), I was wheeled by a nurse from the clinic, across two streets (in enclosed walkways), and into the hospital admitting office.

The next least aggressive treatment, after riding it out, is irrigating the bladder with saline solution continuously for as many days as it takes to flush out dead and dying tissue. Irrigation works because the virus invades cells, multiplies, kills the cells, and then spreads to neighboring cells when the cells fall apart. If you flush the dead tissue, you flush the virus before it has a chance to infect more cells. Of particular concern is that the virus can get into the blood or travel into the kidneys.

Irrigation is not painless, but it is less painful than riding it out.

The first step in irrigation is having a way to get fluid into and out of the bladder, continuously. One word: catheter. It's a two-lane catheter, with half of the tube heading in and half heading out. Then it splits into two larger tubes, one coming from the saline bag hanging from an IV pole and the other running into a bag collecting the outflow.

Overall, the catheter is about the diameter of a cheap ballpoint pen, a little thinner than a standard pencil. Getting the catheter into position is a painful but thankfully quick procedure. There's a numbing, lubricating gel involved, but, in my fortunately limited experience, it only numbs and lubricates up to but not including the sphincter at the bottom of the bladder. Yeowch!

[That's today's installment of Joe vs. BK. More will dribble out—ha!—in days to come.]

Posted by Joseph Seeley at 8:01 PM

Monday, January 30, 2012

My Good Luck Charm Comes Through Again

Today I had my regular Monday clinic visit with my doctor. After my last one, two weeks ago, I went straight from the clinic into the hospital to deal with my bladder infection. Since I was in the hospital last Monday, I didn't have a clinic appointment.

I went with my mom, who has been my Chicago caregiver for a week and will be here one more week. Over the course of dealing with this disease, now exceeding one year, my mom has been my good luck charm. When she is visiting, things go well. Maybe it's the cooking.

My doctor came in, smiling and remarking at how much better I looked than I had looked two weeks ago. She told us my blood counts were looking very good and showed us the printout she was carrying: white blood cells at 4.0 (normal), platelets at 71 (low, but enough of an increase to signify improvement instead of noise), hemoglobin roughly the same as last time. All encouraging, but what really matters is the biopsy results.

Then, and this felt like an afterthought, she reached into the pocket of her white lab coat and said, "Oh. I have more good news." She had the results of two tests carried out on my Day 30 bone marrow biopsy—the XX/XY breakdown (because my donor is female, this is a useful measurement), and the count of cells carrying deletion 7, a chromosomal abnormality that marks my leukemia cells.

The XX/XY breakdown is 100% / 0%, which is actually a teeny bit better than the corresponding result after my first transplant (99+% / <1%). I am woman, hear me roar!

The deletion 7 test claims it found a few cells (3 out of 400), but this is considered a negative (good) result. The test typically has a little noise, and anything under 8 out of 400 is treated as equivalent to zero. My doctor hypothesizes that the testing process itself generates a few deletion 7 false positives. Another way of thinking about it is that my deletion 7 test results are indistinguishable from those of someone with no leukemia.

So, great news! On the other hand, across my celebratory mood lies the shadow of knowing I have received the best possible news before, after my Day 30 biopsy following my first transplant, and it wasn't good enough. On the other, other hand, I can't do any better than I'm doing, so I might as well celebrate—I had sparkling grape juice with dinner.

Posted by Joseph Seeley at 5:55 PM

Friday, February 3, 2012

Rash Behavior

On Wednesday, I noticed that my face was a little bumpy. I thought it might be all the missing whiskers trying to emerge, in honor of the spring-like weather. Speaking of the weather, my mom and I have taken advantage of Chicago's extremely mild winter weather this week to take some lengthy walks.

On Thursday, the skin on my face had a texture somewhat like the surface of a bowl of oatmeal, and the top of my bald head was bumpy, and my neck was a little itchy. During the night, into Friday morning, my neck got very itchy. As did my face, and the top of my head.

This morning (Friday), everywhere that had been bumpy or lumpy or oatmealy or itchy is still that way, and the rash has spread to my lower legs. I call my doctor, who tells me to arrange a visit to the clinic to get it checked out. I get an appointment in the early afternoon.

The first step at the clinic turns out to be lab work. When I take off my fleece to expose my arm for the blood draw, I see that both arms are covered with small raised red welts.

It's itchy and unaesthetic, but I'm thinking it's probably a good thing. One manifestation of graft-vs.-host disease is a skin rash, and having some GVHD correlates with better transplant outcomes. GVHD indicates a solid immune response from the graft (donor) cells. If the new immune system is attacking an organ like the skin, the thinking goes, there is a better chance that it is also attacking any lingering leukemia (graft-vs.-leukemia). Too much GVHD can be very bad, and even fatal, but a skin rash like the one I have, which is relatively mild, is not life-threatening.

My appointment is with a physician's assistant (PA) who works with the On-cology team. The last time I saw her, she was performing my most recent bone marrow biopsy, and I was about to re-enter the hospital because of my bladder infection.

She checks the skin on my face, back, arms, chest, back, legs... She is confident it's GVHD. She asks about any pain (none), intestinal issues (none), eye issues (a little irritated). If there is a dermatologist available on this Friday afternoon, she would like to get a skin biopsy to get absolute confirmation that this is GVHD, but she determines that none is available, and she's quite sure anyway.

After consulting with my doctor, the PA prescribes a couple of steroid ointments, one that is too strong to use on the face, and a second that I *can* use on the face. She also recommends an over-the-counter antihistamine for itching, and eye drops.

By the time I get home, several hours later, I'm ready for a nap. I'm itchy, so I take an antihistamine and apply my ointments. Both ointments behave as if they have a petroleum jelly base, and applying them is like applying Vaseline on my head, face, back, and arms.

Unlike lotions, which sink in, ointments just sit grossly, greasily on the skin. If someone were trying to catch me, I would be hard to hold on to. If I were trying to take a nap, and I am, I would feel pretty disgusting, and I do. But I fall asleep anyway.

= = =

Before my appointment was over, I got preliminary lab results. The last three labs (Thursday 1/26, Monday 1/30, and today 2/3) show solid increases in the main three types of blood cells.

White blood cells: 3.6, 4.1, 5.8
Hemoglobin (standing in for red blood cells): 10.4, 10.6, 11.2
Platelets: 59, 71, 84

I think these numbers, and the onset of GVHD, are both good signs.

When talking with my doctor this morning, I learned that the consensus on the transplant team (when they met yesterday) was to take me off my immunosuppressant medication (which would probably trigger GVHD) and do another bone marrow biopsy pretty soon instead of waiting for day 100 as is typical. Now that I appear to have GVHD at the current immunosuppressant dosage, that plan may get revisited.

Posted by Joseph Seeley at 6:45 PM

Thursday, February 9, 2012

Ambling Along

Monday's appointment was upbeat.

My blood counts were a little lower than before the weekend, but that can be caused by either GVHD or sampling error. My doctor seconded the earlier visual diagnosis of my rash being GVHD, saying it had a classic appearance. By then the rash was still visible over much of my body, but it wasn't itchy enough to cause me to lube up, and it has continued to subside.

A week ago, on Thursday, the transplant team had discussed my case and was preparing to take me off the immunosuppressant drugs in order to trigger GVHD, possibly as soon as this week. On Friday, I showed up in the clinic with GVHD, so we're going to stick with the current dosage.

I am no longer getting magnesium supplements, which are given intravenously, so I will have my PICC line removed this coming Monday. This will be a big step toward normalcy. I can forget about the line dangling out of my arm for long periods of time, but it creeps into my consciousness at night when I change sleeping positions, and it makes showering difficult because it has to be kept dry. I won't miss it. Potassium levels are also OK, which means one monster pill a day I no longer take.

Today, when I pulled my arm out of my long-sleeved T-shirt so that my brother and I could flush the PICC line, the hairs on my arm—just about the last part of my body to have hair—looked like they were dusted with frost. It was enchanting for the second or two it took me to realize the frost was dead skin cells that had accumulated since I got up in the morning. I assume the rash has caused more than the usual number of skin cells to slough off. (Note to self: Wash the sheets.)

My brother the professor has been my minder this week. For now, he has more hair on his head than I do. He is taking the week between his school's January term and the start of the spring semester to keep an eye on me, keeping up my family's superb support. He does his professor stuff, prepares meals, shops, cleans, and takes walks with me. I do a little work, eat, sleep, take walks. This week's new walk was to get all the way to the lakeshore from the apartment. It was dark, so we got to see downtown Chicago's skyscrapers all lit up, off to the north.

My next minder is Jan, for a whole week. I feel well enough that it should feel like a couple spending time together instead of a patient being cared for by a round-the-clock nurse. Sounds good to me!

Posted by Joseph Seeley at 6:35 PM

Thursday, February 16, 2012

Valentine's Week: Cowboy Monday

Jan, my favorite minder, is here this week. It's the first time we've been able to spend days and nights together in four months. This is good!

On Monday, we go to my weekly appointment with my doctor. My blood counts are roughly the same as the week before, and probably a little suppressed by GVHD. My rash has mostly faded, so my doctor decides it's time to poke the hornet's nest a little. She describes what I'm going to do as tapering my immunosuppressant, although skipping one day, taking it one more day, and then stopping altogether seems too abrupt to be called "tapering." In any event, we are discontinuing the drug more than a month earlier than the typical schedule.

On the other hand, I already have (just barely) sub-therapeutic levels of the medication in my blood, so in that sense stopping completely might not be a drastic change. It might be enough to trigger another round of GVHD—maybe of the skin (symptom: rash), or of the intestines (symptoms: diarrhea, cramps, vomiting), or of the liver (symptom: jaundice [maybe vomiting, too]).

My doctor reminds us that a little GVHD is good, not for its own sake, but because it indicates that my donor cells include some T cells that recognize me as "other," which offers hope they also recognize leukemic cells as "other." On the other hand, as she further reminds us, too much GVHD is life-threatening, and I don't need any more of that. If any of the symptoms get too serious, I can go back on the immunosuppressant and/or take some steroids.

When do I get to go home? Not yet. My doctor would like to see how I handle the medication change. She even seems a little superstitious, as if going home is asking for trouble, the way not having an umbrella causes rain. All I know is that I am one day closer to going home.

When the nurse stops by near the end of the appointment, my doctor tells her she's taking me off the immunosuppressant. She says something like, "I'm being a bit of a cowboy."

Giddyup.

Posted by Joseph Seeley at 10:10 AM

Sunday, February 19, 2012

Valentine's Week: Nose-talgia Tuesday

Tuesday is Valentine's Day. We celebrate by returning to the clinic to meet with the ENT surgeon who excavated my sinuses a couple of times back in November. I don't know what we're going to do today—could be just a chat, could be a scoping. I'm hoping for a chat.

It's a 12:15 appointment, but the doctor is running well behind schedule. I fill out a questionnaire, including a review of my medications. I get in some walking while waiting. A nurse then calls me into a room, takes my vitals, and reviews my medications on the computer.

Then a doctor comes in. I remember him from my hospital time. He asks a bunch of questions about my sinuses. He also reviews my medications. (I also reviewed my medications during my clinic visit on Monday. They're very thorough about the meds!) We are then shepherded to another room, and the doctor says, "You can see from the tower what you're in for." This means I'm getting scoped. He speaks softly, in a tone that I think he intends to be comforting. It doesn't work.

He numbs my sinuses by spraying something into each nostril. It drips down the back of my throat, tastes terrible, and numbs my throat to the point that it feels like I can't swallow. "This will wear off in half an hour," he tells me. He leaves.

My wife and I continue waiting, wondering if the surgeon is going to show up before the numbing effect is gone. About 20 minutes after the spraying, she enters, sprays some decongestant up each nostril, and gets right to it. Jan was prepared to leave, but the surgeon assures us nothing upsetting is going to happen. I know that should relax me, and in fact it goes quickly and doesn't hurt at all, but I notice that I am clenching *very tightly* some gauze pads they gave me to wipe my nose after the spraying.

The scope is a stiff, narrow metal tube with a light and a camera at the tip. The camera image feeds into a monitor on the tower next to my chair, and the surgeon is taking pictures and conducting a guided tour of my sinuses for the nurse, and maybe for Jan, but Jan has her head turned *and* her eyes closed, as do I. "This is where we took out [some bone]. Look how nice and open it is *here*. And over here ... Hmmm..."

Hmmm? What does *that* mean?

At the end of the tour, some pictures spill out of the tower and land on the floor, a sequence of circular images, mostly pinkish and fleshy, the "After" photos for the makeover of what used to be Joe's Fungal Chambers of Horror.

Meanwhile, the surgeon sits in a chair and fills out a form with her findings. I'm still wondering what *Hmmm* meant when she looks up and says, "I'm very happy." In that case, so am I! Everything looks good to her. Yay! Pointing to some of the current photos, she tells me that some of my corresponding "Before" photos are posted for other surgeons to see, for educational purposes. Um... yay?

"That was a scary time," she says.

(Yes. When your oncologist tells you you're entering "think about how you want to spend what might be your last few weeks" territory, that is a scary time.)

The surgeon continued... Some ENT surgeons would not have operated on me, due to my lack of an immune system and platelets at the time. Luckily, she was the surgeon on call the night it was determined that I had the fungal infection in my sinuses. And, luckily, her résumé included several years working at a hospital with a lot of transplant patients, so she was used to, as she put it, just "hanging some bags" (of platelets, on the IV pole) and going in. In cases like mine, waiting until the conditions are right for surgery saves a lot of work, because the patient dies.

But they didn't wait back in November, and I get to celebrate Valentine's Day with my Valentine.

Posted by Joseph Seeley at 6:13 PM

Wednesday, February 22, 2012

Valentine's Week: Birthday Thursday

Thursday, February 16, was Jan's birthday. Her best friend, Maggi, sent her a very dense chocolate brownie cake and an elaborate balloon bouquet. (No flowers allowed for post-transplant patients.) Only one balloon died while being liberated, with a knife, from the plastic bag keeping them all together. She also got some candy and some tea and cards and calls. I got her a ... um ... I owe her.

Jan's birthday is my opportunity to remind her that she married a younger man. "Cradle robber" doesn't really apply, since I'm not that young, so these days I go with "cougar." A week's difference in our ages doesn't really qualify, but that doesn't stop me.

Turning 50 hadn't been so bad, but Jan wasn't that happy about turning 52. I, on the other hand, am quite happy about it. As they say, getting older beats the alternative.

Posted by Joseph Seeley at 8:19 PM

Now Playing With a Full Deck

(I'd like to thank childhood friend Peter for the title. And my mother and father, without whom this would not have been possible. And... what? The playing-off music already?!)

My birthday was last Thursday, February 23. I made it to 52.

On Monday, my friend Jeff drove me to my weekly check-up. My doctor gave me a report of steady blood counts and an overall thumbs up for how I'm doing. She did not give me preliminary biopsy results (I'll get them tomorrow) or permission to go home, yet. She did give me, in case I had forgotten, another reminder that getting here was far from certain.

How far from certain? I believe her words were, "You are a miracle." Huh. I have to give her credit for communicating enough of the gravity of the situation, back in November, that I had a reasonable sense of what I was up against, without making the odds seem so bleak that I might lose hope. Not being a believer in miracles, I don't know how I would have handled being told something that amounted to, "You need a miracle." Probably not well.

Fortunately, you don't have to believe in miracles to be the beneficiary of one.

The rest of the week brought my mom; chocolate chip cookies, chocolate cake, candied ginger, and chocolate-coated ginger; and cards, calls, and countless e-mails and Facebook messages, confirming, inescapably, that I am again the same age as Jan—that would be 52, Jan—and I don't get to use my stupid "cougar" joke for another year.

Looking forward to it!

Posted by Joseph Seeley at 7:54 PM

Part 4

Late Birthday Presents

This is the happy time, when Joe seems to be in re-mission, more so than after the first transplant. There are problems ranging from inconvenience to serious pain, generally resulting from graft-vs.-host disease. But there's also good news and a sense that, this time, the stem cell transplant is really going to work.

Reading back through these posts, I'm struck by the effort that went into them, Joe describing his condi-tion so precisely for his growing list of followers. I remember that spring looking forward to reading the next one, which I got used to expecting would be not only a good read, but good tidings as well.

Over the course of Joe's illness, we became aware of some of the limitations he might face. Would he have to take more care about being out in the sun? Would he be able to swim in the lake again? How well would he recover from the neuropathy, and what would it do to his mobility?

The prospect of these losses saddened me. They seemed to cut away part of who Joe was, casting a shadow over the image of him heading off for a care-free afternoon run along dirt roads and then jumping in the pond when he got back.

(continued)

Had we known how this would all play out, we—and Joe—would have gladly counted those limitations a victory.

—Karl Seeley, Joe's brother

Bob, Karl, and Joe: Indiana University, 1989

Late Birthday Presents

Today's regular Monday checkup was scheduled for 2:30, and we got there well ahead of time so that I could have my labs drawn enough in advance that some results would be ready by the time we met with my doctor. We were through with the lab and in the waiting room by 1:30.

I take advantage of the extra time to get in a walk, up and down the corridor. It's actually a scenic walk, with attractive architectural features, looking out over an airy atrium.

My mom inquires whether I could have my monthly inhalation treatment while waiting. A nurse goes into the back to check and comes back with a negative answer.

I finish walking at 2:20 and join my mom in the waiting room. It's clear my doctor is running late, based on how many times a nurse comes out to talk to people other than me about how there isn't a room ready yet.

Around 3:15, a nurse calls me in and takes my vitals.

The doctor comes in around 3:45. "Do you want some good news?" Always.

She hands me a sheet of paper with the results of the test for "deletions of 7q31 and loss of chromosome 7," which is the genetic marker of my leukemia. Out of 400 cells, zero cells had the marker.

"Do you want some more good news? Actually, it's all good news today."

The next sheet contains results for the XX/XY breakdown of cells in the marrow. Out of 400 cells, 399 were XX (donor cells from Mara). One lone male cell does not concern my doctor.

In addition to those pieces of good (great) news, my main counts are stable, my organs are functioning normally, and I'm slowly gaining weight.

All of which adds up to: I get to go home, somewhere I haven't been in more than four and a half months.

Then my doctor is surprised and annoyed to learn that I hadn't done my inhalation therapy (to fend off pneumonia) during my long wait to meet with her. Her recollection of her conversation with the nurse was that she emphatically stated I should take my therapy before my appointment, not after. Anyway, I have an anticlimactic post-appointment appointment with a mask hooked up to an oxygen tank and a small vial of vile liquid, and we don't leave the clinic until 5:00.

= = =

And now I am home! It's great to be here.

Posted by Joseph Seeley at 7:45 PM

At War With My Skin

I mentioned a few weeks ago that I had a rash caused by graft-vs.-host disease (GVHD). I still have the rash, off and on. It is rarely itchy, but it does lead to dry skin, all over. Very dry skin.

How dry is it?

It varies, depending on the day and how recently I have applied my various ointments.

On a bad day, I notice flakes of skin falling into my food as I eat. When I take off my shirt, the flakes swirl around me as if I were inside a snow globe. The joe-flakes settle around me on the couch in drifts. I feel like the *Peanuts* character Pig-Pen, surrounded by a constant cloud of dead skin. It's disgusting.

To prevent these blizzards, I have a full assortment of ointments and cremes, both over-the-counter and prescription. When the rash stopped being itchy, I switched from the steroid ointments to the OTC variety. However, they weren't keeping up with the dryness, so my doctor switched me back to the topical steroids. The problem with dry skin, aside from the gross-out factor, is that the skin is a significant barrier against germs and other microbes. If it gets so dry that it cracks, those cracks open up a whole new front in the fight against infection.

While the dry skin is gross (and dangerous), prevention is also unpleasant. The ointments are based on petroleum jelly, so they don't work into the skin like a creme or lotion. They just sit on the skin, glistening and slimy. Since the rash is all over, I need to apply the ointments all over: feet, legs, groin, arms, hands, torso, face, scalp.

If it's a sunny day, I spread a beach towel in front of the patio door and lie in the sun for a while in my running shorts, pretending I'm at the beach. This is as close as I'm going to come to sunbathing for a long time, maybe for years, due to long-term skin sensitivity for stem cell transplant patients.

Eventually, I need to put on a long-sleeved shirt and long running pants so that I can move around the house and sit on furniture without greasing it up. The clothing sticks to the ointment, leaving me feeling clammy. Yuck. But better than getting an infection because I let my skin get too dry.

Not only is my skin dry, but so is my mouth. This is also a GVHD manifestation, as the disease can attack the salivary glands. The dry mouth makes eating some foods challenging, especially bread and cookies and similar stuff. If I'm not ready with something to drink, I end up with a chewed but unswallowable mass of food in my mouth. Yum.

So, woe is me. I'm either flaky or oily, and my mouth is a dysfunctional desert. All of this makes my doctor very happy. She keeps reminding me that I had none of these symptoms after the first transplant, which did not lead to remission. GVHD indicates that my donor cells contain T-cells that treat my own skin cells as the enemy, which is bad, but which increases the probability that my donor cells will also treat any leukemia as the enemy, which is good.

(Eventually, researchers will figure out how to give a leukemia patient T-cells that only attack leukemia.)

There's no predictability to how long the GVHD will last. Days, weeks, months... who knows. As long as it's going on, I'll be lubing up and both cursing and thanking my new T-cells.

Posted by Joseph Seeley at 5:56 PM

Sunday, March 18, 2012

The Skin War Continues, With Other Skirmishes

I haven't been as (literally) flaky for the past week, because I have been more aggressive with the ointment. I am now applying the ointment twice a day, once in the late morning (my sunbathing time) and once before going to bed.

However, I think I'm losing the rash battle at the moment. When I was first prescribed the steroid ointments, a few applications cleared up the rash. Now, despite the twice-daily ointment, the rash remains on my arms and legs and elsewhere. Sometimes it itches, and sometimes it hurts.

It is especially bad on my hands, which are red and swollen, and the skin is cracking. This makes it hard to do a lot of things—prepare food, use a computer, brush teeth. Not impossible, but definitely uncomfortable.

Adding to the rash's discomfort is muscle inflammation, mostly in my arms. If I extend my arm to, for example, remove a glass from a cupboard, I get a sharp, searing pain between my armpit and my elbow. When the nurse tried to take my blood pressure at the clinic last Monday, the constriction from the cuff was so painful I tore it off. Some nights, it's hard to sleep because there are no comfortable positions for my arms.

I also have some numbness running up my arms, though I can't tell whether it's related to the rash or the muscle inflammation. It could also be a delayed side effect of chemotherapy. The inflammation is probably another graft-vs.-host affliction. Hooray.

I might be reaching the point where we need to treat the GVHD systemically, even though doing so would interfere with the graft vs. leukemia that we hope is happening. As in so many aspects of dealing with leukemia, there are tradeoffs and often no right answers.

Posted by Joseph Seeley at 6:58 PM

Wednesday, March 21, 2012

Spring?

The calendar says spring arrived yesterday. The bulbs and flowering shrubs and trees say spring arrived weeks ago, about a month ahead of schedule.

Meanwhile, inside, we're having a taste of winter. I'm having another round of swirling joe-flakes, as my latest bout of skin rash has progressed to the peeling/shedding/molting phase. The rash was worse, so the peeling is worse. My doctor has described the GVHD skin rash as similar to having a chemical burn, and it feels like I think that would feel this time.

It's especially bad on the palms of my hands. There's an entire layer of dead skin to get rid of, as if I had dipped my palm into molten wax, except I can't just peel it off. It can only come off when it's ready, or, more importantly, when the skin underneath it is ready, to avoid infection. My hands feel sunburnt.

The palm peeling process takes days. First fissures form at the lines that a palm reader would read. Then the skin turns yellow at the edges of the fissures and starts to peel away from the new skin underneath. It's tempting to pick at the jagged edges, even though I shouldn't, and I'm not good about resisting the temptation. After two days, my palms are about one fifth peeled.

I got a prescription for a stronger topical steroid yesterday. It is a creme that comes in minuscule tubes clearly intended for a small, localized rash and not a rash covering 60% of the patient's body. It takes a long time to apply the creme, several times a day.

Tomorrow I have a bunch of appointments in Chicago: dermatology and oncology to look at my rash, a pulmonary function test, and the famous 100-day bone marrow biopsy. After the first transplant, it was the 100-day biopsy that brought the first indication that all was not rosy, which started me down a rocky road to the second transplant. There is reason to hope for better news this time, in particular because of the GVHD that's tormenting me after this second transplant.

I have mixed feelings about the summerlike weather we have been having: sunny, highs in the 80s, evening temperatures in the 60s or even low 70s. The warmth and sunlight and early flowers lift my spirits, and my spirits can use the lift. The downside is that I want to but cannot get out into the yard to mulch and weed and prepare planting beds. Yard work is prohibited—too many malicious molds out there.

I do get out for nightly walks with Jan, which are uncharacteristically sultry and floral for mid-March. On balance, the summer weather is a good thing.

Posted by Joseph Seeley at 6:52 PM

Friday, March 23, 2012

I Have a Weight Problem

The last time I saw my doctor, the main task she assigned me was to gain weight. Don't worry about eating healthy foods, have as much ice cream and french fries as I can tolerate, and put on some pounds.

I have lost weight. I think I went into this second round of treatment, back in October, weighing in the mid-180s on a 6-foot frame. It fluctuated a lot while I was in the hospital, with some extended periods during which I couldn't or didn't want to eat, and other periods when I was pumped full of IV fluids.

Since leaving the hospital, I have mostly weighed in the mid-170s (fully clothed, including shoes, wallet and cell phone) during my clinic visits. Recently, my clinic weigh-ins have been trending down to 170 and then below, which is what prompted my doctor's orders about 10 days ago.

Since then, I have been tracking my daily food intake using an online program. 2,000 calories per day should maintain my weight, under normal circumstances. I have been eating 2,500 to 3,000 calories a day, which should add between 1 and 2 pounds a week.

At the clinic yesterday, I got on every scale I could find, and I weighed between 160 and 162, a loss of 5 to 7 pounds in 10 days. Our scale at home (naked weight 155, down from 161 a week before) yields a comparable weight loss. Maybe I am a little dehydrated, but it's clear I am not gaining the weight my caloric intake would predict, and clear I need to take in vastly more calories than I have been. Roughly 5,000 calories per day should be enough to maintain my current weight!

My doctor has mentioned that GVHD can speed up the metabolism, but this seems extreme. Apparently, any time I have left between napping and applying ointments will now be spent preparing and consuming food.

= = =

Update: To avoid large surprises at weekly weigh-ins, I now weigh myself daily.
Friday: 155   Saturday: 153.5   Sunday: 152

Not encouraging! Those numbers suggest it would take around 8,000 calories per day just to hold steady. I need to set up a cot and sleeping bag at Denny's.

Posted by Joseph Seeley at 2:10 PM

Saturday, March 31, 2012

Attacking the GVHD

My dramatic weight loss and widespread skin rash convinced my doctor that it was time to address my graft-vs.-host disease directly, so I started taking prednisone on Tuesday. I will begin taking sirolimus next week. Both drugs are immunosuppressants, so I will have an increased risk of infection.

Also, I will be suppressing some (maybe all) of the anti-leukemia behavior of my donor cells. I have to hope that they have done what they needed to do —I will get my most recent report card in a few days, when I get the results of my last bone marrow biopsy.

The fact that it was the 100-day biopsy that brought the first bad news after the last transplant makes me apprehensive. The fact that I have had significant GVHD after this transplant makes me (and my doctor) hopeful.

My weight loss has stopped, and my appetite is better, in the days since I started taking prednisone (a steroid). I can't say the rash has improved much. It no longer covers half of my body, but that change had already happened before I started with the new medication. It feels like I'm chasing it around my body with ointment—it's clearing up on my chest and legs, but getting worse on my arms.

My weekly blood tests have been very good. White blood cells and hemoglobin are at normal levels, and platelets have climbed slowly but steadily toward normal.

Posted by Joseph Seeley at 12:04 PM

Tuesday, April 3, 2012

Celebrate?

Last summer, my 100-day biopsy provided the first indication that I was relapsing after my transplant, leading to a longer and more difficult road to a second transplant. The second time through has been harder in many ways, physically and mentally, and that difference extends to the recovery.

One hundred days after my first transplant, I weighed around 190 and I was training for a 5K. I was working well over 50% time. My hair had come back.

One hundred days after my second transplant, I weigh less than 155 and I am not able to run at all. I am working less than 25%, and I can't open the dryer with my right (dominant) hand or jars with any hand. And my skin keeps falling off.

But...

Where it counts, I'm way ahead of where I was at this point the first time. Yesterday, I got the results of the 100-day bone marrow biopsy for my second transplant.

Out of 400 cells examined, *none* carried the deletion-7 genetic marker of my leukemia. 0%!
Out of another 400 cells, *all* were XX (and therefore from my female donor). 100%!

Perfect scores!

My blood counts continue to be very good as well, and I have started gaining weight since beginning prednisone a week ago. And while I still have some new rashes, the percentage of body in a rashy state is lower than it was a week ago.

This is all great news. In fact, it is the best news I could have received regarding my leukemia.

But...

I thought I would be in a more purely celebratory mood if I got this news. Instead, I'm happy, *for now*. I'm beating leukemia, *for now*. This is a big difference between rounds one and two. I've gone from thinking of leukemia as something you can beat to thinking of it as something you can beat, *for now*.

If you're lucky, it stays beaten for long enough that if it comes back, the treatments have improved so much that beating it again has become routine and precise and effective and a lot less dangerous to the patient. And, eventually, something else kills you, years down the road. Victory!

In the meantime, I am celebrating, in my way. I live *for now*. I literally stop and smell the flowers. I don't care what passersby think of the bald man sticking his nose into every flowering tree and shrub he can find. When Jan and I take evening walks, I try to track down the various perfumes that waft our way. It's been a strange spring, with lots of blooming schedules pushed earlier and on top of each other, but it's been a great spring for a guy with a nose that's hungry to smell them all.

Posted by Joseph Seeley at 8:02 PM

In the PredniZone

I am two and a half weeks into my own personal Steroid Era, and it's great!

I started taking prednisone 18 days ago to manage out-of-control graft-vs.-host symptoms: dramatic weight loss (despite 3,000 calories per day), persistent full-body rashes, and muscle and tendon pain that prevented me from fully extending my arms. I needed help opening my special drinks (Boost, Ensure). I was also generally weak and tired.

Since beginning the new medication, I have gained about 14 pounds! A couple of days ago, for the first time in months, I had no active rash! My arm muscles are still tight and painful, but I can fully extend them! Recently, I opened a Boost drink without even using my special rubber gripper cloth!!!

Any downsides? Well, I'm writing this at 3 in the morning. Difficulty sleeping is one of the common side effects, along with increased appetite (check), feeling of a whirling motion, indigestion, increased sweating, mood changes, and nervousness. Two out of seven isn't bad, especially when one of them (appetite) is a benefit at this point.

Maybe I should count mood changes, too, but I think "mood changes" would be ups and downs, whereas I'm just up.

I read that an "exaggerated sense of well-being" is listed as one of the serious side effects requiring medical attention. So if I get *too* excited about walking down the stairs without holding the railing, or *too* pleased with myself for how my Asian coleslaw turned out—and who wouldn't pat himself on the back for going all out and toasting the sesame seeds and the slivered almonds?—we might have to call the doctor.

In the meantime, I'm going to enjoy being in the predniZone.

Posted by Joseph Seeley at 8:07 PM

In Remission

It has taken me a couple of weeks to realize that all those perfect numbers from my last bone marrow biopsy mean that my leukemia is *in remission*.

That two-word phrase is very useful for providing a short answer to people who ask about my health. It captures having achieved the treatment goal while acknowledging the potential impermanence of the new state.

Notes from yesterday's appointment:

▶ I have traded diseases, leukemia for graft-vs.-host. I consider this an excellent trade, like trading a homicidal roommate for one with some extremely annoying habits.

▶ My platelet counts fell dramatically since the previous week. This may be due to ongoing GVHD, but my doctor isn't sure. She tells me not to worry about it, and she tells me she knows I will anyway. She's right. Next week, we will do blood tests to look for causes.

▶ My doctor says few patients do as well after their second transplant as I am doing.

In remission. Weak, with a confused and misguided and suppressed immune system that provides woefully inadequate defense against infection while still managing to mess with my skin and who knows what else. But *in remission*. Sweet words.

Posted by Joseph Seeley at 9:53 AM

Tuesday, April 24, 2012

Start With a Smile

I have noticed that I smile when I wake up in the morning. It's not the result of a conscious thought, and it happens every day. It's a quick, small smile, a ripple on a pond hinting at an unseen fish.

Notes from yesterday's doctor's appointment:

▶ My platelets are significantly down, again. The last four readings have been 105, 96, 46, and 32. (150 is the start of normal.) 105 was the peak of a consistent increase since my transplant, and 96 was the first reading after starting sirolimus to combat GVHD.

▶ Sirolimus causes reduced platelets in 30% of patients, so it's a likely culprit, and I will no longer be taking it. If this change causes my GVHD to rage, I may start taking tacrolimus (ProGraf) again. I took tacrolimus after each transplant. The two drugs are closely related.

- Everything else is good: weight's up, hemoglobin and white blood cell counts are normal. I have less rash than last week, though it still pops up here and there. Yesterday, I had an intense outbreak on the backs of my hands. Bright red and painful. Today, it's gone.

Posted by Joseph Seeley at 8:16 AM

Wednesday, May 2, 2012

Family Matters

We had a wonderful weekend. My parents and both sisters came out from the Boston area. Older son Jake gave up one of his last weekends at college to be in Champaign, and younger son Paul gave up being a testing-the-limits teenager and instead went with helpful and pleasant young man. Cousins Aimee and Jess came down from Chicago. Brother Karl couldn't make it, but his wife did her part by continuing to challenge (beat) me regularly in online Scrabble (most of the time).

The occasion was the Illinois Marathon, of which Jan is one of two co-directors. I am on the race committee as the webmaster, plus other duties as assigned. The race is in its fourth year, and it is a very big deal in our little Midwestern community.

The weekend was a chance for my family to share in the excitement and to help out as needed. And we put them to work: parking, hospitality suite, race number pickup, portapotty line wrangling, sag wagon driver... When they weren't volunteering for the race, my parents and sisters worked through a list of yard work: pruning, weeding, mulching... The yard looks great! We also got a black bean soup and a blueberry pie out of the sisters.

It was so nice to have my family here all together, for fun, rather than one by one to look after me as they have so often since the start of 2011.

Most enjoyable of all was to watch Jan in full event director mode. She and her co-director have built a great team that puts on one of the best marathon weekends in the country. The whole team works hard, but Jan and Mike out-work everybody else. An event of this size is not just a weekend or weeklong commitment, either. The planning and the work go on all year, building to a crazy peak over the final month.

And, for the last two years, Jan has managed to do this with one hand tied behind her back: a sick husband stuck in Chicago for months at a time and unable during those times to help much with the race, or household chores, or parenting.

It's a little scary to think of what Jan will do when she is able to put even more of her energy into the race next year. Can't wait to see it.

Notes from Monday's appointment:

▶ My weight continues its steady increase, up 2 pounds in the last week, for a total of 19 since the low point a month ago.

▶ Platelets are on the way up (32 the previous Monday, 30 on Thursday, 38 this past Monday).

▶ I am still in the study I thought I was dropped from, since the protocol includes "stop taking the sirolimus if it looks like it's doing bad things to you." When my platelets reach a safer level, we might resume the sirolimus at a very low dose. Or maybe not.

▶ I tested positive for platelet antibodies, which alone could explain the drop in platelets. However, given the way my platelet count has correlated with my sirolimus dosage, my doctor thinks it is more likely a combination of the antibodies and the drug that is responsible.

Posted by Joseph Seeley at 5:11 AM

Thursday, May 3, 2012

Not Quite Ready to Run

Last summer, I was training to run a 5K in the fall, and my training was on track for something in the neighborhood of 30 minutes. My leukemia, however, had other plans.

These days, I walk almost every day, but not very fast. Weakness is part of the slowness, but the main issue is neuropathy, or nerve damage. I have had some mild peripheral neuropathy since last spring, in my feet. It showed up a month or two after my first transplant, a slight numbness in my toes and forefeet. Neuropathy can be a delayed side effect of chemotherapy, and that probably explains mine. Last summer, my neuropathy was mild enough that it had no effect on my mobility.

During treatment leading up to my second transplant, which featured four rounds of chemotherapy, my neuropathy got noticeably worse. My feet were more numb than before, and a mild numbness extended past my ankles and partway up my lower legs.

I have received different answers from doctors about the future of the numbness. My doctor says it's unpredictable. Another doctor said it usually heals, but very slowly. A third said he's never encountered a leukemia survivor who complained about numb feet. I don't know whether this means that it eventually resolves, or that his patients have all been relatively sedentary people who don't care about numb feet, or that when you survive leukemia you just don't get that worked up about your feet being numb.

I *am* bothered by it, because it prevents me from running. There is the lack of perception, which makes for unsteady foot plants. Worse, I don't have full muscular control over my feet. My right foot, in particular, has recently started slapping down with each step, especially when I try to walk fast. I also can't raise my right forefoot past the 90-degree point, which makes it easy to stub my toes on flat surfaces.

This past Illinois Marathon weekend included a 5K on Friday night, and I entered it. My goal for the 5K was to break an hour, slightly faster than 20 minutes per mile. Walking with me were Mara, my father, and Jake. Once upon a time, I used to line up on the very front line of 5Ks and occasionally win them. This time, we started at the back. Not near the back, but at the very nobody-behind-us back. It's a different look.

And off we went. Step, slap, step, slap, passing a lot of people. We didn't time the first mile. The second mile was around 16 minutes. (Once upon a time, I would have already finished a 5K by the time 16 minutes had passed.)

With about a half mile to go, I was still feeling good. Step, slap, step, slap. I tried a little bit of jogging, about 20 yards. It felt good—easier than walking. After some more walking, another interval of jogging, cut short by a spectacular tumble as my droopy right foot caught the pavement and spilled me hard onto the concrete.

An EMT who happened to be walking at my pace stopped to tend to me, and another walker offered some wipes to stanch the bleeding from my hands. My knees and right ribs hurt, as did my right ankle. After sitting in the middle of the street for a few minutes, I was ready to finish my 5K, with my hands wrapped in wipes and a sore ankle adding to the unevenness of my gait.

I crossed the finish line in 55:18 (17:48 pace, 153 out of 168 in my age group). Post-transplant PR!

Then I headed straight to the medical tent, providing just about the only action they had all night. The medical volunteers joked as they washed and bandaged my wounded hands that Jan sent me there to test their readiness.

Dad, me, and Mara at the finish.
I am the one holding the wipes.

The price for my first running steps since September was bruised and bloody hands; bruised shoulder, ribs, and knees; a sprained ankle; and a scolding from my doctor.

Worth it!

Posted by Joseph Seeley at 7:05 PM

Tuesday, May 15, 2012

Graduation

Older son Jake graduated from Haverford this past weekend. It was everything a graduation should be: beautiful weather, family, and a graduate who has found a passion to pursue and who got about as much out of the college experience as it is possible to get. Money well spent!

The medical, blog-related aspect to this event is that I got my doctor's permission to attend. Crowds are dangerous, but much of the activity was outdoors and I was able to surround myself with a lot of fresh air. My father flew out to Champaign so that we could drive to the Philadelphia area for the graduation, since plane travel is still off limits. (A hundred people in a sealed container for a couple of hours—not a good idea for people in my condition.)

Not much to report otherwise, medically. My blood counts from a week ago Monday were very good, with the platelets jumping nicely from 38 to 61 in a week. A large amount of rash, but that has since moved into and through an extraordinary amount of shedding, and currently all seems quiet on the GVHD front.

Posted by Joseph Seeley at 10:53 AM

Blueberries

I started the day picking blueberries in the backyard. We have three small but mature bushes, which have been producing about a half cup a day for a couple of weeks now. Unlike last year, the birds are leaving the berries for us. The bushes would be more productive if properly pruned, but I've been otherwise occupied during the last couple of winter pruning windows. If I skip a day of harvesting, I bring in a cup and share them with Jan and Paul.

A half cup a day isn't enough to make a pie, but it's enough to make a classy upgrade to breakfast. I don't know that I could tell the difference in a blind taste test, but it seems like the berries I bring in from the backyard taste better than any other blueberries. I do know I enjoy them more.

It's been fairly quiet on the medical front for the last several weeks. I continue to have a little bit of rash and dry skin. The contractures (muscle and tendon pain) have been diminishing. I did call my doctor once, after a bloody stool, but it ended up being an isolated incident, and I didn't need to go up to Chicago for testing.

At my last appointment, my platelets were down from the previous visit, after a long stretch of climbing. Why? Who knows? My next appointment is Monday, and I'm hoping the platelets are on the way back up again.

Posted by Joseph Seeley at 1:42 PM

Wednesday, June 27, 2012

Trying Not to Think of the Elephant in the Room

I had several tests on Monday: pulmonary function, blood counts, and a bone marrow biopsy.

My pulmonary function test results are very good. Volume, diffusion... all indicate that my lungs are doing well and that my blood is taking up oxygen as it should.

My blood counts are not so positive. My platelets continue their steady decline, and for the first time in months my white counts have also slipped below normal. The hemoglobin counts are fine, which is consistent with my pulmonary function results. The neutrophil count is good, providing decent infection protection. The low platelet numbers are not a surprise, since my legs are covered with tiny red dots and larger red spots, both signs that capillaries just below the surface of the skin are leaking.

Why are the counts dropping? We don't know. The last time I visited my doctor, she said she didn't know. My doctor is currently on vacation, so I was seeing an APN, and she wasn't inclined to make a guess. She did say that she didn't think sirolimus was a likely culprit, an earlier hypothesis, since it has been quite a while since I stopped taking it.

What other explanations are there? GVHD, though my symptoms have been receding. Or an autoimmune response that targets platelets, which is supported by positive tests for platelet antibodies. Or the return of leukemia.

I don't want to think about the last possibility, but I can't help it. It is not my doctor's style to hide bad news, but maybe she has chosen to spare me a disturbing suspicion until she has actual news to talk about. I'm disturbed anyway.

I would be on edge even without the negative blood counts, since I am waiting for biopsy results. The edge has been sharpened by the last few blood counts and the recent don't-know-what's-going-on stance of my caregivers.

I have another blood test tomorrow, and I may get preliminary biopsy results today or tomorrow. Depending on the results, I will either be tentatively relieved (while awaiting the more comprehensive results in early July) or forced to think about what I am unsuccessfully trying to not think about.

Posted by Joseph Seeley at 10:47 AM

Part 5

Inside the Silver Lining, a Dark Cloud

We learned that my father was out of remission on my 22nd birthday. The devastating news interrupted what had been a relatively carefree summer—a summer that began with Dad in the audience at my college graduation. He may have driven rather than flown to Pennsylvania, in order to protect his fledgling immune system, and he may have been dressed in all white during the ceremony, in order to protect his recovering skin, but the fact that Dad was there at all felt reassuringly normal. Then came week after week of improving blood counts and an apparent victory over graft-vs.-host disease. I was all too willing to forget the lesson of the failed first transplant.

Within a few weeks of my birthday, I was flying home to Champaign instead of across the country to start grad school, and I felt overwhelmed with a strange relief. Being away at college for the majority of Dad's illness had been a guilty privilege; from that distance, I could occasionally forget that someone I loved had long odds against a deadly disease. This was impossible for Mom and Paul, of course, who were stationed on the front lines for the entirety of Dad's battle

(continued)

against leukemia. As Dad keenly observed, it felt right for me to finally be able to help at a time when my family needed it.

I don't think anything could have prepared me for how painful it was to be at home for the last phase of Dad's illness. Even so, the way time seemed to stretch out for those final few months living with Dad felt like a gift.

These last blasts are also a gift—the parting thoughts of a man who knew so much about how to live a good life, and how to die a good death.

—Jake Seeley, Joe's son

Joe and Jake, December 2002

Inside the Silver Lining, a Dark Cloud

On the outside, encouraging news. My skin rash was nearly totally under control, my muscle contractures were gone, and I was gaining weight. In other words, I was getting over the GVHD.

Inside that silver lining was a dark cloud. My 180-day biopsy preliminary results show that the leukemia has returned. (The other results that take longer won't change this conclusion. They will just provide additional information about the extent of the return.) This was not a surprise, given the recent downward trend in blood counts, but I didn't have to face it and cry about it until yesterday, because it wasn't confirmed.

The two events—GVHD goes away, leukemia comes back—are, I assume, linked. Given a choice, I'll take the GVHD, thank you.

Jan and I are going up to Chicago Monday to talk about next steps: maybe trying to trigger graft-vs.-leukemia; maybe another transplant, perhaps with a different donor; maybe something else we haven't heard of previously.

After the first transplant, I was thinking "cured!"

After the second transplant and the clean report card at 100 days, I was of course hoping for long-term remission but mentally prepared to fight again in a few years, perhaps when treatments were more effective and less dangerous. Instead, we're back at it six months since I left the hospital and four months since I was able to come home.

These recent months of nearly normal life have brought me a lot of simple joy, and I am grateful for that. It's painful to think about merely going back into the hospital, let alone the other darker possibilities.

I was trying not to think of the elephant in the room, without success. But even if you manage to avoid thinking about the elephant in the room, it can still crush you.

Posted by Joseph Seeley at 9:45 AM

Hints of Sunshine

We went up to Chicago today to discuss potential paths forward.

All of the paths start the same way, getting off prednisone as quickly as possible without triggering a dangerous amount of GVHD. I started the weaning late last week, and I am starting to have a little skin rash at the current dose of alternating 20mg and 10mg daily. The rest of the week will be at 10mg, followed by a transition to 5mg daily. The current weaning schedule will have me completely off prednisone in a couple of weeks, subject to adjustment based on the amount of GVHD.

Taking the prednisone leash off my immune system could slow the progress of the leukemia, or maybe even start to reduce it, though I don't get the feeling that the latter outcome is likely.

Once I am no longer taking prednisone, and if the number of blasts in my marrow is still too high to make a donor lymphocyte infusion worthwhile, there are a couple of promising new chemotherapy protocols that might make sense for me to try. Both treatments involve outpatient visits to the clinic and were described as well tolerated (minimal side effects).

Like weaning myself off prednisone, the chemotherapy might be enough to give my new immune system the upper hand.

If not, and as long as the chemo reduces the number of blasts in the marrow sufficiently, then we might try a donor lymphocyte infusion. A DLI is yet another way to tip the scales in favor of the immune system, again with the risk of triggering too much GVHD. When my sister donated stem cells, the team also collected lymphocytes and froze them, just in case we needed them at some point in the future. I guess it's good to know my medical team was more prepared for a relapse than I was.

Along with a rough plan, we got the following news:

▶ My platelet count did *not* fall between Thursday and today, which meant I did not need a transfusion.

▶ There are no blasts in my peripheral blood, which suggests that the blasts are not proliferating as rapidly as they might.

I'm also delighted that I don't need to pack a bag for another hospital stay in the immediate future. This is what passes for good news, under the circumstances. We'll take it.

Posted by Joseph Seeley at 9:03 PM

Triple Sibling Infusion

We typically visit New England in the summer, shortly before school starts. Our parents and siblings all live in the Northeast, with almost all of them in the Boston area. The trip almost always includes time in New Hampshire, where my parents and sister Lauren have vacation homes, just as the blueberry season begins there. We thought we would be able to do it again this summer, though we expected it to involve driving instead of flying to accommodate my still-compromised immune system.

With my relapse, there's no way I should be getting that far away from my doctors or getting exposed to extra people, so I will be staying in Illinois for the first summer in a long, long time. Maybe even for the first time since moving to Illinois 25 years ago. Paul will fly to Boston, and Jake is already there for the summer, so they will have to be our representatives at the annual summer family gatherings.

Since I had to cancel my summer travel plans, and to help ease the shock and pain of learning my leukemia was back, all three of my siblings flew out for a long weekend of hanging out, cooking, and yard work. And blueberries.

There is a U-Pik farm not too far west of town. Last year was their last year of being officially open for business, but they still let you come and pick and pay on the honor system. There are lots of weeds, and the bushes have not been pruned, and it's a little sad. It was also just shy of 100 degrees and very humid. But the late afternoon light was beautiful, making the scene look like a painting of an Italian landscape. And, of course, there were blueberries! Writing the perfect metaphor about finding beauty and sweetness in a day's dying light, in a blueberry patch succumbing to weeds, is left as an exercise for the reader.

Mara tames some tomatoes.

Karl and others picking...

Paul picked the most.

Joe holds Paul's bucket
while Paul takes the picture.

I did not pick, an extension of my doctor's orders to avoid yard work. I roamed the rows finding bushes that were relatively loaded. It has been so hot and dry for the last week and a half that the berries were smaller than expected. However, they pack the flavor of a larger, plumper berry into a smaller volume, so they should make a good pie.

Mara flips Karl's famous
pancakes, some of which got
to be blueberry pancakes.

As expected, the pie turned out great. I should
have worn a hat! I forgot that I don't need
much hair to have a bad hair day.

Posted by Joseph Seeley at 3:49 PM

Tick Tock

The past week featured two trips to Chicago, two visits to the local cancer center for platelet transfusions, and a decision to bring our older son Jake home for the rest of the summer and the fall.

Monday

The Monday trip to Chicago, with Jan, had the usual blood work and a meeting with my doctor, now back from vacation. My blood counts continue to drop and are now at dangerously low levels across the board: red, white, and platelets.

The gist of my doctor's message was that most people in my position would choose to keep seeking treatment, but we should think hard about how I want to spend what is, statistically, not a lot of remaining time. How much of that time do I want to spend in Chicago, maybe in the hospital, maybe suffering painful battles with infections, and all for a less than likely positive outcome? Where do we want to draw the line? That is a very hard question to answer, and we have not yet done so.

Then a nurse brought in a consent form for participating in the clinical trial we had heard about earlier, which is the only treatment option that the leukemia team thinks has some chance of success for me.

The drug is SGI-110. The protocol doesn't sound so bad: an injection a day for five days, with frequent blood draws on the first and last days, and a bone marrow biopsy on the last day. Then three weeks at home, waiting and watching blood counts. Then we repeat the cycle if there is any sign that it's helping. The main potential side effects are not anything that I'm not already experiencing: lowered blood counts, feeling tired, high risk of life-threatening infections. The injections are done as an outpatient, so the main drawback for us is the disruption of being in Chicago for five straight days.

Since the alternative is waiting at home for some disease or infection to take advantage of my weakened immune system and do me in, we decided that the treatment falls on this side of the line we haven't drawn yet. It may or may not work, and the odds are not in my favor, but it's worth a shot. So we signed the forms. The nurse was unsure whether I would be able to start in one week or two—the timing depended on the length of time since my last dose of prednisone, and she didn't recall whether that gap needed to be one week or two.

That was a sad ride home from Chicago. We talked to my parents and to Mara. We decided to ask Jake to come home from his summer job at Harvard, and to delay the start of his graduate work at Berkeley so that he could be home this fall. No matter how this turns out, it will be better for all of us to be together.

Tuesday

On Tuesday, we talked by phone to the doctor running the clinical trial. That raised our spirits, as she recounted some of the success stories they have had. She didn't sugarcoat the odds, but she did second our opinion that there's little harm in trying. We also heard from the nurse coordinating the trial that we would be starting the first cycle next week (July 16), which was another boost to our spirits. We made arrangements to stay in Chicago for four nights at the same place we rented in January and February, when I was out of the hospital but needed to stay close.

Wednesday

On Wednesday, I told my supervisor at work that they should be prepared for me to stop working. I have been working about 50% time lately, mostly designing user interfaces for web and smartphone apps. It is enjoyable work, and it keeps my mind occupied in a good way. They were already planning to hire an additional person to keep up with anticipated extra work. Now they can conduct that search with a different perspective about their future needs.

I went to the local cancer center for a platelet transfusion. My platelets were at 11 on Monday, and the Chicago team felt I should get some more in preparation for my Thursday biopsy, part of the screening tests for the clinical trial.

At the end of the day, we learned that I could not start the clinical trial for another week, on July 23. The nurse thought I had stopped taking prednisone a week earlier than was the case. This was discouraging. The longer we wait, the more time the leukemia has to build, and the greater are the chances of an infection taking hold.

Thursday

A friend drove me up to Chicago for screening tests for the clinical trial: a couple of heart tests (MUGA and EKG), some blood work, and a bone marrow biopsy. We won't get any results from this biopsy. Some of the samples go to the drug company that is sponsoring the trial, and the rest get frozen at the Chicago clinic for future research.

The nurse practitioner who performed the biopsy gave me her professional opinion on the return of my leukemia: "This sucks." So true! She also prescribed an additional antibiotic and, at my request, some sleeping pills.

Friday

Another platelet transfusion at the local cancer center, accompanied by my son Paul. I don't get the same boost in platelet counts that most people get from a transfusion. So not only am I not producing enough platelets because of the leukemia, but I'm also losing the ones I do make or receive, for some unknown reason.

The outward manifestation of my low platelet count is that my lower legs are densely covered with tiny red dots called petechiae. My low red blood cell count causes me to be more tired than I have been recently. My low white cell count causes me to worry about every sniffle or ache—is this the start of some killer infection?

= = =

Was the account above hard to read? That seems fair—it was hard to write.

It is not easy to be realistic and optimistic at the same time. Realistic, because we have to prepare for the worst. Optimistic, because a positive outlook correlates to better outcomes, and because hope feels better than despair. On the positive side: I have some symptoms of GVHD, indicating that my immune system might still have some useful fight left in it, if the new treatment can slow down the leukemia.

The odds are against me, but that has been true before. The last time the odds looked especially bad, late last fall, I was in a hospital bed in Chicago battling a deadly sinus infection and leukemia at the same time. This time, I get to be at home: grilling on the patio, watching the Tour de France and movies with my family, doing useful work, taking walks in the neighborhood, holding and being held by my wife. This is better.

Posted by Joseph Seeley at 5:29 PM

All Together (Nuclear Family Version)

Jake arrived Tuesday, cutting short by a few weeks his planned stay in Cambridge, where he was working at Harvard with his Haverford thesis adviser. He may continue to work for his thesis adviser into the fall. Having Jake at home will be good for each of us, in different ways.

Paul will benefit from having his big brother around: someone to play tennis or kick a soccer ball with, and someone to talk to about things he isn't comfortable talking to his parents about. The talking could have happened by phone, but it's more likely to happen, and to happen more often, when they're under the same roof.

We will all benefit from having another adult around the house: an additional cook, an additional shopper, an additional driver, an additional listener.

Jake will benefit from being able to help at a time when we need help.

There is only so much friends and family can do when they are one or two thousand miles away. We know they wish they could do more and be around more. We wish so, too. Most of our extended family lives near Boston, and it would certainly be easier on everyone if we were not the Midwest outliers.

Posted by Joseph Seeley at 6:11 PM

Wednesday, July 25, 2012

Buying Green Bananas

I am three days into the five days of injections that begin the first 28-day cycle of the clinical trial. So far, so good.

The day before the trial started, I had an uplifting experience and a scare.

The uplifting experience was a Meeting for Worship with a concern for Healing held by the local Quakers (my religious community). Since I am in isolation, my family participated via Skype. We had some technical difficulties during the hour, but it was good to see all those familiar faces doing the Quaker silent worship thing on my behalf. I heard afterward that when the meeting was over and we had signed off, the gathered Quakers hung around saying nice things about me, some of which were relayed to me. It was like being eulogized while still alive, which seems more useful than the usual practice.

The scare was a fever that climbed as high as 99.7. If it had reached 100.5, I would have had to go the emergency room, and my participation in the trial would have been postponed until the fever was controlled. Fortunately, the fever went away as quickly as it appeared, and we were able to begin the trial on Monday.

Monday was a long day. It started with Jan and me leaving Champaign shortly after 5:00 in the morning so that we could get to the clinic in Chicago by 8:00. Jan's best friend Maggi flew in from California for a much-appreciated 24-hour visit, joining us at the clinic not long after we arrived. I had a blood test, which confirmed that my counts continue to approach zero. I had another EKG. Then I was called back to a reclining chair—chair 18—in the infusion therapy room, which is a large room with a lot of chairs separated from each other by curtains. There are a few private infusion rooms, some with beds, but I guess I didn't rate. I spent about eight hours in that chair, except for bathroom breaks.

We heard that it took a couple of hours to prepare the injection, and we expected the injection to take place around 10:00. This would allow for the eight hours of blood draws we agreed to in the consent form. It took about four hours for the injections to be delivered from the pharmacy, so we only had time for six hours of blood draws before the clinic closed, at the same time that I was receiving a bag of platelets and a bag of red blood.

Ouch! Times two!

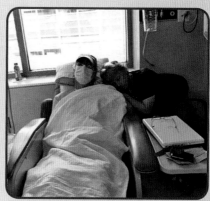

A nap with Jan was one of the best parts of a long day in chair 18.

After a final blood draw around 6:00 p.m., the three of us headed to the apartment Jan and I rented for the week and ordered dinner from a Mediterranean restaurant. It was wonderful to be able to spend the day with Maggi, especially for Jan.

Maggi left at 7:00 a.m. on Tuesday. We were back at the clinic at 8:00, scheduled for another bag of red blood and the second day of injections. I got chair 18 again. There was no order for blood, so it took a while for the blood to show up, and it again took several hours for the injections to arrive from the pharmacy. We left the clinic a little before 1:00. Leftovers for dinner, and then a lovely walk along the lakeshore around sunset.

Wednesday was easy. We arrived at 8:30 and were done around 10:00, again in chair 18. It didn't make the injections hurt any less, and they are pretty painful, but it's nice not to spend so much time in the clinic.

Thursday and Friday may be a little longer, depending on what transfusions I need and when, to get me through the weekend before I return to the clinic on Monday to visit my doctor. I will probably get more transfusions Monday, and the current plan is to have a line inserted into my arm to make it easier to draw and receive blood.

If we're lucky, there will be more blood tests and transfusions in the coming weeks and months than the veins in my arms can handle. Having this procedure is an act of optimism, like buying green bananas.

Posted by Joseph Seeley at 7:47 PM

Sunday, July 29, 2012

Lentius, Inferius, Infirmus...

We have been enjoying hours and hours of Olympics. Seven channels!

At the moment, I am living a sad inversion of the Olympic motto: Slower! Lower! Weaker! I walk more slowly, my blood counts can't get any lower, and simple tasks (like taking a shower or climbing the stairs) leave me winded.

Unfortunately, the symptoms of progressing leukemia and the side effects of the clinical trial are hard to distinguish right now. So we can't tell if I'm benefitting or not. At some point in the next several weeks, we might see a turnaround in the blood counts. It would be great if it happened before the end of the Olympics, so that I could experience some Faster-Higher-Stronger of my own, with the right sound track on television. It would not take much.

Posted by Joseph Seeley at 7:26 PM

Healthy Dreams

My Olympic fortnight has so far been filled with refillings of my tank: sometimes platelets, sometimes red blood cells, sometimes both. Last week, I received transfusions each day from Monday to Friday. That wasn't the plan, but scheduling problems kept turning what would have been a long day of transfusing into two only slightly shorter days. Fortunately for the sake of time, all but the Monday transfusions happened locally instead of in Chicago.

Ideally, I would only need transfusions every other day, and maybe even just three times a week. *Ideally*, I wouldn't need transfusions at all, but where we set our sights depends on where we are.

On Sunday, another planned long day of transfusions turned into what is now a hospitalization of three days and counting. Toward the end of the session, I started running a fever above the standard threshold of 100.5. That temperature means automatic admission when you are neutropenic and have as few white cells as I do, because an infection can easily get out of control.

After admission, I started getting an additional antibiotic, and we converted another medication that I had started having trouble swallowing from tablet form to intravenous. They also started testing for various infections: lungs, blood, urine. So far, nothing has turned up.

The hospitalization hasn't been bad. I'm at the local hospital, so it's easy for family to visit. Jake and Paul are back from their annual summer family visit to New England, and my parents are also in town, so there's plenty of family. And the nightly interruption schedule is more sleep-friendly than it is in Chicago.

There are usually two criteria for release from the hospital when you have been admitted for a neutropenic fever. The first is to be fever-free for 48 hours. I keep running up over 100 in the evening, so that 48-hour clock keeps resetting. The second is for the neutrophil count to get up to a level that offers some protection. It's been weeks since I had that many, and it will be weeks before I get that many again, if ever. Therefore, we're waiving that criterion, and I only need to meet the fever rule.

When I am not being transfused, and even when I am, I usually feel like sleeping. I wonder how much is the push from being anemic and otherwise quite unwell and how much is the attraction of being asleep. I don't remember most of my dreams, but the ones I do remember feature a me who is healthy. I'm running alone or with friends, on trails or on the track. I'm trying to figure out how to unlock the gas tank on a bizarre foreign car. I'm being shooed out of the kitchen as I forage during meal prep. It's a relief to not be sick, even if only for a few hours at a time.

I'll take those dreams as visions of the future and not just fever dreams.

Posted by Joseph Seeley at 6:50 PM

Tuesday, August 14, 2012

Out

I was released from the hospital Friday evening, after managing to keep my temperature (just) under 100 for a couple of days.

I still spent most of Sunday at the local hospital getting transfusions, and most of Monday going up to Chicago and back, but at least I got to sleep in my own bed.

In addition to the comfort of being in my own bed, I also got to sleep with the windows open on some really great nights for sleeping: cool, light breeze, crickets and other night chirpers, a gentle rain one night. The hospital can't provide any of that.

Posted by Joseph Seeley at 8:33 AM

Thursday, August 16, 2012

In

Due to a fever on Tuesday night.

I don't want to talk about it.

Posted by Joseph Seeley at 11:16 AM

Now I Can Talk About It

Still in the hospital. The fever that landed me back in the hospital has been under control for the day. So that's good.

But we're also dealing with several varieties of bad.

For this hospitalization, I have been designated a fall risk. I don't know how they determined that, but I don't blame them for being cautious on my behalf. As a fall risk, I have a bed alarm that would go off if I got out of bed to use the bathroom without assistance, or tried to make a break for it. I also wear yellow socks and a yellow "FALL RISK" wristband, in case I disable the alarm and make a break for it. When Jan is here, they turn the alarm off so that she can get in bed with me. Usually, she sits at the foot of the bed so she can look at me. Sometimes, she curls up there and takes a nap.

I have trouble keeping food down. I'm taking Marinol to enhance my appetite and Zofran to manage nausea, but the vomiting comes on so unexpectedly and without any preceding nausea, that we can't time the Zofran to be reliably ahead of it. Besides being unpleasant, regularly throwing up interferes with my nutrition, which further weakens me.

Medically, the worst of the bads has to do with my vulnerability to infection. I was scheduled to start cycle 2 of the trial this coming Monday, but it's too soon to stop the intravenous drugs that are addressing the undiagnosed infection(s) behind the recent fever. So maybe the week after, if no fevers return. And the fevers have to stay away during the week of treatment. And with my immune system in its current state, that's a shaky proposition.

More bads, psychologically, are the unknown length of the treatment and the low odds of success. My previous treatments, no matter how unpleasant the side effects, always had relatively short durations (maybe a couple of weeks) and the confidence of my medical team. It's a lot easier to tolerate distress when you can count the days. This treatment could take months to show signs of success, and more often than not, it doesn't.

All of the above has caused us to step up the pace of learning about palliative care, which is what you do to remain as comfortable as possible once you decide to stop treating whatever is killing you. Which, unfortunately, is a decision we may have to make soon, especially if I can't shake the fevers or if some other complication shows up, like one of those killer fungi I had each of the previous rounds of treatment—there won't be any emergency surgeries this time. I am having a bone marrow biopsy early next week to try to gather additional information. It won't make the decision about continuing or discontinuing treatment easier, but it may make it clearer.

In the meantime, my plan is to stay in the hospital receiving IV antibiotics for as many days as possible, with a discharge right before my next chance at starting cycle 2. It's not all bad. Jan spends a lot of time here. We reminisce, we cry, we just hang out without saying anything. Best part of my day.

Posted by Joseph Seeley at 8:00 PM

No day can be all bad when I have this gorgeous woman on my hospital bed.

Sunday, August 26, 2012

No Happy Ending

The biopsy results trickled in over the course of Thursday.

First result: Only 2% blasts! That sounded really good, since I had been at 20%. We were warned that it might not be all that good, especially if the marrow was essentially empty (hypocellular).

Second result: Less hypocellular than before! Lots of immature cells. Maybe things are moving in the right direction, depending on where those immature cells are headed.

Third result: Almost all of those immature cells carry the deletion-7 abnormality that marks my leukemia. We have lost.

Fourth result: Due to some miscommunication between my local and Chicago doctors, we hang a shred of hope on the belief that the deletion-7 number is premature. But it isn't.

If we hadn't done the biopsy, we wouldn't know it was over and we would be hoping for a highly unlikely five-day break in the fevers at just the right time to get in another (fruitless) cycle of the clinical trial.

Instead, we get to plan my final days, to the extent possible, and think of ways to celebrate my life. Not everyone gets to do that.

Once we figure out the hospice arrangements, I'll leave the hospital and head home. I can keep taking my medications and going in for transfusions, until a fever sets in. If my time in the hospital is any guide, that might not take long. The fever precludes transfusions, and I won't be coming back into the hospital for IV antibiotics to try to get it under control.

My parents are already in town and have been since I re-entered the hospital. My younger brother and his wife had already been planning to visit this week, so they'll be here. My sisters are coming, too. The more family, the better.

We'll do our best to make me comfortable by controlling the fever and taking various narcotics. At some point the infections or a stroke or some other failure will be the end. I am strongly hoping it's in my sleep, without drama or trauma. We've had enough of that.

I have mood swings: acceptance, melancholy, peace, grief, gratitude. They come and go, sometimes within just a few minutes of each other. No anger.

Acceptance is usually highest in the morning, for some reason. Maybe I've been having those pleasant dreams in which I'm healthy, so I'm more open to the it's-all-part-of-life and we-all-get-here-eventually outlook when I first wake up, and less so as the day goes on and I have more time to think about the sadder sides of my current reality.

Posted by Joseph Seeley at 11:20 AM

Thursday, September 6, 2012

In Between

I have been home just over a week, since the Wednesday before Labor Day. It's so much better than being in the hospital.

I have not been in a writing mood. No, that's not quite right. I have wanted to write—letters to family; blasts to keep telling the story. But I have serious writer's block.

= = =

All of my siblings, plus my brother's wife, Kate, came to town the day before I came home and stayed as long as their schedules allowed. They brought some pictures from our childhood to help us reminisce, which generated some smiles. We got in a live game of Scrabble with a few of the regulars from our family gatherings in New England, which was also fun, even if I did come in third of four, and Kate won as usual.

Unlike the last sibling infusion in early July, this visit was a good-bye, so there was a lot more crying.

= = =

This is a very strange time, the days after the last day on which I could see many more years forward in this life, no matter how unlikely.

I know people have enjoyed and admired my positive outlook, humor, and willingness to share what's going on, often in great detail. About all I'm willing to share right now is that I'm not feeling much like that person these days.

That, and my gums have recently swollen to the point that I need to take in liquid foods only. We're trying to see if there's something short of extracting teeth that we can do to ease the problem. Extracting teeth doesn't feel right for someone where I am in life—it would mean going back into the hospital, the wounds would probably never heal because of my immune system, it would open up additional avenues for infection. At this point, I'm aiming for the best possible days, not as many days as possible.

= = =

The response to my previous blast, in which I laid out the path as we know it, has been humbling and comforting. Thank you.

Posted by Joseph Seeley at 8:29 AM

Sunday, September 16, 2012

Liquid Diet

A flap of gum has grown over the lower wisdom teeth on each side of my mouth, so I cannot chew. (My previous statement that my gums were swollen was incorrect.) After consulting with oral surgeons and my other doctors, we have decided there is no good solution under my circumstances, or at least no solution better than living with it.

So far, I have been relying heavily on thinned hot cereals, pureed bean soups, banana ice cream shakes, yogurt and fruit smoothies, and a commercial nutritional drink with a lot of calories, protein, and fat. Though I'm generally in favor of real food, the commercial drink is very convenient and very chocolatey.

I have been feeling sorry for myself about needing to get all my nutrition in liquid form from now on. I miss eating solid food a lot.

Then I saw that people with broken jaws face the same problem. This gave me hope that I could find a tasty variety of nutritional drink/smoothie/shake recipes.

Some of what I found sounded terrible. For example: pizza, hamburgers, Chinese food, or Mexican food, plus some extra liquid, put in a blender and then strained. Also, baby food. I have been having problems with nausea and vomiting, and I get queasy just thinking about these. But if I get desperately bored with what I'm doing, I might have to give them a try.

I did learn about some promising additions like nut butters, hemp and flax seeds, and tofu. Those are probably where I'm going next to boost the nutrition of what I'm doing. Vegetable juice, too.

If you have some clever ideas for drinkable, nutritious, and tasty foods, please pass them along.

Posted by Joseph Seeley at 7:53 PM

Saturday, October 13, 2012

Rest in Peace, Joe Seeley

Joe's 21-month fight against leukemia ended Saturday night. He was surrounded by our sons, his parents, Paul's best friend Andy, and me when he passed peacefully. Last Friday, Joe had moved into hospice care at home, after receiving final transfusions at Carle, so we knew we didn't have much time left with him. Each day this week was a treasured gift.

A ceremony to celebrate Joe's life will take place on Saturday, November 17, at 10:00 a.m. at Faith United Methodist Church on Prospect Ave. in Champaign. We hope many of you can join us. Joe has written a final blog entry that we will read at that ceremony and then post on Joe's Blasts.

To carry on Joe's long-time commitment to youth soccer in Champaign-Urbana, we have established the Joe Seeley Scholarship Fund with the Illinois Futbol Club (formerly LISC). In lieu of flowers, donations can be made to "Illinois FC" with "Joe Seeley Scholarship Fund" on the memo line of the check, and checks can be mailed to the following address:

Illinois FC
Attn: Joe Seeley Scholarship Fund
2310 N. Willow Rd.
Urbana, IL 61802

We are so grateful to all of you who have faithfully followed Joe's blog during his journey. Your comments about Joe's posts meant a great deal to him, and buoyed him during his toughest times.

We are also grateful to Joe's doctors at the University of Chicago Medical Center and for the care he received recently at Carle.

Lastly, we cannot thank enough everyone who has supported Joe and us during his illness. Your many acts of kindness helped us more than you may realize.

Jan Seeley (the shorter half of "Team J")

= = =

Posted by Jan Seeley at 10:36 PM

Saturday, November 17, 2012

Last Blast

Joe's Last Blast was read today by good friend Jeff Rubin at Joe's Celebration of Life Ceremony at Faith United Methodist Church. Thank you, everyone, who came to remember Joe.—Jan and family

****

This is not the final blast I hoped to write.

My plan was more like this: When I had been in remission for a few years, I would wrap up this writing project with some carefully crafted post about lessons learned, how going through these troubles had made me a better person, blah blah blah. It would have been witty and full of insight and written while on vacation with family in New England. Maybe it would become a book and I would go on tour.

Instead, I have to come up with something much sooner than planned, and I have to write from a very different place. I'm afraid it's going to fall short of my earlier aspirations for quality.

I am grateful for what I learned about myself and about living and about how much love and support that was in the hearts of so many who know me and my family. I do feel that the lessons would have been just as effective without this particular ending, so my gratitude is tempered.

I am happy that my writing found an audience that found it valuable. Many mentioned how much my writing about my experience with leukemia helped them or changed them, and it feels good to know I was able to do that.

Some mentioned that they didn't know I had such a great sense of humor. That hurt a little, since I always thought I was funny.

The many messages I have received all along and especially during the final phase of my illness make it clear we affect many more lives than we know. Some of it is intentional—teaching, coaching, parenting, working—but much of it is incidental, based on how we live.

I can't write a last blast without thanking the many friends, both recent and from way back, whose support has made these hard months since January 2011 much easier for me and my entire family. My family and I are so thankful.

And I am thankful to have such a supportive family, from the sibling visits (and stem cells!) to my parents practically taking up residence in Illinois as needed. And to have seen my two sons develop for an extra couple of years, and to see in both of them the ability to succeed at whatever they put their minds to.

And above all I am grateful that Jan overlooked the clumsiness of my marriage proposal, and the substitution of a treadmill for an engagement ring, and accepted me for what turned out to be 26-plus years of a rich marriage. I could not have found a better match: common interests, shared goals, different strengths, and unconditional love. She definitely got the short end of the "in sickness and in health" clause, but she has handled it beautifully.

I have noticed the coincidence between how long we've been married— 26-plus years—and the length of a marathon, an event that has percolated

Last family photo: Carle Hospital, August 2012

through our life as a couple and, in the last few years, has given Team J a lot of time working closely together, a source of joy.

26-plus... as many years as a marathon has miles, though it felt as easy as a 5K. If only we had been working on a 50-miler.

I don't know what else to say.

Enjoy the blueberries.

Posted by Joseph Seeley at 7:34 PM

Postscript

Family, Friends, and Followers Share Their Thoughts With Joe

(after Joe's August 26, 2012 blast *No Happy Ending*, pages 256–257)

Joe, I can't think of anything to say except that I love you and Jan and Paul dearly. You have meant so much to me and to Andy. He has become a man under your watch and I admire your work. You have proven to be a man of strength, dignity, love, and (we have found out through your blog) humor.—Janelle

Our hearts and souls hurt for you all. We're praying for peace and comfort in the time to come. Thank you for being so willing to share this journey with us. We have learned so much from you and feel blessed to know you.—Eileen and Danny L.

Your family is in our thoughts and prayers! As my brother recently traveled a similar journey to yours, you made my days a bit brighter by getting a glimpse of what he may have been feeling and thinking. Thanks so much for sharing!—Jackie and Karl Newman

Thanks for teaching my son to play soccer and for sharing your difficult journey with us. You will be remembered.—Trish and Josh Gulley

We are really sad. Thank you for sharing your most difficult and tender times with us. We missed out by not knowing you better, but got a glimpse of your wit, humor, and charm through this blog. I think we are living our lives somehow better, with more awareness and even with more love, because of your journey. We'll be here with that love for Jan and the boys if and when they need us.—Lisa and Rick

Dear Joe, We are so sad. Thank you for sharing all of what you have gone through on your blog. I wish I had been a follower earlier. Thank you for being a friend. It has been 7 years since I have seen you, but it feels like just weeks ago. I have admired and respected you from the first time I met you; your intelligence, creativity, kindness, and thoughtfulness are an inspiration I've carried with me. Sometimes people touch you in a way you only hope to pass along to others. Love,—Leigh Gordon

Dear Joe, Jan, Jake, and Paul, I'm at a complete loss of words and for me that doesn't happen very often. Jill and I are incredibly saddened by this latest news but know that you all continue to be in our thoughts and prayers! Thank you Joe for sharing this difficult time. Your strength and gratitude for life has and will continue to lift me for the rest of mine! May God bless you and your family!—Dick and Jill

Joe, It is with tears in my eyes I write to you to say how sorry I am to read your blog this morning. Your amazing courage and strength has been something for everyone to learn from and your family/friend support system is certainly a wonderful testament to the man you are. Those who have the privilege to know you well, I wish I were one of them, will undoubtedly be there for you as these days progress and I know that will bring you and your family comfort.—Sue O.

Oh Joe, and Jan, and family…our hearts ache for you. Thank you for sharing your journey with us. We will be praying for you all in the days to come. Warmly,—Jill

Joe, I am so sorry. I have learned so much from your journey about you as a person. It has been an honor to witness your fight and to learn about your amazing family that you have been fighting with and for. You are an inspiration. I have read the comments before mine, and I don't know what else to say that hasn't been said. Thank you for being so brave and fighting so hard because, should I ever have to face a similar situation, I want to be just like you! My heart goes out to you and your family. The prayers will not stop. I will pray for peace and comfort for you and strength for your family.—Lynn Z.

Joe and Jan, words can't convey how sad I am right now. I have not stopped thinking about you since I read this last night. Thank you so much for sharing your story. It has meant so much to me. I am inspired by your humor, strength, optimism and courage.—Alex

Joe: I am so glad to have reconnected. Your life is indeed one to be celebrated; thank you for your candor, your tenacity, your courage. You and Jan and Jake and Paul are seldom far from my thoughts.—Molly

Joe, It seems we are all without adequate words in the face of this devastating news. And yet there you are, giving us the words that must have been very difficult to write. Please know that even back when we were teenagers in high school, I always liked and admired you so much. Following your battle the past couple of years has only magnified that admiration and affection. Your marvelous family, your clearly beautiful relationship with Jan, as well as your strength, wit, grace, and eloquence throughout are, to me, the very definition of a life truly well lived. May you enjoy and take comfort in the presence of your family who love you so much. I will be thinking about you all. Love,—Sarah Longson

Joe: Jerry and I pray for your comfort and peace. You are a very special person in the hearts of many.—Jerry and Dalene Reeder

Joe, May you find comfort and peace in your family and friends. Your strength and courage in facing this difficult journey has inspired us. It is a privilege to know you.
    "May the road rise up to meet you. May the wind be always at your back. May the sun shine warm upon your face. May the rains fall soft upon your fields and until we

meet again, may the Lord hold you in the palm of His hand." (Old Irish Blessing)—Jim O'Neill

Joe, I write this as I sit here crying. You have taught me so much—how to live, how to face grave illness, and how to face the end of life with grace, dignity, and even humor. There are so many people whose lives you've touched. I am so grateful to know you and Jan. You were there when I needed help and I will never forget that. And also all the fun times—visiting, trips, board mtgs. I have you in my thoughts and prayers every day. You have a wonderful family. I'm glad they are or soon will be with you. And Jan, Jake, and Paul…who love you so much, as you love them. You are a righteous man, Joe Seeley. I am blessed to know you. And to know Jan, too. Love,—Freddi

My heart goes out to you and your family, Joe. I am so sorry about the news. Thank you for being a great running partner when I was working at HK, even when the weather wasn't great. It has been a privilege to know you. I will always remember you as an inspiring and very strong person, and runner, and writer, with a wonderful sense of humor, even in the very difficult times. Thank you for sharing your journey and for being the person that you are. Prayers are with you and your family.—Valeria

You're such a good man, Joe Seeley. My thoughts are with your family. Your open sharing amazes me. Simply, thank you.—Brendan

Much love, Joe. Thanks for helping me qualify for Boston all those years ago. One last hill.—Blaise

I am so sorry to hear this sad news, Joe. I am so thankful that I had the chance to meet both you and Jan. I enjoyed the short time we had, working together and running at HK. As I already do, I'll continue to think of you on cold winter runs (there is no such thing as bad running weather!). You, Jan, and your family will be in my thoughts and prayers.—Kelsey

Joe, you should know that just this weekend Bridget and Noah visited us in Denver. We were talking about you and how much we loved our HK lunch runs together. You and Jan are 2 of the nicest people I've ever met. I am crushed by this news, and wish you nothing but comfort, happiness, and peace with your family and friends. I'd like you to know that I am running a marathon in September and it is dedicated to you and our 1-year-old cousin who is battling leukemia. I have tears streaming down my face as I write this, and that's a true testament.—Aaron

Dear Joe, I found you and your blog through Hal Higdon. I was following one of his training programs when I found out I needed to start chemotherapy. I asked Hal if he knew of any runners who continued to train while undergoing treatment. He shared with me a link to your blog and said how much he admired you. Following your journey has helped me immensely, Joe, and I hope you can take some comfort in the knowledge that you have given me (a stranger) the strength to fight my disease with a bit of dignity. Thank you, Thank you, Thank you.—Judy

Joe, I'm so sorry. I always enjoyed the times we ran together at HK, even though calling it "together" would be charitable since you would dash off into the distance with ease (regardless of the weather!) while I plodded along in the back. But you were an inspiration then, and you have continued to be an even greater inspiration in being so positive and open about fighting your illness. You, Jan, and your family have so much strength and courage, it's just amazing. A bunch of us from HK have formed a team for the Crazy K on September 8, and we're dedicating our race to you.—Ray

Joe, I would like to speak for all the girls in your class at Newton South High School and thank you for showing us at a young age that a boy could be smart, athletic, tall, handsome, musical, and NOT a jerk. I don't know how you did that. It was like a magic trick. I can't think of anyone else from that time with your talent and abilities who was as graceful and sensitive and kind. You know we all had crushes on you. Still do. Love,—Nell Scovell

"There's no such thing as bad soccer weather, there's just the wrong clothes." Quoted by my sons every time it rains for the past 4 soccer years since first heard from the fantastic U8 Coach Seeley.—Laura

Some years ago I attended the "living visitation" of a dear friend losing his battle with prostate cancer. Fully anticipating this experience of saying goodbye to someone still quite alive to be very uncomfortable and somewhat morbid, I was surprised to find how comforting and peaceful it was to express sorrow, share memories, and have some laughs in person. Reading through these posts it is wonderful that you, and all of us, are able to have that experience here now. A celebration of you, your life, of all the lives you touched and all the people who love you. (including the girls from high school who still have crushes on you?! Wow, Joe!) I have mostly known you as the Man Behind Jan—imagining you behind the scenes holding down the home fort and making sure she stops going long enough to eat and sleep. Ha! (btw, if you have a Jan Manual, make sure Bonnie gets it, she's the only one tough enough to use it). Thank you for sharing so much of your personality, wit, reality and experiences in your blog—although I wish you could simply write the "happily ever after" ending, post it, and that is how it would be. Our family is holding you and yours in our thoughts and prayers. Peace.—Peggy

Dear Joe, Jim O'Neill shared your blog post. Haven't spoken in many years—probably since we were in college. But, I will keep you and your family in my thoughts and prayers. Thanks for sharing your struggles. Best,—John Wysolmerski

I so wish the news had been different. I'm all too familiar with the emotions you're experiencing—they come whenever there's a scare about my numbers. I hope that your dominant feeling will be a sense of peace and connection to all living things, in every sphere, and that you will experience more happiness than anything else in the rest of your life. And should you feel well enough, I wish you days of total disso-luteness, all stops pulled out. And I'm not talking just deep fried Twinkies!—Love, Athena

Joe, Rather than repeating all of the wonderful things that have been said much bet-ter than I could ever say them, please know that you have made an impact on all of your readers. You have changed us for the better. Thank you.—Jeff Loeb

Mr. Seeley, I'm so sorry to hear this news. I've been quietly following your blog for a bit now and it has been a true inspiration to read your stories of humor, poignancy, and patience. If I tried to think of all the ways you have helped and taught me in my life, I would be at a bit of a loss since there are so many ways, but I can come up with at least a partial list.

-You taught me how to play soccer as a young kid.

-You taught me how to play Risk and Scrabble.

-You drove with Paul, Andy, and me to Six Flags; that was a blast! Maybe it was less of a blast for the guy driving 5 or 6 hours round-trip, though.

-Many, many other anecdotes.

-You have always been patient and welcoming to me, having me over at your house very often, cooking food, spending time with me, especially when I was in elemen-tary and middle school.

-When I was younger, you and your family were like a second family to me. I cannot possibly thank you and your family enough for everything you have done for me.

-You are a model parent and a standup guy; if I ever have children, I would like to raise them the way you and your wife raised your sons, and the way your family has always treated me.

Thank you so much for everything. With much love for you and your family.
—James Boyle

Joe, I love you man!—Charlie (Strange) (Never was a writer...)

Joe and Jan, You have both touched many lives in countless ways, as I have sensed from afar but witnessed again through your blog, Joe, and the responses to it. Your stories and your love for each other, for your sons and family will continue to have that impact for years to come. While I don't know your extended families and closest friends, I understand also that they have, are now and will continue to surround you with their loving presence, in the days, weeks, and years to come. Please know that I hold you all close in my thoughts and prayers, and that I too am grateful to take a place in your circle.—Janet Morford

It's not often I find myself with nothing to say. I have enjoyed the very brief time we shared over the last three years. I've missed seeing you but I appreciate you encour-aging me as I changed my own life. Thanks.—Mike Stemle

Joe, Your more eloquent friends have spoken already, and Nell covered the high school girl sector. I'm just speechless. Thinking about you and your family with love.—Susan

Joe, I haven't seen you since we left school but I just wanted you to know that I am thinking about you with hope and strength. My husband is in the last stages of prostate cancer and I was truly touched by your blog and your struggle with your emotions. I hope you can gain strength from the knowledge that there are so many that love and care for you—that is something that never goes away. My thoughts and prayers are with you.—Margie (Dao) Miller

Joe, About 12 years ago, you and I gave speeches at a beautiful reception following a beautiful wedding on a beautiful farm outside Seattle. People said we were funny and touching; I know I thought you were. And in following your blog (silently) over the past couple of years, I see that you are still funny, touching, insightful and incredibly positive. I recently spent a lot of time with a friend who was on a journey similar to yours. No fun, but we managed to find fun and enjoyment and happiness in the little things, as it is clear you have. It is really all that you can do. I wish you and your family peace over the coming days.—Steve McConnell

Joe, To all that everyone else has said so well, let me add my thanks for your generosity in choosing to share so much of the last few years with us. Your grace through it all has been inspiring. Wishing you and your family peace, and may your dreams continue to bring comfort.—Bill Glaser

Joe, I was very lucky to grow up across the street from your family. So much gratitude for all of you. So many great memories. I will always remember the hiking trip to the Southern Presidentials; you helped me go past my limits. You brought so much humor to so many situations, and always made us laugh. You are an amazing person, and you have been extraordinarily brave. I am sending love and light to you, and Jan, Char, Bob, Mara, Lauren, Karl, and your extended families…—Sarah Lance

Joe, We've followed the ups and downs of this journey you've shared with us through your blog. While appreciating your wit and grace, imparted through your words, we've had our fingers crossed so hard that you and your family would get your happy ending. You and Jan were instrumental for getting the girls and me into longer distance running. They thought you were the coolest parents, with your working, coaching, getting the Illinois Marathon off the ground, and introducing so many people to the joys of finishing a half marathon or marathon. I made the mistake of trying to follow you during the first and last 8-mile Soaring Eagle race at Kennekuk, because you claimed you were going to run at an easy pace. I quickly learned we had vastly different definitions of "easy pace." But, you made it look so easy! It's been a privilege to know you and our thoughts are with you, Jan, and the boys in the days ahead.—Beth Scheid, Bruce Hajek, Brittany and Brianna

Dear Joe, I was going to send this by snail mail for privacy sake, but I fear it may not get to you before you cross over to the other side. Rhys and I met you when we were teaching at Hotchkiss. I was in awe of you—smart, athletic, and not afraid to speak your mind. While Rhys and I romantically snuck around campus, a bit of a hide and seek with Security, you confronted the administration about the ban against adults spending the night together in the dorm faculty apartments.

While I was focusing on honing my athletic training skills by treating young athletes, you were coaching them to be great runners and challenging their math skills. When I was nervous about my computer skills prior to going to graduate school, you were patient enough to teach me PASCAL, allowing me to be part of your class. You were willing to let me take the final exam. You were sensitive enough to NOT share the results of my exam with me. I am certain I didn't do very well on the exam, but I learned enough about the thinking process to feel confident in programming in FORTRAN for my graduate thesis project.

You and Jan celebrated our wedding with us in 1990. Jan was pregnant with Jake. We were so happy to have you two (three) at our rehearsal dinner table. Our families did not communicate much during the year but started getting together at Christmastime when you returned to MA to visit family. We shared meals with your whole family, pasta from Vinnie T's, dessert, and ginger tea. We discussed heady topics and played games with you and the boys into the evening and then looked forward to our next annual meeting. Your boys have grown up smart and caring and well-adjusted. It has been too many years since we last saw you.

I have always admired the way that you and Jan prioritized the important things in your life and stayed focused on them. You have carried this focus through your illness and now into your dying. You have educated the readers of your blog about oncology and the medical system and your efforts to improve it. You have shown the full range of emotions that many of us hide. You have been full grace. I am thankful for your sharing it all.

I pray your death is as you hope it will be. You will be missed by so many people. Rhys and I will keep you, Jan, Jake, and Paul, and the rest of your family in our prayers. I hope that we will see them again soon. Peace be with you.—Becky Snow

Joe, I am so sad at this news and so admiring of your courage, your words, and your amazing spirit. You and Jan are inspirations and such an amazing couple, such an amazing family. My thoughts and prayers are with you, Jan, the boys and your entire family.—Nancy McCarty

Thank you for sharing this journey in your words. You are an amazing person. Thinking of you, Jan, and your boys.—Susan A.

Oh Dear Joe and Jan (and family), I am so very very VERY sorry to read these latest posts. Who ever really knows what to say in this situation (but Nancy McCarty did a great job and so did others), but I really appreciate your sharing this roller coaster ultra-marathon that you have been on. It was always so good to see the "good" posts and nice to know what was happening, no matter whether bad or good. You are one courageous, brave and funny man. I hate to think of your loved ones' lives without you! You are loved by many—including me and Laura—and will be remembered fondly!! All my love.—Tracy

Joe (and Jan), My thoughts are with the entire family. You are all awesome human beings. Wish I could be of more help…know that the entire running community (and beyond) is with you. You inspire a lot of people.—Chris Migotsky

Joe, Please know that your life has had a positive impact on the lives of so many others. Champaign-Urbana (and the rest of the world!) is a better place because Joe Seeley has lived here. Paul and I feel privileged to be able to call you our friend. May God's love and peace uplift you and your family.—Lori and Paul

Dear Joe, Your latest blog message was one we hoped we'd never have to read. But as you have done during this entire ordeal, you have gracefully dealt with a situation more difficult than any of us hope to ever deal with. We have followed your blog and prayed that you would overcome the obstacles that you have faced. We have been inspired by your courage and determination and pray that you will be pain free while being surrounded by the family that has been there for you every step of the way during this difficult time. Thank you for your strength and determination and for sharing your thoughts with everyone; they have truly been an inspiration for all of us. And lastly, thank you for being a part of the HK family and for the terrific contributions you made over the years. Our thoughts and prayers are with you, Jan, the boys, and all of your family.—Rainer and Julie

Your courage and grace have made me a different person. My perspective on life has been shifted by following the entries on this blog. Prayers and love for you, Jan, and the boys. Thank you for sharing something so personal.—Michelle Grindley

Joe and Jan, So deeply saddened to read this. But as others have said, your courage and peaceful attitude are inspirational. You are in my prayers and thoughts.—Lucia Alzaga

Joe and Jan, Our thoughts and prayers are with you, just keep enjoying. We love you. —Tim and Meg Collins

Joe, We've spoken and yet you, Jan, and the boys remain in the forefront of my mind. I needed to reflect on this entire experience and hope to offer some words of comfort. In reviewing your website I'm struck once again with how courageous, tenacious, generous, and inspiring—to say nothing of humorous—you have been as you've shared your journey. The fortitude with which you have fought for life is testament to the human spirit's will to survive. But the grace with which you've surrendered to what was in Divine Order is testament to your faith.

In celebration of you and this life with which you've been blessed, I am compelled to say that we die the way we live. My hope for you is that you have a sense of fulfillment and satisfaction about your life and that you will be peaceful and comfortable and surrounded by those you love in your final moments. If your blogspot and the comments offered after the most recent entry are any indication, yours has clearly been a life well lived. The world is a better place for Joe Seeley having been in it. In fact your life spirit is so strong I don't have a sense that you're going anywhere other than passing over into another dimension. You will be terribly missed here, but many who have passed over before will be there to greet you. Big party. I believe that.

Joe, you have and will continue to touch the lives of many through memories, stories, inspiration, example, modeling, photos, conversations, etc. Every time your name is invoked (trust me, it will be invoked many, many times in the years to come) will be testament to the fact that you remain very much alive in the places that matter—the heart and mind. And just look at the gifts you and Jan have bestowed on the world in Jake and Paul. What a legacy! Know that all three will be well cared for. Like you, they are quite beloved.

During the Olympics we prayed for the thrill of victory in your treatment. We prayed that you would cross the finish line. In my book you are going to cross that finish line the same way you've done everything else—with a world class Gold Medal performance! Fact is, though, you're not finishing. You're about to begin the adventure of a lifetime—eternal glory. If we all follow the example you've set, we may be fortunate enough to join you one day.

Thank you for letting us celebrate your mortal life while we still can. You and your loved ones will remain in our thoughts and prayers. The Force will be with you, always. In peace and light.—Rich & Rhonda

Joe & Jan, Much love to you and your family.—Jeff Haas

Joe, Been following your journey. Very sad—heart hurts for you and Jan and Jake and Paul. Tears, Prayers, and Peace.—Joan Hammond

Dear Joe, It has been inspiring to read your humorous and heartfelt posts. I am saddened to hear the latest news. You, Jan, the boys, and Bob and Char are in our thoughts.—Mike & Kristy Powell

Dear Joe, Thank you for being my friend. I will always remember how you were there when we were deciding to live in England last fall. Your words of encouragement and support meant a lot to me. Thank you for being my teammate. I learned so much from watching you and there are still times where I feel as if I'm merely channeling the questions that you would ask, through me. Thank you for all your humor and kindness. I am so lucky to have been a part of your life, and you a part of mine. In my mind I'll always remember you as someone who was strong, and kind, and patient…and with slightly mussed up hair. :) As you fall asleep and leave this world, I hope that you are filled with warmth and knowledge of how much you are loved by so many. All my love and respect.—Lisa Swanson

Joe, you are someone worth knowing, and I don't say that about many people. I am so grateful I got a chance to meet you. Thank you for being you.—Letitia Moffitt

Joe, I am so sad about this news. But I greatly admire your courage in writing about your journey. You've inspired so many people, both in running and in how you've faced your illness. You've done so much for this community, and we're grateful. I'm thinking of you and Jan and your boys.—Jodi Heckel

Dear Joe, Like many others, I didn't know what to say after reading your last post, after I read it Sunday night. Second Wind has given me so many opportunities to be around Jan, and I'm sure we crossed paths a time or two. You, Jan, and the boys are in my thoughts. Thank you for sharing your journey.—Tricia Crowder

Dear Joe, Jan, Jake and Paul, This sucks!!!—Ann O

Joe, Looking back to meeting you first as neighbors, I've always been in awe of yours and Jan's ability to approach parenting, work, running, and life with passion, purpose, and humor. I was equally impressed with your patience when you coached both of my daughters in micro-soccer, which led to a love of that sport. And now through this journey, you've inspired so many people near and far. We are all better people for knowing you. Praying for you, Jan, and the boys.—Jayne DeLuce

What a special person you are, Joe. I've been touched by your openness in sharing your journey and now by the many, many tributes that keep coming in. So few of us will have the opportunity to feel that kind of love and support. Our thoughts and prayers are with you and all the Seeleys.—Mary Ellen McConnell

Joe, Jan, Jake, and Paul, We were hoping and praying for a different outcome. I have no words of my own for comfort, but I've always found comfort in these words from William Penn (from More Fruits of Solitude): "They that love beyond the world cannot be separated by it. Death cannot kill what never dies. Nor can spirits ever be divided, that love and live in the same divine principle, the root and record of their friendship. If absence be not death, neither is theirs. Death is but crossing the world, as friends do the seas; they live in one another still. For they must needs be present that love and live in that which is omnipresent. In this divine glass they see face to face; and their converse is free, as well as pure. This is the comfort of friends, that though they may be said to die, yet their friendship and society are, in the best sense, ever present, because immortal." Your grace, dignity, and humor through this whole ordeal have been an inspiration. We will continue to hold you all in the light. —Rebecca, Ian, Matthew, and Heather

Joe and Jan, We are thinking about the wonderful time we had with you in Bermuda and glad we got to share that time. We are sad that your inspirational struggle is ending this way. We know that you and your family are strong but this will take the ultimate strength. Please know that our prayers and love are with you.—Marcia and Derek

Joe, Jan, Jake and Paul, My heart goes out to all of you, the rest of your family, and the many many friends that will miss you. Joe, I have been constantly amazed by your blogs, amazing grace, wit, and humor throughout such a long painful process. I am truly blessed to have known you all these years. I pray for peace and strength for you and family —Kathy Meyer

Joe, Jan, Jake and Paul, We are praying for all of you. Joe, your sense of humor and courage through this very difficult ordeal is just amazing! Thank you for keeping us informed through your blog. We pray for peace and strength for the family. God Bless You.—Brenda, Ed, Michelle, and Peter

Joe, Words seem inadequate in expressing the joy in celebrating a life so fully lived, and yet the sadness of you soon leaving the rest of us here to miss you. I pray for strength for you and your family, to continue doing as you have done for what I'm sure seems like such a long time. To care and cherish each other even in the midst of pain. Thank you for sharing yourself and your journey with us.—Michelle Maloney

Dear Joe, Although our paths at HK never intertwined deeply, I am very pleased to have had the chance to get to know you and Jan. Outside HK, I was able to see you in action from the sidelines during my daughter's brief foray into youth soc- cer and again through the ups and downs detailed so poignantly through your blog. Through it all, I have held in deep regard your heart, humor, candor, intelligence, and strength. Even from afar, you are an easy man to admire. I wish you and yours peace and patience.—Bill Johnson

Joe, I may have my voice back but my eyes are still full of tears. I do want you to know what a fabulous person you are and what a wonderful family you are a part of.

You and your family have been an inspiration to Stephen and me in more ways than one. Soccer of course, it was always great to see you on the field with your team, and your boys playing on their teams; all the energy Jan and you put in to helping the boys get to Sweden and Denmark. We always enjoyed the times we could share drives and enjoy the company of your kids, the chance to catch up, share a meal, take a walk.

Know how many lives you have touched, and continue to touch each day. Know what a special family you are and will always continue to be. We admire you so much, your strength and openness to share your feelings. We love you and are speechless at the moment. Love, hugs and strength—always!—Deborah and Stephen

Dear Joe, You have been such a great friend to us and such an important extension of our family through the wonderful friendship that Jake and Jacob have had through high school, college, and now grad school. Our collective hearts are breaking because there is no happy ending to your brave story that you have been so generous to share with all of us. Please know that the Olshansky-Tylers will be there for Jake (and of course Jan and Paul) through what we know will be a brilliant life and career. We love you all and our thoughts are with you. Thank you for everything. Peace and love.—Libby, Rob, Jacob, and Alex

You never know when something is going to stick in someone's mind. While we were all staying in a rental house overlooking the Up Harbor Marina on the quiet side of Maine's Mount Desert Island, I remember Jan asked Paul what seemed like an eminently reasonable question. Paul answered annoyedly to the effect of "How would I know?" Sitting in a big chair in a corner of the living room, you said to Paul ever so matter-of-factly, "You know stuff." Nothing more—just "You know stuff." I'm not a parent and I don't play one. But those three words struck me as the perfect response. Supporting but gently upbraiding. Vernacular, but accurate. The kind of thing your ideal dad might say to his very smart teenage son. These several years later, Claire and I still use your phrase just about every week in our domestic life. I expect we always will. At a quiet dinner yesterday, Claire and I agreed that there isn't a single other person whom we could imagine displaying the strength of character and pointed good humor that you have. Plus you're a damn good writer. And you know stuff.—Uncle David

Joe, it has truly been an honor and joy to get to know you. I'm simply in awe of all the loving, heartfelt words and testimony from your many friends and associates. Your courageous and proactive approach to your struggle has been inspiring, a very fine model of how to deal with such a traumatic situation. You've set a high, high standard for living up to the twin terms, Friend and friend. Holding you in the Light. —Buz

Joe, I have always been one of your blog stalkers but not much of a poster. I have laughed and cried reading your updates over the past year and a half. I admire the courage you have to keep others updated during this terrible journey. I wanted to let you know how much we have enjoyed hosting your family. They are all wonderful people. I have also enjoyed working with Jan and developing a friendship as well as a working relationship with her. I wish you peace as you continue this struggle. Please know we will always be there for you, Jan, and your family.—Susan Jepsen

Dear Joe, I think we've known each other ever since our kids played soccer together, and I will always treasure running Soaring Eagle with you. You are a good man, and you and your wonderful family have touched my life. Thank you for sharing your journey with us, my friend.—Judy Tolliver

Joe: I always looked up to you. You are an awesome uncle. You will always be in my heart. You told me such great stories. You would always come to visit in New Hampshire in the summer & I enjoyed when we walked to Squam Lake & u made those little leaf boats. Love you tons.—Izzy

Dear Joe and family, Having stalked your blog for a while, I have gotten to know you better than you know me. I have learned much from your blogs—not only about cancer and chronic illness, but also about love, determination, sharing, families, honesty, integrity, dignity, and the value of a good sense of humor. You have given much to many, in so many different ways. Thank you. Your sons are an incredible testimony to you and Jan. There are many of us who want to support Jan, Jake, and Paul in future days, months, and years. I wish you peace as you transition.—Ann O.

Joe, You are a blessing to so many people & have influenced & touched many lives. Your courage & grace are inspirational. Your family is fantastic. God bless you all now & in the future!—Amy B.

Dear Joe, While I've been blissfully ignorant of what you've been facing so bravely the last couple of years, let my ignorance serve as a sort of testimony to the man that you are. WITHOUT knowledge that this world was in danger of losing Joe Seeley, and without having really crossed paths with you at all for the last couple years, I have actually reflected often on your wit, wisdom, and graciousness, and have considered you as a model for philosophy, attitude, and behavior when facing stressful situations in the workplace or at home. I've made my own lame efforts to apply the sort of gentleness and optimism to my dealings with the world around me that I have seen and admired in you since I met you and had the pleasure of working with you so many years ago. My deliberate attempts to copy you have made me a better person. I know that many others must feel this way about you. You have been and will continue to be a powerful model for how to approach life. It should not surprise me that even through this blog you are leading the way into the unknown, still with that same wit, wisdom, and grace. I thank you and I thank God for the impact you have on so many lives, Joe, past, present, and future. I am praying fervently for your continued gentle strength and for God's hand to be with you and your family always.—Dean Hixon

Joe, I don't think we have spoken since I left HK about 5 years ago, where we used to share an office wall. Dean told me about the article in the News-Gazette today, and I went to get a copy so that I could read it. That led me here. I am incredibly sad to hear about your fight with leukemia and even sadder to hear that the leukemia has won.

We named my 7-month-old son Joe. Before my son, I have only ever known two Joes in my life, and you are one of them. They say that people have trouble naming their child a certain name if they know anyone by that name that they dislike. I can obviously report that I had nothing but positive impressions of you :)

You and your family will be in my thoughts over the next few weeks, and I wish you peace.—Amanda Palla

Joe, I was incredibly saddened to read this post. I wish you much peace, rest, and love in the arms of your family. I struggled with the idea of calling you; however I don't want to take away from the time with your family. Please know that you all are in my thoughts and my prayers, and I will continue to carry you in my thoughts. You have been an inspiration to me, and my life is changed having known you.—Broch

Afterword

Joe: simply stated, Jake and Paul carry you with them every single day of their lives.

You live on through them and with them. When they run in the cool, crisp air of fall, you are there. When they eat a sumptuous meal, you are with them. Certainly when they savor the succulent, sweet taste of a blueberry, you are with them.

The Seeley clan lost a wonderful soul, teammate, lover of words, and keen observer of life. They carry you each day to work, to the grocery store, to the New Hampshire cabin, and sitting at the kitchen table talking, laughing, joking.

The cross-country girls' team at Hotchkiss feel your presence when they take to the roads for a run; my goodness, you even bought each one a set of spikes before the 1986 New England Prep Cross-Country Championship. And there's the Not Your Average Joe Race and the Joe Seeley Blood Drive—people giving the blood from their veins in hopes that another shall live.

The Little Illini Soccer Club (now Illinois Futbol Club) boys and girls scamper about on the soccer pitch in your honor, so proud to wear the jersey of the larger-than-life man you are to the club. Your scholarship fund allows them to play the wonderful game that brought you and your boys so much joy.

Your Majesty Sugar Maple tree stands strong at Crystal Lake Park, enduring the harsh winds and cold of the Champaign winter each year, renewed in the spring with lush leaves symbolizing rebirth, renewal and the cyclic nature of life.

We miss you, Joe, but we carry on in your spirit, strongly, and every day. We look up to the moon each night and take notice of the miracle that is the moon's phases, how the light glows down and speaks to us, how sleek and slender and strong is the crescent, even a supermoon this year.

In the dark of the early morning, coursing through the cornfields, yes, you are there too in the feeling of the swift and easy glide and effortless movement that is darkness running. Jan feels you most, enshrouded in darkness, her being the shorter half of Team J.

Team J goes on as you always told me it would—yes, with pain and sorrow, but also with ease and joy. Twenty-six years of marriage to Jan, same as the distance of the marathon. Too bad you weren't training for a 50K.

Resilience—keep the eyes trained forward—that's all there, too. An indelible mark you have left in the hearts and souls of so many, as sharp a mind and wit as any of us have ever known. Grace and grit in the face of an overwhelming opponent, living each day to the fullest and taking notice of the small moments of each day, so seemingly insignificant and yet strung together to make a lifetime.

A wonderful lifetime was yours, Joe, and to that we give thanks, now and forever.

—Maggi Smeal, college classmate and friend

L to R: Maggi Smeal, Jan, Dan Jorgensen, Joe,
Sally Strauss, and Paul Lewis: Scarsdale, New York, May 1982

Acknowledgments

The seed for *Joe's Blasts* becoming a book was first planted by his Human Kinetics colleagues. As a gift to me a few months after Joe's death in the fall of 2012, Jill Wikgren, Kim Scott, Angie Snyder, and Keith Blomberg undertook the gargantuan task of assembling all of Joe's blog posts and photos to design and print a single hardcover "book." I will remain forever thankful to these wonderful friends for giving me one of the nicest gifts of my life. I was too raw at the time to revisit Joe's words, so I set the gift aside. Over time, though, I dipped back in. What I quickly realized was this: If I wanted to hear Joe's voice or laugh at his wry sense of humor or feel his deep love, the blog was where I needed to go. Friends and acquaintances that had followed the blog, or were reading it for the first time, encouraged me to publish it for a wider audience. The nudges grew more frequent, to the point where I sensed that Joe was in on it too, so thank you, Joe. Thanks to Bob, Char, Lauren, Mara, Karl, Jake, Lucy Godley, and Maggi Smeal for the pieces they contributed to help me make Joe's blog into a *real* book. I mourn the passing of Joe's dad, Bob, on November 30, 2016, mere weeks before this book came into print. Finally, thanks to Jill Wikgren for her guidance throughout the production and printing process. There isn't a better person than Jill to have your back.

Praise for *Joe's Blasts*

"I read this as Joe was writing it and again four years posthumously. Still captivating, LOL funny, deeply moving, and inspiring. Joe's gift reminds us to live every moment with grace and courage and appreciate the little things in our lives."—*Mary McGrew, grateful friend*

"I cried then I laughed then I cried again. But reading *Joe's Blasts* taught me to strive to be a better person and to appreciate every aspect of every day." —*Mary McGrath, Jan Seeley's running partner and friend*

"Every once in a while, perhaps once in a lifetime, you come across an individual who can shape your way of thinking, your approach. Whether you had the pleasure of knowing Joe Seeley or not, his story transforms the importance of how to look at life. How to appreciate it. How to laugh at it. And how to love those around you. Thank you, Joe Seeley . . . may we each always enjoy the blueberries!"—*Janice McAteer, fellow runner and lover of blueberries*

About the Author

Joe Seeley was born in 1960 to Bob and Char Seeley and grew up in Newton, Massachusetts, along with sisters Mara and Lauren and younger brother Karl. The Seeley family experienced many adventures away from Boston during Bob's sabbaticals; at various times in his childhood Joe lived in Holland, Italy, Seattle, Peru, and Mexico.

Joe majored in economics at Yale, where he was also a track standout and team captain in 1982. He continued running after college, completing 10 marathons and countless road races. He also coached and cajoled many others into running faster and farther than they ever imagined.

After college, Joe taught math and computer science at The Hotchkiss School in Lakeville, Connecticut, before moving to Champaign-Urbana in 1987 to attend graduate school in computer science at the University of Illinois.

The year before, he and college sweetheart Jan Colarusso were married. Joe and Jan have two sons: Jake and Paul.

Joe was a passionate youth soccer coach for many years in the Illinois Futbol Club (formerly Little Illini Soccer Club.) He was also very active in the local Second Wind Running Club and was the webmaster and key team member for the Christie Clinic Illinois Marathon. At the time of his death, Joe was the Usability Architect for Human Kinetics in Champaign, Illinois, where he had worked for over 10 years.

Joe was not a simple man, but he did enjoy the simple pleasures in life, like picking blueberries, tending his garden, or tapping the maple trees in

his yard for sap, which he would boil down into syrup and give away at Christmas.

In his blog, Joe's Blasts, Joe wrote honestly and humorously. Even the title was a joke of sorts. "Blasts" referred simultaneously to his blog posts and to the leukemia cells that ultimately took his life. Joe's insightful writing inspired family, friends, and even the many strangers who stumbled across his blog during his 21-month odyssey. This book presents those blog posts and additional material from his family.